W9-BSW-072

Historical analysis in geography

WILLIAM NORTON

LONGMAN
London and New York

Longman Group Limited
Longman House, Burnt Mill, Harlow
Essex CM20 2JE, England
Associated companies throughout the world

*Published in the United States of America
by Longman Inc., New York*

© Longman Group Limited 1984

All rights reserved; no part of this publication may be
reproduced, stored in a retrieval system, or transmitted
in any form or by any means, electronic, mechanical,
photocopying, recording, or otherwise, without the
prior written permission of the Publishers.

First published 1984

British Library Cataloguing in Publication Data

Norton, William
Historical analysis in geography
1. Geography, Historical
I. Title
911   G 141
ISBN 0-582-30104-1

Library of Congress Cataloging in Publication Data

Norton, William, 1944–
Historical analysis in geography.

Bibliography: p.
Includes index.
1. Geography, Historical.   I. Title.
D21.5.N67 1984   911   83-747
ISBN 0-582-30104-1

Set in 11/12 pt Linotron 202 Garamond
Printed in Singapore by
Selector Printing Co (Pte) Ltd

FOLD, TAPE, AND MAIL

NO POSTAGE
NECESSARY
IF MAILED
IN THE
UNITED STATES

BUSINESS REPLY MAIL
FIRST CLASS PERMIT NO. 50745, NEW YORK, N.Y.

FIRST CLASS POSTAGE WILL BE PAID BY

LONGMAN INC.
1560 BROADWAY
NEW YORK, N. Y. 10036

COLLEGE DEPARTMENT

LONGMAN INC.

1560 BROADWAY   NEW YORK, N.Y. 10036

FREE DESK OR EXAMINATION COPY FOR

| PROF Y SAUERESSIG
UNIVERSITY OF DELAWARE | 095300
C0607 36-01
PUB DATE 83-01 |

QTY	NUMBER AUTHOR AND TITLE
1	301041 NORTON HIST ANALYSIS IN GECGRAPH PR

IS THERE AN ASSOCIATE OF YOURS WHO SHOULD EXAMINE A
COPY OF THIS TITLE. IF SO, PLEASE FILL IN THE NAME
AND ADDRESS IN THE SPACE PROVIDED BELOW.

NAME AND TITLE

COMPANY OR INSTITUTION

DIVISION OR DEPARTMENT

LOCAL ADDRESS

CITY STATE ZIP CODE

WE HOPE YOU WILL FIND TIME TO USE THE SPACE BELOW TO
GIVE US YOUR OPINION OF THIS TITLE AND LET US KNOW
ABOUT YOUR PLANS FOR ITS USE IN YOUR COURSES.
MAY WE QUOTE YOU   YES//OR NO//

Contents

Preface

I have enjoyed writing this book and I appreciate having an opportunity to express thanks to those who have, either directly or indirectly, helped me in the task. Many scholars have unwittingly influenced the writing of the book and especially the approach which it adopts. As a graduate student at Queen's and at McMaster I was particularly impressed by the teaching and writing of Ed Conkling, Lou Gentilcore, Les King, Bryan Osborne and George Papageorgiou, and I have in some way blended ideas from each of them in this book. In a more practical sense I wish to thank those who have typed successive drafts of the manuscript, notably Evelyn Gaetz who has a happy knack of placing problems in their correct perspective. Marjorie Halmarson is responsible for the cartographic work and I am grateful for her skills and conscientious attitude. The staff at Longman proved continually encouraging and I thank my publisher for supporting this work and improving the finished project in many ways. The book was appraised by two readers and their contributions are much appreciated.

Finally, I recognize a somewhat perplexing contribution. I am sure that without the inspiration, or was it cajoling, of Pauline the book would never have been conceived and yet I suspect that, once started, that same person delayed completion substantially. Despite the final observation I gratefully dedicate this book to Pauline and to two other delaying factors, Philippa and Mark.

WILLIAM NORTON
Winnipeg, Manitoba
October, 1982

Acknowledgements

We are grateful to the following for permission to reproduce copyright material:

Academic Press Inc. (London) Ltd for our Figs 9.1, 9.2 and 9.3 from Figs 21, 26 and 29 (E. Pawson, 1977); Almquist & Wiksell International for our Fig. 8.1 and Table 8.2 from Fig. 4 and Table 1 (W. Norton & E. C. Conkling, 1974); Association of American Geographers for our Figs 5.1 (D. W. Meinig, 1972) and 7.3 (J. A. Alwin, 1974); the author, Prof. H. Carter for our Fig. 7.4 from Fig. 13.4 (Carter, 1978); Clark University, Massachusetts for our Fig. 9.6 from Fig. 1 (C. G. Sargent, 1972); Wm. Dawson & Sons Ltd for our Fig. 8.4 from Fig. 39 (A. J. Christopher, 1976); The Geographical Society of New South Wales for our Fig. 8.3 from Fig. 1 (J. C. R. Camm, March 1976); Geographical Society, Portsmouth College of Technology for our Figs 9.4 and 9.5 from Figs 1 and 4 (G. J. Ashworth & J. B. Bradbeer, 1977) and our Table 8.1 from Table 1 (S. Leonard, 1976); The Journal of Interdisciplinary History and the M. I. T. Press, Cambridge, Massachusetts, Copyright © 1978 by the Massachusetts Institute of Technology and the editors of *The Journal of Interdisciplinary History* for our Table 7.1 from Table 2 (G. Rozman, 1978); the author, Dr. R. J. Ross and London School of Economics for our Fig. 10.2 (R. Ross, 1975); Royal Scottish Geographical Society for our Fig. 7.2 from Fig. 2 (W. Norton, 1975); University of Nottingham for our Table 10.1 from Table III (R. Hall, 1974); University of Oklahoma Press for our Fig. 8.2 from Fig. 1 (C. B. Lewis, 1979) and Fig. 10.1 from Fig. 4 (H. L. Lefferts Jr., 1977); Copyright 1979 and 1977 by the University of Oklahoma Press; the author, Prof. J. R. Walton for our Fig. 8.5 from Fig. 9.1 (Walton, 1978).

Introduction

Recent years have witnessed a remarkable growth of interest in historical geography as evidenced by the emergence of a specialist newsletter in 1971, a specialist journal in 1975, a profusion of journal literature and a host of books focusing primarily on specific regions. For North America Conzen (1980: 549) identified the 1970s as a decade of 'explosive growth', a term which can also be legitimately applied elsewhere. It is with these developments in mind that this book attempts both to discuss and appraise historical geographic methodologies and applications. There are few book-length accounts of historical geography which are not regional discussions, and it is this gap which the present volume attempts to fill.

This book has two basic aims. The first is to present and discuss the methods of historical geography, both as they have developed within historical geography and as they relate to the methods of the broader fields of history and human geography. A principal consequence of this discussion is the elaboration of an approach which is subsequently exploited in order to achieve the second aim. This is to discuss the literature of historical geography within a framework which provides a comprehensive account of the emergence of human landscapes through time. The two aims are thus closely related.

This book emphasizes the historical as being one approach to geography, and historical geography is interpreted as being primarily concerned with geographical change through time, the development of landscape and the evolution of spatial form. Geographical change through time is one of the two traditional modes of analysis in historical geography and is particularly associated with the work of Andrew Clark, until his death in 1975 probably the premier historical geographer in North America. The development of landscape relates specifically to the work of historically inclined cultural geographers following the pioneering work of Carl Sauer. The third idea, spatial form evolution, is at first sight little more than a contemporary phrase for the first two ideas. In actuality it is much more, for this idea draws explicitly from the recent advances in human geography, and to a lesser degree in economic history, in arguing for the temporal or historical analysis of process to form relationships. Studies which emphasize spatial form evolution represent a valid approach to historical geography. The discussion of literature in this book embraces a wide variety of historical approaches, but the basic framework imposed on the literature relates to the evolution of spatial form and to the related ideas of geographical change through time and landscape development. The majority of discussion centres about North American examples, a reflection of the available literature. However, other areas of new settlement such as South Africa, Australia and New Zealand, are also well represented. Examples from, and discussion based upon, Britain and Europe are also included where appropriate.

This book is divided into two separate but closely related parts. The first four chapters tackle the especially hazardous task of discussing methodological developments. Undoubtedly readers will find much to disagree with, and yet it is hoped that these chapters will open up the whole question of approaches to historical geography in a way which encourages comparisons and assessments. The initial discussions focus, perhaps surprisingly, not on historical geographic literature but rather on history and economic history. The author feels strongly that an appreciation of these related disciplines is valuable to the historical geographer, and it is argued that new economic history in particular has much to offer with respect to problem formulation and research methods. The relevance of these first discussions becomes especially clear in Chapter 4 which evaluates specific approaches and is also evident throughout Chapters 6 to 9 which discuss landscape evolution. The consideration of historical material is followed by a discussion of the perceived need for temporal explanations in what is essentially the spatial discipline of geography. Chapter 3 is a discussion of the methods and techniques of historical geography. This chapter uses a basic tripartite division into past geographies, change through time and the past in the present and incorporates literature from a wide variety of countries. The fourth chapter utilizes material from each of the first three chapters in presenting a discussion of the contemporary character of historical geography including recent non-positivistic emphases. This fourth chapter also states and explains the basic assertion of the book, namely that historical geographers are able to contribute to explanations of change, an assertion which is both supported by the material presented in the first three chapters and which is exploited where appropriate in the succeeding material. In many respects Chapter 4 thus contains the most crucial arguments presented in this book.

Chapters 5 to 10 summarize and use literature to demonstrate the prevailing interest in studies of change, to indicate the potential for new areas of research and to present an essentially chronological account of human landscape evolution in areas of new settlement (North America, South Africa, Australia and New Zealand) and in more established areas (Britain and Europe) where appropriate. Chapter 5 considers three areas of continuing interest – regional historical geography, cultural analyses and the perception of new landscapes. Chapters 6 to 9 focus on the emergence of the economic and cultural landscape. Chapter 6 considers the processes of migration, in movement and the concept of the frontier. Chapter 7 focuses on the process of rural and agricultural settlement evolution and the emergence of an urban network.

Land occupation and agriculture, including the significance of subsistence and commercial developments, are the subject-matter of Chapter 8. Chapter 9 completes the discussion of landscape developments by considering transport network evolution, urban historical geography and industrial growth. The tenth chapter focuses on population and social aspects. These chapters are thus concerned with the literature of historical geography and particularly with the evolution of the human landscape from an essentially empty area to one with a well-developed economic and social infrastructure. A brief concluding chapter attempts to indicate new directions and perspectives for historical geographic researchers.

The discussions in the book thus accomplish the two aims, the earlier chapters focusing on methods, the later chapters focusing on practice. Together these combine to afford an insight into the evolution of the human landscape by means of a, hopefully, clearly articulated and justified methodology.

In addition to the above content the book offers discussions of several issues rarely developed in either book or article form. These issues include: the use of process to form analyses, previously well discussed in the context of human geography by Amedeo and Golledge (1975); the technique of simulation in historical geography, previously discussed briefly elsewhere, for example Haggett (1965); the explicit use of counterfactuals, not previously discussed in any substantial form in historical geography; the decision-making process and the location of settlers; subsistence and commercial agriculture at the frontier; the process of settlement and the diffusion of agricultural innovations, these final four having been previously discussed primarily in journal articles.

This book will have achieved its primary purpose if it succeeds in generating discussion about methods and about applications in historical geography among all participants, from undergraduates to academic faculty and researchers. It may leave much unsaid and many dissatisfied, but if it causes some thought and questioning it will have been well worth writing.

CHAPTER ONE

Developments in history and economic history

The primary purpose of this chapter is to review and appraise the methodological interests of both history and economic history in an attempt to understand the ways in which these disciplines structure explanations. The selection of history and economic history for detailed consideration reflects their close and continuing methodological ties to historical geography. Further, both disciplines have derived benefits as a result of recent inputs from other disciplines, with historians turning to anthropology, sociology and psychology while economic historians continue to utilize advances in statistics and economics. In rather similar fashion historical geographers tend to borrow from such disciplines for the purposes of developing new approaches and, indeed, identifying somewhat different problems. Although historical geography has a wide variety of ties with other disciplines, the closest remain with history and, to a lesser extent, economic history. The historian and the historical geographer share a number of major methodological issues and it is instructive to consider the views of historical writers. Despite their common interests historical geographers have demonstrated only limited concern with the work of historians, perhaps a consequence of the view that history is a somewhat scientifically retarded discipline. Methodologically, history most certainly is not retarded as evidenced by the emergence of journals such as *History and Theory* (American) in 1960 and the arrival of the socialist *History Workshop Journal* (English) in 1974. In short, historians continue to debate a multitude of conceptual issues relating to the methods of history, and their experiences, and those of the economic historians, are most instructive for the historically inclined geographer. This chapter focuses on the issue of explanation which is one component of a most developed controversy, that concerning the relationships between history and science.

EXPLANATION IN HISTORY

The facts of history are necessarily selective for, of the total number of past facts, only some are known to the contemporary writer. Further, known facts are themselves open to interpretation and are therefore subjective. Viewed in this light the facts of history are nothing more than propositions. Berkhofer (1969: 20) saw the process of producing history as comprising two stages. First, the collection and analysis of available evidence to produce relevant facts. Second, a synthesis of these facts into a written history. Both stages in this process are highly dependent upon the aims and abilities of individual historians. Accordingly, then, a piece of written history needs to be viewed as but one selective account of a possible past.

The use of narrative

Regarding the writing of history as an exercise in synthesis implies some procedure for explanation, and the critical question which emerges concerns the types of explanation which historians can legitimately utilize. Problems of historical explanation have received much attention and perhaps the most important single issue debated concerns the relationships, or lack of, prevailing between history and science. Not unlike geography, history has a well-developed tradition of being non-scientific, primarily a consequence of a preoccupation with apparently unique events. Certainly, there are many possible reasons for not regarding history as a valid scientific study, including the suggestion by Buckle that it tended to attract inferior minds. One level of explanation proposed is the *narrative*. Indeed, some have argued that history is narrative while others have suggested that one form of history narrates (Dray 1971: 153). Gallie (1963: 193), for example, contended that a narrative is an explanation and that historical understanding is the ability to follow a story or historical narrative. In rather similar fashion Louch (1969: 55) argued that narrative provided a viable alternative to scientific explanations. However, as Arthur (1968: 203) noted, the procedure of following a story to a conclusion is not equivalent to arguing that the conclusion follows. The debates reflected in the above sentences are a response to a relative decline of narrative historical writing and the disrepute into which it has fallen.

The concept of history as narrative was strongly advocated by nineteenth-century historicists who regarded history as genetic. The basic arrangement of a narrative is descriptive not analytical and the emphasis is on man not circumstances. Stone (1979: 5) proposed two reasons for the decline of this traditional historical method. First, narratives appeared only to answer what? and how? questions. Second, historians became exposed to both Marxist ideology and social science methodology with the inevitable consequence being an increased interest in more scientific approaches to history. The various forms of scientific history all employed analytical rather than narrative styles. Despite the growth and dynamism of the more scientific approaches there is evidence of a revival of narrative, a revival which Stone (1979: 8–15) attributed to a variety of factors including a dissatisfaction with the economic determinist model of historical explanation, the mixed record of quantitative analyses, the replacement of sociology and economics by anthropology as the most relevant and stimulating of the social sciences and, finally, the asking of new historical questions relating to such matters as past thoughts and past circumstances. Such factors are not adequate for many historians, but they are suggestive. There remains considerable controversy both as to the relevance of narrative and as to the ability of a narrative to explain. Wisdom (1976: 266) argued for a narrative impregnated with generalizations. Indeed, examples of revived narrative are methodologically distinct from the earlier version and Stone (1979: 19) noted the following changes. First, new narrative writings focus not on the great figures of the past but on the lives of the poor and more generally obscure. Second, analysis is as integral to the new narrative as is description. Third, the use of novel data sources is characteristic. Fourth, use of the new narrative involves exploration of the subconscious rather than rigid adherence to literal facts. This fourth development is a reflection of an interest in anthropological analyses. Finally, practitioners of new narrative employ the procedure in order to investigate the character of a past culture by means of the analysis of but one person or one event. These five differences between new and old styles of narrative demonstrate that new narrative is much more than a mere reintroduction of an established, if somewhat neglected, procedure. Indeed, the term 'new narrative' is perhaps inadequate for a development which clearly incorporates a variety of non-scientific procedures including, for example, aspects of idealism.

History as science

A discussion of the role played by historical narrative, particularly by the revised version, introduces the main issue debated in the literature dealing with explanation in history. This issue relates to the relative validity of the two apparently dissimilar approaches of the *idealist* historian and the scientific historian deriving his stimulus from the *covering law thesis*. The relative merits of these two approaches continue to be discussed and, although the content of the debate has broadened notably, the principal conflict continues to refer to the nature of history and its relationship to science in general. Idealists maintain the human studies are fundamentally different to the natural sciences and reject the suggestion that, while there may be differences, all are sciences and can accordingly rely on a standard form of explanation. A principal justification employed by idealists is the continuing suggestion that history is concerned with unique events and is therefore an idiographic discipline. Of course everything may be regarded as unique, with non-uniqueness resulting from procedures of classification. A second justification for separating history from science is the suggestion that natural sciences are objective while history is subjective. Gilliam (1976: 233–41) divided critical historiography into two parts, namely, realism and including empiricism, positivism and materialism, and, idealism. Two contrasting views were noted. First, realists allow facts to speak for themselves and do not volunteer any interpretation, so far as this is possible. For the idealists it is past thoughts which become facts. Second, realists tend to isolate causes. Idealists use motives rather than causes, and motives are essentially indeterminate because they are on an individual basis. However, realists

3

and idealists are not easily distinguished according to the degree of determinacy nor according to their relative emphasis on the general and the particular. The seminal paper (Hempel: 1942) advocating a natural science methodology for history, in the form of the covering law thesis, appeared at a time when the idealist approach was relatively well established. The earlier development of an idealist methodology was, in turn, partly a reaction against nineteenth-century positivism, a reaction which stressed the humanistic factor and the assumed unsuitability of a natural science methodology.

Idealist approaches

The idealist approach to history is one associated particularly with Dilthey, Croce, Collingwood, Oakeshott and Dray. Briefly, the emphasis is as follows. Historians are urged to reconstitute the past on the basis of available evidence, and also the historian is to govern the selection and interpretation of facts. Emphasis is placed on historical understanding, on re-experiencing or rethinking the past. This emphasis on intuition is seen by Lubasz (1963: 5) as guesswork and Carr (1961: 27–52) is critical of Collingwood, noting that one historical interpretation is not necessarily as good as another. Further criticisms of the idealist approach noted that the emphasis on discovering the thought behind the action may be unsatisfactory in that the thought behind a particular act is not necessarily the thought of an individual actor. In general, idealists both oppose all attempts to regard history as a science, on the grounds that the subject-matter of history is conscious human actions, and explicitly state that there are no general laws in history. Hence the concentration on thoughts. The use of 'rational explanation' has been advocated by Dray (1964) as one detailed variant of the idealist stance. This involves a connection between reason and effect with the assumption that the act was rational. To achieve a rational explanation, then, the historian needs to know what the past actor believed to be the facts of his situation and, also, what it was that he wished to achieve. Both of these requirements are very demanding.

The covering law thesis

Two very general criticisms of the above idealist position are the difficulty of distinguishing normal from eccentric actions and the problem of interpretation. It is this second problem, concerning the subjectivity involved in an idealist study, and indeed, in narratives also, which was partially responsible for the emergence and acceptance of more objective scientific procedures. Stone (1979: 5) identified three versions of scientific history. First, the marxist economic model with history moving in a dialectical process of thesis and anti-thesis. Second, the ecological or demographic model which suggests that the key variable in history is shifts in the ecological balance between food supplies and population numbers. Third, the approach of the new economic historians which utilizes models, economic theory and inferential statistics. A common feature of all three of the above scientific histories is their emphasis on analysis. None

4

of the three derive directly from the pioneering work of Hempel (1942) and yet this work merits consideration as it has been at the centre of much methodological writing. The basic contention, that causal explanation in history needed to be subsumed deterministically under general laws, has frequently been regarded as too extreme. McClelland (1975: 93), for example, favoured the general position, but with the proviso that the law-like statements were probabilistic. Hempel's early argument has proved to be very much against the actual practice of historians, and attempts to apply strict Hempelian logic have been largely unsuccessful (Porter 1975: 298). Donagan (1964: 7) was critical on the grounds that neither Hempel nor Popper, who developed similar arguments, offer to demonstrate the validity of the proposed methodology by example. The basic version of the covering law thesis is as follows:

always, if $(C_1, \ldots, C_n)$ then E, where C refers to cause, E refers to event.

McCelland (1975: 95) noted that Hempel was aware of the limitations of this initial formulation and a probabilistic version of the above is as follows:

probably, if $(C_1, \ldots, C_n)$ then E.

Certainly the chance factor in history has frequently been acknowledged and Carr (1961: 98) suggested that history was a chapter of accidents. Major opposition to either version of the covering law thesis has typically centred on a perceived overemphasis on the similarity between history and the natural sciences. Passmore (1962: 111–22), for example, argued that a good historical explanation was closer to that of everyday life than to those developed in the natural sciences. Another basis for criticism of any proposals for theory and law incorporation in historical studies has been 'the appalling precedent of Spengler and Toynbee' (Anderle 1964: 43). However, the ambitious theories and laws of such authors are not laws in the natural science sense and are not, therefore, a reasonable basis for criticism.

Some alternative modes of explanation

It is probably somewhat artificial to set the idealist and covering law versions of historical explanation as opposite views, but it is fair to say that they represent radically different interpretations of historical explanation and that much controversy has centred on their differences. There is, however, much more to the issue than is indicated by a simple comparison of these two. Pechuro (1965) was highly critical of what he saw at the time as a rising trend towards an idealist and positivist controversy for, from a marxist viewpoint, neither group seemed to grapple with the basic issues and too much emphasis was being placed on the definition of methods. In addition to the principal themes noted so far, namely the narrative, idealist and covering law emphases, there are a variety of other approaches advocated as viable alternatives. Several of these have strived to demonstrate that the supposed differences between idealist and scientific approaches are not as significant as has often been assumed. Beer

(1963), for example, argued that, while there are differences, the two approaches may be employed together and that the supposedly opposed views were in fact interdependent. Gilliam (1976: 241) suggested the writings of Max Weber as being a reconciliation of the two approaches while Berkhofer (1969: 291) saw both as necessary and capable of producing different levels of explanation. In rather similar fashion Fain (1970) argued that narrative is not necessarily opposed to scientific explanation. It seems clear, then, that much controversy in history has focused on the relative merits of various modes of explanation with particular attention placed on the idealist and covering law positions. But, in addition to both the proponents of one or the other of the two and those who seek a compromise stand, there are proponents of other often quite different approaches. The narrative approach, which has already been discussed, is one viable alternative, particularly those newer forms which have ties with idealist thinking. A number of further proposals for historical explanation are now considered.

One criticism of the idealist approach involves the difficulty of distinguishing between sensible and relatively eccentric actions. Accordingly, a mode of explanation which can be used for either variety of action was suggested by Forrester (1976). Given an act, it is inferred that, of all the likely effects, one is the reason for the act being accomplished. If, however, it is difficult to regard one of the likely consequences as being the reason for the act then the historian can argue that the act was irrational. This is a novel form of explanation for distinguishing between rational and irrational actions. The difficulty of assuming rational decisions is also investigated by Adelman (1974) in a discussion which makes four points. First, both Hempel and Dray were criticized for having proposed unsuitable examples of their ideas. Second, Hempel and Dray are seen to share the assumption that the procedure of rational explanation is based on a particular paradigm of decision-making, namely, that of a rational decision to select the best of the available alternatives. Third, analysis of the examples offered by Hempel and Dray actually suggested that the appropriate paradigm was one of opportune decisions rather than best decisions. Fourth, this paradigm of opportune decisions is, then, the appropriate one to exploit in historical explanation.

A sophisticated attempt to develop an alternative form of explanation, involving an integration of the genetic narrative and covering law approaches, has been made by Porter (1975) by means by applying Whitehead's idea of process to historical method. A fundamental issue relates to the situation whereby historians are attempting to achieve two different goals at one time, aspiring to be empirical scientists and striving for literary creativity. The suggested resolution to this apparent dilemma involves use of Whitehead's arguments whereby events may be regarded as actions extended in time following a process of genetic development and the resultant genetic structures may be analysed. Such an argument might facilitate understanding of the changing relationships between causal conditions and the determination of particular events. Use of such a procedure demands the development of a narrative. Such process-oriented explanations would not appear especially different from causal explanations and Porter (1975: 313) acknowledged that the task of accomplishing such an explanation was 'a formidable one'. Interestingly, this methodology implies that the historian considers alternative propositions to those known to be real, that is counterfactual propositions. The need for their explicit use stems from the necessity of demonstrating the importance of actual events.

In a very different manner Todd (1972) has strived to show that the conflicts regarding historical explanation may be resolved. A new methodology was developed, a methodology which succeeds in achieving both the needed discovery of facts and the type of historical understanding desired by idealists. A review of twelve pieces of historical writing showed that, in all cases, the authors employed both counterfactual assertions, defined as any hypothetical statement which has a false antecedent, and evaluative judgements. Todd (1972: 161) also showed that historians employ reasoning comparable to that of science and that they rely on implicit psychological laws. It is the lack of precision concerning these laws which obliges the historian to practise imaginative re-enactment. Reconciliation of the two views of history as science and as *Verstehen*, or complete intellectual fulfilment, followed an analysis of the role played by models and games. Models were regarded as simplifications which necessarily involve the use of counterfactuals and which are operationalized by the use of simulation. The procedure of historical explanation therefore involves the gathering of facts, explaining by means of models utilizing counterfactuals, and using the technique of sympathetic identification. Todd (1972: 180) argued that historians analyse social science problems in the past, but that history is distinct from the social sciences in the respect that historians use rather than develop laws. Laws are used for model construction and for facilitating sympathetic identification with persons living in the past. This view that historians employ rather than discover laws was argued by Joynt and Rescher (1961: 154–8). Although the views expressed by Todd (1972) rely heavily on a social science methodology presently losing favour, the arguments remain persuasive and the analysis of historical writing is convincing.

Probably the most convincing development in history which represents a viable alternative to both idealism and the covering law thesis relates to the many and varied advances associated with the *Annales* school. Founded in 1929 by Febvre and Bloch in the form of a journal entitled, *Annales d'histoire, économique et sociale*, subsequently retitled *Annales, économiques, sociétés civilisations*, the school began to exert a dominant influence in western Europe by the mid-1950s. This movement is convincing because it incorporates new attitudes, new methods and substantive application of these new attitudes and methods. In many respects the controversy as to whether history is a science or otherwise has fallen into oblivion because of the clearly demonstrated relevance of much *Annales* work. Quite simply, history has become as scientific as any other science. The relevance of this school is difficult to explain briefly for it incorporates a variety of new approaches and these approaches have been subject to change. Fundamentally, a much richer notion of historical time is advocated, a notion of time which is dependent on the social sciences, and the object of study moves from the individual to the total social fact (Ricoeur

7

1980: 9). In turning to the social sciences for inspiration the *Annales* school closely paralleled development among United States historians in the late 1950s and 1960s. For Barraclough (1979: 43) the central achievement of the school is a closer alignment with the social sciences in general, including geography. A reflection of the concern with the social sciences is the increasing recognition of varied data sources, and for the *Annales* historian all the artefacts of man became data. The general programme of this school involves a reassertion of the scientific character of history as contrasted with an earlier, essentially German, historicist approach and its focus on intuition and subjectivity.

It seems evident that this discussion of explanation in history is but part of a much wider issue. It is also evident that many of the issues introduced so far have parallels in human or historical geography. This section concludes with consideration of these two themes.

Explanation in history – an appraisal

A principal issue identified concerns the extent to which natural sciences and history are able to utilize common modes of explanation. Some historians have maintained that all are sciences with similar explanations. Others argued that natural sciences are nomothetic and objective, whereas history is necessarily idiographic and subjective. Although important and although essentially unresolved this debate has broadened appreciably. Topolski (1976: 536), for example, identified five ways of interpreting the task of historical explanation. First, explanation by descriptions; second, explanation by pointing to origin; third, explanation by pointing to the relevant place in a structure; fourth, explanation by offering a definition; and fifth, explanation by indicating a cause. For Topolski (1976: 539) only causal explanation was explanation in the strict sense of the term.

The different approaches of the positivist and the idealist have been emphasized and the rise of idealism as a move against nineteenth-century positivism is evident. Opposition to positivism also led to the rise of structuralism which does not aim at explanation by either discovering the purpose of human action or by identifying causes preceding events. Rather the main explanation constructs are the structures which reflect the non-empirical properties of the human mind. Explanation involves the discovery of the necessity of the explained element in the structure. Anti-positivistic tendencies also help explain the emergence of marxist emphases in much historical writing. Judt (1979: 66–79) condemned contemporary social history because of a constant striving for scientific status, because of the use of concepts such as modernization theory, because of the use of models and statistics and, most fundamentally, because of the absence of any genuine problematic or question. Topolski (1976: 230) suggested three ways of interpreting historical facts, namely, postivistically, structurally or dialectically. A dialectical interpretation is primarily concerned with a study of the development of society. Marxism undoubtedly has provided a relevant alternative to historicism. A principal reason for the growing significance of marxism is that it does offer a legitimate approach to the rational ordering of the complex facts of human society (Barraclough 1979: 17). Despite some similarities there is no real evidence of a combined marxist–*Annales* approach (Stoianovich 1976: 154).

The central issue, relating to the status of history as a science, and the various secondary issues remain unanswered. Movements away from positivistic approaches are closely tied to an emerging humanistic emphasis in history, but this emergence, in turn, raises new issues and rejuvenates old issues. Argument by selective example, for instance, is not necessarily persuasive. The difficulty of distinguishing normal from abnormal past events remains unresolved. Most crucially, the very real difficulty involved in subjective interpretations becomes evident. Stone (1979: 23) identified a number of changes which were perceived to be occurring. These included a declining interest in the circumstances surrounding man and a correspondingly increasing interest in man in circumstances; a change from group to individual subject-matter; changes from analytical to descriptive style and from the scientific to the literary emphasis; and, finally, a decreasing stimulus from economics, sociology and demography and an increasing stimulus from anthropology and psychology. Economic historians and others continuing to advocate and employ a variety of scientific procedures remain committed to such procedures despite the above perceived changes. In a series of essays Le Roy Ladurie (1979) noted various advances in history with a particular emphasis placed on quantitative and related developments. The ability of a computer to accommodate any approach or ideology was noted and the value of statistical analyses in investigating traditional topics, such as *ancien régime* societies, was emphasized (Le Roy Ladurie 1979: 4–12). Accordingly, contemporary historians are in disagreement regarding the best approaches to be adopted, and these disagreements are reflected in both methodological and empirical writings.

Explanation in history – some parallels with historical geography

Historical geographers have been exposed to many of the same influences and have debated comparable issues as have historians. The major themes of twentieth-century historical methodology – including issues about narratives, idealism, the covering law thesis and relationships to science – all have their counterparts in historical or, more generally, human geography. The historical geographer shares the problems of limited and often unreliable data. Past facts are open to interpretation whether they are being used by a historian or a geographer. Narrative methods have close parallels to the regional approach in geography with a shared tendency to emphasize facts and to focus on description. Both narrative and regional geography experienced something of a decline as a result of the impact of social science methodology, followed by a questioning of that methodology and contemporary proposals for a revived narrative (Judt 1979) and a revived regional geography (Guelke 1977; Gregory 1978c). There have been similar discussions concerning the uniqueness of phenomena and the subjectivity of history and historical geography compared to the objectivity of other disciplines. The rise of scientific approaches in history may be

9

likened to the quantitative and spatial analytic developments in geography, and related debates about deterministic and probabilistic reasoning arose in both disciplines. More generally, historians and historical geographers share the problem of distinguishing between relationships and cause-and-effect relationships. The parallels are both numerous and close and it is evident that the historical geographer is able to increase understanding of several issues by reference to the history literature. Not surprisingly the links have been most evident in the work of the *Annales* school which has borrowed from human geography, in addition to other social sciences, in a rather similar fashion to the recent and contemporary borrowings of historical geographers (Billinge 1976). Indeed, work from the *Annales* school now receives frequent, and usually favourable, comment by historical geographers.

THE NEW ECONOMIC HISTORY

Any discussion of methodology in history needs to consider those developments which have occurred in economic history since the mid-1950s, developments which are essentially scientific in character and which may be regarded as one part of wider historical changes. These developments are evident in both the United States and in France as a part of the *Annales* school. Economic history is being considered separately because it is here that these changes have been both best conceptualized and best applied. There are similar, if less well articulated, developments in social, political, urban and rural history (Bogue, Clubb and Flanigan 1977; Kulikoff 1973; Sharpless and Warner 1977; Swierenga 1973). The changes in economic history have given rise to an entirely new type of research, variously labelled new economic history, econometrics and cliometrics. The academic debate fostered has been at times quite bitter, as reported by Fogel and Engerman (1974: 11–19), and sweeping criticisms continue, as evidenced by the remarks of Judt (1979: 74). Three features are characteristic of new economic history: first, a rigorous use of quantitative procedures for both descriptive and inferential purposes; second, an explicit use of available economic theory; and third, a deliberate use of counterfactuals. All three of these features are evident, but to a lesser degree, elsewhere in history. Use of quantitative procedures is not unusual in social history, historical demography and electoral history, and a number of specialized quantitative texts are now available (Aydelotte 1971; Aydelotte, Bogue and Fogel 1972; Dollar and Jensen 1971; Floud 1973; Floud 1974; Rowney and Graham 1969; Swierenga 1970). An increased use of mathematics has been proposed by Rashevsky (1968), a proposal which has met with little response. Use of theory is less evident in the wider historical realm. Increased adaptation of theory into history was proposed by Anderle (1964) but, as indicated by Hollingsworth (1974), the impact has been minimal. Use of counterfactuals is little evident outside of the new economic history although Todd (1972) discussed their use in a wider context.

10

The origins of new economic history in the United States are usually seen in the pioneering work of Conrad and Meyer (1957) which urged economic historians to begin the testing of propositions by means of statistical inference. The response was dramatic and, by the mid-1960s, new economic history was well established (Fogel 1966: 642). The aim of this new economic history is not towards universal laws or complete explanations but rather towards an increasingly closer approximation to reality (Aydelotte, Bogue and Fogel 1972: 8–11). This aim and the means by which it was pursued have not been without their critics. By the late 1970s, however, the literature was little concerned with the supposed conflicts between the established and the relatively new. As early as 1960 Goodrich (1960: 538) argued that the two approaches needed each other and more recent literature within new economic history is largely concerned with identifying internal limitations and advocating improvements rather than any continued defence of the basic ideas and practices. Fishlow and Fogel (1971: 30–1) argued that the use of counterfactuals and rejection of the doctrine of uniqueness have facilitated better interpretations of nineteenth-century United States developments, although they noted two major shortcomings: first, a tendency for empirical analyses to be too narrowly focused in space and time, and second, an overly narrow range of theoretical constructs. Further research into the demographic and spatial dimensions of economic history was favoured by Swanson and Williamson (1971) while North (1974) argued that too much of the research was destructive and there was insufficient emphasis placed on long-run transformations. More specifically North (1977: 193–7) noted several limitations imposed by the emphasis placed on neo-classical economic theory including, first, the assumption that there are zero costs involved in operating the economic system, and second, the emphasis placed on market rather than other forms of resource allocation. The second of these two is fundamental to North (1977: 195): 'The basic tension between population and resources is the very heart of economic history, and the failure of neoclassical theory to be able to deal with one of these variables keeps it from coming to grips with the most basic of all issues in economic history.' New economic historians have also been unable to cope with the difficulty of producing sequential discussions using neo-classical theory and with the difficulty of dealing with irrational actions in a theoretical framework of economic man. Neither of these two difficulties are peculiar to the economic historian.

The origins of the new approach in France are one part of the *Annales* school. The origins of French quantitative work go back to Simiard in the 1930s and Labrousse in the 1940s. These authors borrowed quantitative methodology from economics and utilized the notions of trend and structure. The result was an economic history dominated by the history of prices. For later scholars history has consisted of structures or geographical time, conjunctures or social time and events or individual time, with the first two assuming more importance. Viewing history in this light required new methods and an awareness of other disciplines. Of these two developments, the emergence of new economic history in the United States and the focus on economic issues by *Annales* scholars, it is the former which is used as the principal basis for the succeeding discussion as it is the more explicitly focused on economic concerns. For the *Annales* school the quantitative and related developments are but one component of a more general concern.

Quantitative methods

The use of quantitative methods in both history and economic history is well established and, indeed, was so prior to the rise of the new economic history. The impact of this rise was to provide a much firmer foundation for such procedures and to introduce a much wider range of applications. The most visible development has been the introduction of inferential statistics in addition to the traditionally employed descriptive statistics. The introduction and expanding use of inferential procedures is closely related to the increasing scientific content and the attempts at hypothesis testing in the new economic history. Clubb and Bogue (1977: 170) noted that new economic historians 'have been in a class by themselves' as a result of good data sources and a social science background. The attitude adopted towards quantitative developments has varied notably. Again, Clubb and Bogue (1977: 171–2) noted:

The modest improvement of technical sophistication has been greeted with mixed reactions. Neanderthal traditionalists, including some who are ostensibly friendly critics, insist that jargon and an excessive reliance on numbers is destroying the literary quality that, they maintain with considerable exaggeration, has been a fundamental characteristic of historical writing. Quantification, in their view, dehumanizes history and substitutes tables of numbers for humane understanding of the personalities of the past. Less paranoiac scholars recognize that quantitative methods and materials have already contributed to deeper and more precise knowledge and have allowed investigation of the conditions and behaviour of ordinary men and women of the past who were usually neglected by traditional historians. Thus, quantitative approaches have added a humane dimension to history that traditional approaches with their exclusive dependence on elite sources could not provide. These same historians, however, also express concerned recognition that growing technical efficiency is leading to a form of history that cannot be read effectively, much less critically evaluated, by the technically untrained.

Clearly the issue of quantification is much more than 'simply the extent to which historians are willing to substitute relatively precise quantitative statements for the imprecise ones they are in the habit of making' (Rowney and Graham 1969: vii). Objections, or at least reservations, to an increasing use of quantitative procedures assume at least three directions. First, as already noted, there is concern among historians regarding the interpretation of relatively sophisticated analyses. If the majority of historians are unable to comprehend the analysis then how are the results to be evaluated? There is clearly no answer to such a dilemma and perhaps none is necessary, for the growth of specialized interest groups is inevitable and the requirement of some almost universal comprehension is unlikely to be met. Second, few historians have discussed the quality of data or the means by which data are collected and critics contend that research problems are being defined according to data availability. Although generally correct, such an assertion applies to all forms of historical data, not only to the quantitative variety. Third, quantitative history rarely focuses on issues of data classification despite the acknowledgement in social science that classification procedures are one influence on results obtained.

Despite some shortcomings the use of quantitative approaches is certainly a valid procedure for the historian. In the introduction to a collection of essays Floud (1974) discussed simple descriptive statistics, averages, measures of association, correlation analysis, regression analysis, change over time and inferences and samples. Aydelotte (1971) noted that quantitative approaches are appropriate only in certain circumstances and ought not to be applied unless appropriate. Unfortunately, it is not easy to identify the circumstances on all occasions.

The use of theory

The increasing concern with a scientific approach in the new economic history has resulted primarily in the use of existing economic theory rather than in any notable theory development. Aydelotte (1971: 14) commented on the paucity of theory and advocated further use of theory on the logic that chronologically arranged data do not speak for themselves. A similar observation was made by Clubb and Bogue (1977: 173) in a criticism of the overemphasis on quantification without appreciation of the need for conceptual advances: 'Before the data can speak conceptualization is necessary. Conceptual models, frameworks and theoretical formulations are a necessary basis for assigning meaning to observed statistical relationships and patterns and are required to suggest relationships that ought to be present in relevant data if other propositions are to be accepted.' The need for further attention to theory is reinforced by a consideration of the limitations of the typically employed neo-classical ideas already noted by North (1977).

Any discussion of theory in new economic history and, indeed, in history raises the question as to whether or not these disciplines are sciences. For the new economic historian the answer is affirmative and certain. The aim is to develop, test and amend theories as one viable means of achieving explanations. Kahk and Kovalchenko (1974: 217) were quite explicit in this respect and noted that method, and technique were subordinate to theory. For most researchers, however, the issue is not quite so straightforward. Even the most committed of new economic historians questions the theoretical component of the discipline on the basis that there has been a general failure to develop theory. For Hollingsworth (1974: 225) this failure is evident in much social science because of the opposition to the suggestion that concepts must be culture free. It is clear that there is a real gulf between simply using available theory and actually developing theory. Most new economic history focuses on the former. Given that such theories are typically deterministic and that the need is for probabilistic formulations, this state of affairs is especially disturbing. Of the three advances in economic history being discussed it is the theoretical advances which are most necessary and yet which have experienced the least expansion.

Counterfactuals

Within the theoretical and quantitative framework of new economic history one technique predominated in analyses, the technique of the counterfactual. Given that a counterfactual is any statement which is untrue it is only to be expected that their explicit incorporation into new economic history created some early confusion. Redlich (1965: 484–6) was a severe critic for, having separated counterfactuals into two categories, namely, hypothetical statements with a basis in reality and figments with no basis in reality, the second category were chastised for investigating 'what would have happened in the event that something else had happened which could not have happened'. Most interested researchers have viewed such comments as misunderstandings and have emphasized that the only difference between old and new economic history in this respect is in the previously implicit and later explicit use of the technique. While events may be described without any reference to counterfactuals an explanation requires this tool: 'there is in fact no way that cause and effect can be discussed without comparing the observed to the hypothetical' (Davis 1970: 283). Similarly, McClelland (1968: 102–3) noted that to consider cause and effect one is required mentally to remove the cause and speculate on the consequences. A principal impetus for the use of counterfactuals stems from the desire to assess the effects of economic policies by means of a consideration of the effects of alternative policies.

The suggestion that counterfactuals have been employed implicitly in much economic and other history has received compelling support from Todd (1972) who contended that there are two features common to much historical writing with one of the two being the use of counterfactuals. Todd (1972) demonstrated that much historical writing utilized counterfactuals and proceeded to advocate a methodology highly dependent on the modelling of past situations and the inclusion of counterfactuals. Explicit applications in economic history typically involved the analysis of commonly held assumptions regarding the evolution of an economy. Examples include Conrad and Meyer (1958) on slavery profitability, North (1961) on cotton and inter-regional trade, Fogel (1964) on technology and economic growth and Kelley, Williamson and Cheetham (1972) on the American and Japanese economies. Justification for the employment of such explicit counterfactuals was that 'every statement of causation implied the counterfactual proposition that in the absence of the causative factor the event would not have occurred' (North 1977: 189). These uses which analyse cause and effect assume the following character: *If not A, then B*, where A is known to have occurred and B is an assumed consequence. The aim of such an investigation is to question the assumed consequences. New economic historians also introduced counterfactuals with the following character: *if not A, then not B*, where both A and B did occur. In this instance the aim is to stress the relevance of the hypothesis relating B to A by showing that B would not have occurred had A been absent. Both varieties of counterfactual are also capable of generating counterfactual outcomes in addition to that input. Where the original statement is of the, *if not A, then B*, variety, the output is a similar but different B. Where the original statement is of the, *if not A, then not B*, variety, the output is quite different to B.

A third, and somewhat different, justification for the use of counterfactuals relates to the significance of chance factors in the historical process (Carr 1961: 98). Historical outcomes are but one of a number of alternative outcomes. This realization, that other outcomes may have resulted from similar causes, implies that the real outcome may indeed be an unlikely outcome. Given this state of affairs it is valuable to generate non-real outcomes in order to observe their character and similarity to the real outcome. Using such logic the counterfactuals are outputs of analysis.

The debate concerning the validity of counterfactual procedures is not yet resolved. Kahk and Kovalchenko (1974) chose to distinguish between hypothetical models and simulation models. The former were seen as acceptable and described 'potential situations which have not become real due to certain conditions'; the latter were rejected because they imitated 'situations which do not correspond to the real course of development' (Kahk and Kovalchenko 1974: 222). For most new economic historians such a distinction is both unclear and unacceptable. The counterfactual technique is, perhaps, the most original and distinctive component of the new economic history and one which merits imitation elsewhere.

CONCLUSIONS

The above discussions of history and of the new economic history provide compelling evidence of a continuing conflict within both areas of study. Similar disagreements are evident in the areas of social, rural and political history, although these interests are generally of less relevance to historical geography. Kulikoff (1973) reviewed the work of three historical geographers and suggested a number of ways by which they might benefit from an increased association with the ideas prevailing in social history. In particular, social historians 'organize their data in a tighter chronological framework' and also use the biographical approach, 'the systematic collection of various kinds of data on the same individuals' (Kulikoff 1973: 125). Swierenga (1973: 111) identified a 'new rural history' and also expressed hopes of achieving a combined urban and rural history. For Swierenga (1973: 119) a new rural history might arise, 'with the help of the locational theories of economic geographers, the macroeconomic regional agricultural models of the "new economic historians" the community studies and ethnocultural and political research of the behavioral historians, and the population analyses of the historical demographers'. Scholars of the French *Annales* school have successfully extended the frontiers of each of these interests because of their long-standing interest in human and environment interactions, their concern with *genre de vie* or way of life and their awareness of spatial relationships. Indeed French history has progressed further and contributed to issues such as climatic change and plant and animal movements (Le Roy Ladurie 1971).

In history, those who stress scientific emphases and related theoretical and quantitative thrusts remain in a minority. Allardt (1974: 245) observed an increased interest among historians in model-building and related approaches, an interest which meets with 'acceptance by many sociologists and political scientists'. It is not an interest, however, which meets with whole-hearted support within history. According to Barraclough (1979: 3) the majority of historians are sceptical of recent trends in general, with the most important of recent trends being the search for quantity. There is no doubt that the attitude of historians has been profoundly affected by scientific ideas, with some historians now asking scientific questions about historical facts. Similarly, in economic history there remains a substantial divergence of interests between the new and the more traditional approaches. The varying acceptance of scientific orientations is well summarized by a comparison of the editorial policies of the journal *Historical Methods* and the comments from Judt (1979). An editorial in *Historical methods* (1980: 1) observed that 'the concerns of the journal have moved from the periphery toward the centre of the discipline' and the concerns are 'systematic linking of historical evidence, methods of analysis and theoretical perspectives'. The journal focuses on quantitative and interdisciplinary approaches and, during the 1980s, intends to express continuing discontent with traditional history. Quite a different perspective is argued by Judt (1979: 74) who saw an 'obsession with "models" with the abstractions to which they lead, . . .'. The interest in models and related procedures is seen to be a fundamental defect for, 'the interest in numbers and their uses, is clearly linked to the absence of any properly conceived historical question' (Judt 1979: 74). The difference of opinion is total. In addition to this polarization of attitudes there is evident some serious and critical questioning of the meaning of science to economic history. Recent views of science recognize it as being 'inherently messy and complicated' and thus, if accepted, permit a 'messier and broader economic history' (Rutten 1980: 138). The key implications involved in adopting such a view of science are that it is not necessary to insist on methodological purity in economic history, or elsewhere for that matter, and that intellectual curiosity must not be handicapped by insistence on proper techniques.

A discussion of history and new economic history is valuable for the historical geographer. It is clear that many of the recent changes, new perspectives and controversies are similar to those in human and, specifically, historical geography. The subsequent assessment of contemporary historical geography necessarily has greater meaning in the light of several parallels with these related disciplines.

CHAPTER TWO

Temporal explanation in geography

Throughout the twentieth century the academic discipline of geography, although dominated by, first, a regional paradigm and, second, a spatial analytic paradigm, has included a variety of concerns which deal explicitly with time. Temporal interests include cultural geography, innovation diffusion studies, time geography, arguments favouring a process–form approach and historical geography. This chapter focuses on each of these interests, with the exception of historical geography which necessarily merits more detailed and separate consideration. A number of actual and potential links between these several interests and historical geography are emphasized. The basic theme being developed here relates to the presence in geography of a wide variety of temporal interests which are, in principle, valuable emphases for the historical geographer to exploit. This theme is especially evident in consideration of process–form reasoning.

GEOGRAPHY: A SPATIAL SCIENCE

Prior to discussing the temporal approaches it is necessary briefly to review the prevailing twentieth-century interpretations of geography, interpretations which are essentially non-temporal. Until the 1950s academic geography was dominated by a regional approach which effectively excluded explicit temporal analysis. Exceptions to this statement were limited but significant and included the work of Darby (1951), Dion (Prince 1971), the Land Use Survey Reports in Britain (Stamp 1937–47), and Stamp (1964). This latter work focused explicitly on 'the hand of man in shaping the scenery as we actually observe it today' (Stamp 1964: xiii) and recognized that land-use evolution was a continuous process. Responsibility for the collective decision to focus largely on regional matters is typically placed with Hartshorne (Sauer 1941). Hartshorne is considered to have been strongly influenced by Hettner who, in turn, is thought to have been responsible for disseminating the Kantian view of geography as a distinctly different, exceptionalist, discipline which was defined by method rather than by subject-matter. Broek (1965: 14) is quite categorical in this respect: 'From Kant onward, this view has been stated and restated as the fundamental justification for geography. In the United States Richard Hartshorne – following the German geographer Alfred Hettner – made it the cornerstone of his learned treatise.' Two comments are now needed. First, such a view of the development of the regional approach is not acceptable to all geographers (May 1970). Second, there was another discipline which was afforded an exceptionalist position, namely history. History analysed facts as they related through time. Geography analysed facts as they related in space. The legacy of Kant is, then, threefold: a separation of geography from the wider body of sciences which was perhaps responsible for the weak links between geography and other disciplines prior to the 1950s; an explicit emphasis on space which was subsequently interpreted as a regional interest; and a separation of geography and history which reinforced the interpretation of geography as a discipline which neglected time. Although the above remarks are quite general the simple logic appears appropriate. Prior to the 1950s a regional view prevailed which largely omitted time. During the 1950s this view was challenged and overcome by an alternative interpretation of geography as spatial analysis which also largely omitted time. Spatial analysis remains as a dominant view of contemporary geography, although it has been challenged by behavioural and structuralist revolutions, revolutions which have proved unsuccessful (R. J. Johnston 1979: 176–7). Thus, the two interpretations which have effectively dominated twentieth-century geography have both excluded temporal analyses. Reference has already been made to Sauer's (1941: 1) criticisms of regional geography without time and there have also been criticisms of spatial science for the similar fault (King 1969).

Geography, then, has been and continues to be typically interpreted as a regional or spatial discipline. The transition from the regional to the spatial paradigm provided no stimulus for any further growth of temporally oriented geographies. The pioneering article by Schaeffer (1953) maintained the non-temporal stance in geography and an article by Watson (1955) regarded geography as a discipline in distance.

TEMPORAL EXPLANATIONS: AN INTRODUCTION

The principal purpose of this section is to place the above remarks in a proper perspective. It is evident that geography has typically excluded time, but it would be grossly misleading to suggest that temporal concerns have not played a role in geography. Traditional cultural and historical geography have been relatively constant components of the discipline as any historical account emphasizes (R. J. Johnston 1979). But the temporal interest goes beyond these two established, if not dominant, themes. In addition to the interests in innovation diffusion, time geography and process to form analyses already noted, there have also been many appeals made on behalf of a temporally oriented geography. This section reviews such appeals and thus serves to introduce the discussions of temporal interests as well as placing the previous section in perspective.

According to Daly (1972: 77–96) there have been four approaches to the study of time in geography. The first approach identified was labelled 'traditional' and referred to both historical studies and equilibrium analyses. These were not truly temporal for they emphasized the description of past landscapes, with the study of particular things being of prime importance. Daly (1972: 78) noted the use of comparative statics for describing systems at specific times. The second approach was labelled 'time and standard techniques' and involved the use of any standard geographical procedure with the addition of time. Although little used, dynamic programming is one such adaptation. The third approach utilized stochastic processes and treated systems, as they developed through time, as the outcome of probabilistic factors. Markov chains represent one such interest. A fourth and final approach involved time series where the aim was to determine trends and fluctuations from trends in a given set of temporal data. In analyses of time series the aim was to fit a model to the data and to predict future trends; spectral analysis was a suggested technique.

It is possible that few other writers would choose to categorize temporal interests in the manner Daly (1972) has indicated, but it is nevertheless an interesting classification with its recognition of a static historical geography, to be discussed in Chapter 3, and the emphasis placed on probabilistic temporal analyses. This second point has received considerable attention in geographic writing. Wilkie (1974: 9–10) distinguished between structure of change and process of change. The former referred to the analysis of spatial structures at different points in time, whereas the latter implied an analysis of variable interaction in an effort to discover the causes of change in structures. It was this latter approach which was favoured and which was seen to involve probabilistic reasoning. In general, proposals advocating temporal explanations have also been proposals for such reasoning. Pred (1969: 5–8) noted that static conditions never prevail, and that new behaviours appear and previous behaviours disappear. Accordingly, a behavioural matrix was advocated to assist in gaining insight into these changes. In a series of articles Curry (1964, 1966, 1967) has proposed that the time factor is the key to an understanding of spatial forms. With reference to location problems Curry (1967: 237) argued for the intriguing combination of theory and history but noted difficulties:

While it is both profitable and easy to call for a dynamic approach to location theory, it is extremely difficult to answer this challenge. Obviously theory calls for some form of logical structure and although it is possible to conceive a synoptic logical structure for, say, a central place system, there is no reason to believe that this structure could have evolved by any conceivable process. And since today's data has no special relevance in an historical process, the synoptic pattern must be logical at all stages of its growth.

Another writer, Olsson (1969: 219) argued for studies of change and recognized that all spatial forms are subject to continuous change. In similar vein Harvey (1967, 1968, 1969) emphasized that all cultural and economic systems evolved, and produced arguments in favour of a geography concerned with spatial system change through time. Harvey (1967: 549–50) noted the absence of studies of change in human, including historical, geography – an absence which was criticized because form evolution was not haphazard and hence principles of spatial evolution could be developed. One major problem in developing such evolutionary analyses was the scale issue (Harvey 1968).

The above discussion indicates that, while geographers largely exclude time, it is not because of a lack of advice to the contrary. More recent advocates of temporal explanations include Berry (1973), Amedeo and Golledge (1975), Eichenbaum and Gale (1971) and Sack (1972). Many of these arguments have also included an explicit advocacy of process–form reasoning, and hence details are presented later in this chapter. Hopefully, enough has been said to demonstrate the long-standing and continuing interest of geographers, other than those characteristically labelled as historical, in time. The following three sections appraise three areas of geographic concern which focus on time. The first, cultural geography, has always had close links with historical geography and has operated as a substantive part of geography throughout the twentieth century. The second, innovation diffusion, has origins in cultural geography but received a major stimulus from rural sociology and from the work of Hagerstrand (1967). A related theme, time geography, is a more recent interest in geography. The third area of concern relates to those arguments favouring a process–form approach for explanation, an approach which is by definition temporal. Many of the ideas noted in this current section represent the beginnings of such arguments.

CULTURAL ANALYSES

Cultural geographers have traditionally focused interest within five themes according to Wagner and Mikesell (1962). The five were culture, culture area, cultural landscape, culture history and cultural ecology, and two of these themes were concerned explicitly with time. Cultural landscape studies investigated 'a heritage of many eras of natural evolution and of many generations of human effort' (Wagner and Mikesell 1962: 11). Studies of culture history were necessary because 'behind most culture areas of today lies a long succession of different cultures and cultural developments' (Wagner and Mikesell 1962: 13). Subsequent writings have emphasized the interest in cultural landscape; Jordan and Rowntree (1979: 28) included it as one of five themes of interest and noted that, 'much of what meets the eye in that landscape comes from vanished causal forces and circumstances'. Culture history, on the other hand, is somewhat more difficult to identify in recent writing, with the major concerns belonging to historical geography and to more specialized fields such as innovation diffusion. Perhaps the principal contributions to culture history have been offered by Kniffen (1951a, 1965) in a series of studies concerned with the origins and diffusion of selected culture traits.

20

A principal contemporary interest of the cultural geographer which deals directly with change is, then, the study of landscape. This is a long-standing interest which was most clearly expressed in North American geography by Sauer (1963). For many, the study of landscape might be most correctly identified as cultural–historical geography and the usual identification of Sauer with both cultural and historical geography gives weight to this suggestion. Many cultural landscape analyses have also been concerned with the identification and determination of regions. Pioneering work by Meinig (1965) focused on the evolution of the Mormon region of the United States and was convincingly presented in a process to form methodology. A regionalization of the United States by Zelinsky (1973a) was accomplished by means of a discussion of historical factors.

One aspect of this theme has engendered some controversy. According to Harvey (1969: 408–16) the interest in time advanced one step too far with the suggestion that genetic explanations of landscape were the only relevant explanations. The significance of a genetic explanation can only be assessed in the light of stated objectives; if the aims of research are to analyse genesis then clearly a genetic approach is appropriate. Contemporary cultural geography acknowledges the necessary limitations of any one mode of explanation, and the problems of both historicism and of the genetic fallacy are of little significance.

Within geography during the twentieth century the interests of cultural geographers have maintained a consistent emphasis on temporal explanations, particularly relating to landscape studies. A second area of more limited impact has been culture history, although one aspect of that impact has assumed an independent significance resulting from the stimuli provided by particular individuals and by related disciplines. This is the area of innovation diffusion.

INNOVATION DIFFUSION

Studies of innovation diffusion were one component of traditional cultural geography, but received much development during the 1960s in association with the advances in spatial analysis. Several review articles provided a summary of the development of this interest (Brown and Moore 1969; Gould 1969). This section appraises the innovation diffusion emphasis as one aspect of temporal explanation in geography.

The combined spatial and temporal interests of innovation diffusion have often been noted (Brown 1966: 2; Gould 1969: 1). Two types of diffusion were isolated by Brown (1966: 2–3), namely, relocation and expansion diffusion. In both instances the diffusion processes operate in both space and time dimensions. Unquestionably the crucial influence determining the character of diffusion research was the pioneering work of Hagerstrand (1967). Innovation adoption was conceptualized as being the result of a learning process operating through time. This idea was in close accord with developments in the rural

21

sociology literature. Rogers (1962: 17) included time as one of four crucial elements in the innovation diffusion process. There is, however, an important distinction between incorporating time into analyses by virtue of the introduction of temporal processes and actually achieving a clear understanding of the processes involved. The diffusion literature characteristically analysed forms as outcomes of processes or, alternatively, generated forms from hypothesized processes. While the latter technique was clearly superior there have remained a number of difficulties relating to process formulation, form generation and form assessment. More generally, Brown and Moore (1969: 148) stated that a major problem in diffusion research was the role of time and the continually changing role of each variable through time. Thus, although innovation diffusion analyses represent perhaps the most successful incorporation of time into geography outside of historical geography, the research performed failed to handle time with total success. A brief review of selected literature follows in an attempt to illustrate both the achievements and limitations of diffusion research with regard to their temporal content.

All spatial forms are somewhat dependent on previous forms and diffusion studies are able to focus on process. One example of such work is that by Bowden (1965) which closely parallels the work of Hagerstrand (1967) in developing a model of the process and proceeding to simulate diffusion forms. To simulate the location of irrigation wells surrogate data derived from information on long-distance telephone calls and barbecue attendance were employed and the probability of new locations calculated. In a somewhat different vein Pyle (1969) analysed cholera diffusion in the nineteenth-century United States with reference to the frictional effects of distance and the relation to the hierarchy of urban centres. With limited transportation and an embryonic urban system distance friction was critical, while with advancing transport technology and a more sophisticated urban system hierarchical diffusion was dominant. In addition to empirical analyses a number of authors have attempted to conceptualize the innovation diffusion process and all such attempts recognized the temporal aspect of the process (Norton 1974). The close relationship between diffusion and simulation is also a result of the ability of the simulation procedure to incorporate time. Building and running a simulation model enables observation of dynamic behaviour under controlled experimental conditions and the testing of process-generated or theory-generated hypotheses. Any simulation enables the determination of both the long-run state of the system and the sequence of development. Much of the simulation literature in geography, particularly evident during the late 1960s, was related to diffusion or other growth processes. Garrison (1962) advocated simulations of urban growth; Malm, Olsson and Wärneryd (1966) detailed procedures and Morrill (1965a) provided a substantial example. To summarize, simulation presents one viable approach to the modelling of dynamic spatial systems (Marble 1970). Although most recent work in innovation diffusion has departed from the by now traditional route pioneered by Hagerstrand (1967), and has emphasized issues of modernization for example, the contribution of diffusion and related simulation studies to historical geography has been significant. Not only have a number of historical geographic studies employed such procedures (Levison, Ward and Webb 1973; Norton 1976; Walker 1972; Widgren 1979; J. D. Wood 1974) but also the concept of process has been emphasized as an integral component of any temporal explanation.

Relationships between the new interest in time geography and historical geography are limited. Thrift (1977: 70–84) identified three varieties of time; namely, biological, psychological and socio-ecological time and noted their relations to social behaviour, to learning and to the temporal organization of society. Although Prince (1978) has considered the role of time in historical geography, it appears that the basic ideas of time geography have little to contribute to historical geography. The potential benefits of a time-geographic approach to diffusion have been succinctly noted by Carlstein (1978) who advocated viewing time and space as resources affected by innovations and also influencing innovations. This was a novel suggestion for conventional diffusion research recognized but one resource, economic wealth.

PROCESS AND FORM

In general, geographers have been singularly inactive regarding the explicit analysis of process and form. Disenchantment with static theories and static explanations, however, has resulted in an increased demand for dynamic theory. Methods of static analysis are usually unsatisfactory as means of explanation for all forms are necessarily outcomes of both previous forms and processes. 'Reference to spatial process is inescapable in any analysis of spatial structure' (Abler, Adams and Gould 1971: 60). In this sense process and form are circularly causal and a principal objection to a static analysis is the omission of process. Olsson (1969: 220) was especially clear on this point: 'the widespread dissatisfaction with geographic theory may be due to a preoccupation with spatial patterns and a neglect of small scale generating processes'. Theories which include the basic form as given are weak according to King (1969: 593) and it is preferable to develop form as a logical deduction of theory. Static form analysis is also unsatisfactory because static conditions do not typically prevail and because one determinant of present locations is past locations (Morrill 1970: 6; Pred 1969: 5).

Initial attempts to relate process and forms often proceeded by means of, first, a description of form and, second, attempting an understanding of process via form. Such a procedure has met with many objections for it represents a clear instance of the inference problem. Generalizing about process from specific form data is an uncertain route to new knowledge (Berry 1973: 3; Webber 1972: 44). The dangers of such a procedure have been most evident in point pattern analyses. The difficulty of deriving process knowledge from form knowledge was also referred to by Cliff et al. (1975: 81) with reference to the use of spectral analysis. Perhaps the earliest recognition of these issues was by King (1962) in a discussion of the term 'random', in nearest-neighbour analysis. Random forms do not necessarily imply random processes (Getis 1977: 59).

Curry (1964: 146) was categorical on the basic point: 'That a given set of premises contains logical consequences which are in agreement with reality is no guarantee that a model is itself realistic. Several quite different models may give the same result.' The inclusion of time and the use of behavioural assumptions were both firmly advocated by Curry (1967: 31–3). Olsson (1974: 52) has similarly noted that there is not a clear one-way relationship between form and process and that process cannot be analysed via form. A given form may result from a number of different processes and form analysis does not permit the detection of process; thus geographers reject form analysis *per se* and the inferential procedure of deriving process from form. Even in those situations with form descriptions at several points in time it is difficult to detect process. In general it is evident that reasoning from form to process is reasoning from effect to cause. Thus geographers have advocated process analysis but, unfortunately, the meaning of process is unclear. Abler, Adams and Gould (1971: 60 – 1) and Blaut (1961) suggested that process and form are essentially the same thing. Words commonly used in association with process are 'ongoingness' and 'change' and process may be defined as a succession of actions which occur and lead eventually to a result (Eichenbaum and Gale, 1971: 526). Studies of innovation diffusion are prime examples of process-oriented analyses, but Amedeo and Golledge (1975) argued that geographers had little knowledge of process. Processes with spatial ramifications typically generate either clustered or dispersed forms through time (Cox 1972: 197; Getis 1974: 77); however, at any one time several processes may be operating at a variety of scales. The relevance of process to studies of change was emphasized by Berry (1973: 17) with a recognition of system-maintaining, evolutionary and revolutionary processes. The need for process analyses is evident as process laws are the most complete dynamic laws and are explanations of change (Sack 1972: 66–7).

The discussion so far in this section has utilized a diverse body of literature to argue that one valuable means of temporal explanation is to discuss process first and form second. Chronologically, process precedes form. A major problem is that of arriving at the initial understanding of process. A typical procedure is to develop a process as a result of available theory, relevant empirical analyses and possibly form analysis. On the basis of information from these three sources generalizations are derived and are organized into a simplification of the process. This simplification or model is used to generate forms, often by means of simulation. The simulated are compared to the known outcomes and an assessment of the model is possible. Such a procedure is typically stochastic. This type of analysis closely accords with the scientific method as defined by Kemeny (1959); that is, induction, deduction and verification. Such an analysis does not totally remove the inference issue as inference is likely in both model development and model evaluation following outcome comparison. Again, it is the literature on diffusion which best exemplifies this type of analysis, granted with varying degrees of success. Problems of circularity are often evident. To avoid such issues it is necessary to ensure that the model is not directly related to the known forms to be simulated. Colenutt (1971: 140) observed that one major difficulty in a simulation analysis concerns the definition of probability surfaces; actual surfaces of development must not be used in probability calculation. If the process model depends directly on the form to be simulated then the analysis is circular and nothing new is learned. Colenutt (1971: 141) suggested that the urban fringe study by Morrill (1965b) and the commuter study by Taafe, Garner and Yeates (1963) both suffered from circularity and Pred (Hagerstrand, 1967: 317–18) similarly criticized the Swedish settlement study by Morrill (1965a).

A procedure named process–model–pattern was favoured by Boots and Getis (1977). A theory is selected; assumptions which constitute the theory are specified; the output of the process model is evaluated with reference to the real world, thus allowing the acceptance or rejection of the process model. Such a procedure ensures that empirical form knowledge does not influence the creation of the process model.

A number of processes have been discussed by Amedeo and Golledge (1975) including those of marketing, diffusion and economic development. These discussions demonstrated that different processes operate at different scales (Harvey 1968: 71). Scale is also a major problem in form description (Dawson 1975), but it is with regard to process that the situation is least clear. Further, non-random processes may be operating in a given area such that their combined effect is random. An understanding of process, then, necessarily implies an appreciation of all relevant processes. Again, processes change through time; neither form nor process are static. For this reason any construction of a model needs to allow for change within the model through time.

One major area of model construction relates to the use of stochastic formulations ranging from simulation analyses to specific stochastic models (Hepple 1974). This area of research is similar to the social process stochastic models exemplified by Bartholomew (1967) and to the work of Bartlett (1962). In addition there is currently a significant development of space–time modelling (Bennett 1979).

This final section has introduced an important theme and a variety of related issues. It is appropriate to conclude with a summary of the principal points emphasized.

1. Spatial forms may be interpreted as outcomes of processes.
2. Processes and forms are circularly causal. Processes produce forms which then affect subsequent processes.
3. Accordingly, to explain a form at time t_n, it is necessary to refer to both a previous form at t_{n-1}, and the intervening process.
4. Both process and forms are liable to change through time.
5. Processes operate at a variety of scales. Descriptions of form depend on scale.
6. A given form may be the consequence of a variety of processes and it is not possible to interpret process from a knowledge of form (see Fig. 2.1).
7. A stochastic process may generate more than one form (see Fig. 2.2). This

POSSIBLE GENERATING PROCESSES

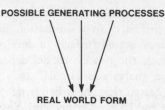

REAL WORLD FORM

Fig. 2.1 Process and form relationships – I

STOCHASTIC PROCESS

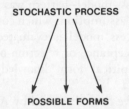

POSSIBLE FORMS

Fig. 2.2 Process and form relationships – II

point has important ramifications for it states that the real world is only one of many possibilities and may, indeed, be an unlikely outcome of the generating process. If we assume that the possible outcomes of a process are normally distributed, then this suggests that the real world may be a poor fit to the generating process. Thus geographers may profitably analyse other, more or less likely, outcomes of the process in order to facilitate comprehension of the process.

8. If a form is analysed there is no reason to anticipate that the form will display regularity in response to a supposed process. Any form analysis is only a stage in a continually changing environment. Thus, ideal states, such as that proposed by Thünen for agricultural forms, are unlikely.

9. The effects of process on form may be subject to a lag factor if the form exhibits some inertia.

10. The developing emphasis in geography which advocates dynamic process-oriented theories for the explanation of form is partly a response to a perceived need for temporal explanations, partly a response to a dissatisfaction with static analysis and partly a response to the recognition of the need for behavioural considerations.

11. A process may be defined in terms of a number of variables, all of which are related to the development of form. Processes comprise variables and an analysis which succeeds in isolating the relevant variables, indicating their interaction with one another, their changing emphasis through time and relative importance, is an analysis which is focusing on process. Specifically, process is interpreted here as a set of rules that transforms map forms through time.

CHAPTER THREE

Developments in historical geography

Historical geography has been recognized as a distinctive and substantive component of geography throughout the twentieth century. As one of many systematic specializations it has always maintained close links with the discipline as a whole and yet, at the same time, has tended to remain somewhat apart from other specializations. During the period when regional geography effectively dominated the discipline the historical geographer represented a different methodology. Again, with the relative demise of regional emphases and the advent of spatial analytic approaches, the historical geographer remained surprisingly unblemished and continued to develop along established lines. Similar remarks might be appropriate for the closely linked area of cultural geography. Notwithstanding this apparent failure to be incorporated within prevailing geographic paradigms, or possibly because of this failure, historical geography has been and continues to be characterized by a surprisingly wide variety of interpretations and methods. This chapter appraises these diverse themes within three general categories – the study of the past, the study of change through time and the study of the past in the present – and concludes with a discussion of relationships with spatial analysis. As there are many good accounts of the nature of the field available it seems superfluous to produce yet another discussion, and accordingly the aim of this chapter is to highlight key themes with detailed discussion being avoided. Considerably more emphasis is given to contemporary historical geography in Chapter 4. Reviews of the development of the field are available in Baker (1972c), Clark (1954, 1972), Darby (1962), Jakle (1971), Newcomb (1969), Prince (1967, 1969, 1971), Smith (1965) and Ward (1975a). Prior to the tripartite categorization being detailed it is appropriate to acknowledge other interpretations evident at various times.

Smith (1965: 120) noted six definitions of historical geography, two of which, the history of geography as a discipline and the history of exploration, were seen as no longer relevant. The four remaining definitions proved difficult to distinguish and were labelled the operation of the geographic factor in history, the evolution of the cultural landscape, the reconstruction of past geographies and the study of geographic change through time. A more developed

Table 3.1   Approaches to historical geography

Traditional	New departures
Temporal cross-section	Man's role in landscape change
Vertical theme	Areal diffentiation of relict features
Cross-section vertical blend	Genre de vie
Retrogressive	Theoretical model
Dynamic culture history	Pragmatic preservation of landscape legacies
Historical regional geography	Past perceptual lenses

(Adapted from Newcomb 1969)

and more complex classification was provided by Newcomb (1969) and included a total of twelve approaches, six of which were regarded as traditional and six as new departures. These approaches are listed in Table 3.1.

A third and final example of a classification of the approaches to historical geography was provided by Prince (1971). This thoughtful and stimulating summary introduced three arbitrarily defined realms of knowledge, namely, real worlds, perceived worlds and abstract worlds of the past. Within these three original categories were included the procedures listed in Table 3.2. The explicit introduction of both perceived and abstract worlds was related to developments in human geography during the 1960s with the acceptance of spatial analysis and the growing recognition of behavioural interests. Despite significant growth in both these categories it is the first category, that of real worlds of the past, which has continued to dominate historical geography.

The three reviews noted convincingly demonstrate the diverse and catholic interests of the historical geographer through to the early 1970s. Rather than utilizing one of the above, or developing a further detailed classification, a more elementary and established tripartite division is employed, a division of research into studies of the past, of change through time and of the past in the present. Studies of the past and of change through time are often regarded as the two major approaches and, further, two approaches which are relatively easy to distinguish, at least in terms of major emphasis (Baker 1972c: 91; R. J. Johnston 1979: 37; Prince 1967: 164). There has also been a tendency, at times misleading, to regard studies of the past as belonging primarily to a British school of historical geography and studies of change as belonging to a North American school. The pioneering book by Mitchell (1954: vii) entitled *Historical Geography* included references to 'a new line of approach' and was essentially a study of the changing human landscape with much emphasis placed on geographic field research. Thus Mitchell (1954: 14–15) embraced both studies of the past and studies of change: 'The great themes of the historical geographer concern then the long lasting, stable elements of the geographical scene. . . . The great themes are also those rapid changes in a region that man's increasing ability to adapt himself to his environment and to modify bring about. . . .'

Table 3.2   Real, perceived and abstract worlds of the past

Real worlds	
Past geographies	*géohistoire*
	urlandschaften
	static cross-sections
	sources and reconstructions
	narratives of changes
Geographical change	sequent occupance
	evolutionary succession
	episodic change
	frontier hypothesis
	morphogenesis of cultural landscapes
	agency of man
	rates of change
Processes of change	dynamics of change
	inadequacy of inductivism
Perceived worlds	
Reading the historical record	reading maps
	translating dead languages
	words and cultures
Historical imagination	reconstructing perceived landscapes
	geosophy
	mirrors for the times
	strange and alien worlds
Value orientations	tides in taste
	antiquarianism
	associations with the past
	preservation
Cultural appraisals	abominations
	hazards
	crowding
	possession
Worlds we have lived in	resources as cultural appraisals
	utility and knowledge
	alternative ways of life
	behavioural and cultural environments
Abstract worlds	
Patterns of spatial interaction	models of interaction
	functioning systems
	testing for connectivity
Deterministic models of process	analogies
	environmental determinism
	economic determinism
	counterfactual reconstructions
	deterministic simulation of processes
Probabilistic models of process	law and order
	orders of probability
	probabilistic simulation of processes
	post-diction

(Adapted from Prince 1971)

THE STUDY OF THE PAST

For Smith (1965: 128) this qualifies as the 'most orthodox view' and for Prince (1967: 168) it is a 'central theme'. A principal reason for the relatively wide-spread acceptance of this theme is that it did not offer any real methodological conflict to the prevailing view of geography from approximately 1920 to 1950 as the study of areal differentiation. Hartshorne (1939: 187) found this view of historical work acceptable, whereas studies of change were less easily accommodated into the regional paradigm. Writing in 1959 Hartshorne (1959: 80) quoted Hettner as follows: 'time in general steps into the background'. It is not difficult to see that a static historical geography was acceptable, a dynamic historical geography relatively unacceptable, in the context of pre-1960s geography. Hartshorne (1959: 102–7) subsequently revised the view that historical geography could not include studies focused directly on change through time following challenges to the earlier view by Sauer (1941), Whittlesey (1945), Darby (1953) and Clark (1954). The arguments of Clark (1954) may be taken as representative in that they included statements to the effect that geographers needed to be interested in past circumstances, that there was no logical dividing line between past and present and that historical geography was readily distinguishable from history in terms of subject-matter. The importance of studies of the past within historical geography was not, however, simply a function of their acceptance as a part of a regional paradigm. Such a view had been argued by Hettner (Hartshorne 1939).

The relatively early recognition of past geographies and their acceptance into the prevailing view of geography help explain the emphasis which has traditionally been placed on this approach. Studies in this category can, in principle, encompass all of the established systematic subdisciplines such that there can be historical agricultural geography and historical industrial geography, to quote just two examples. Major empirical studies included are those by Brown (1943) and Darby (1952). Both of these studies utilized the technique of the cross-section, a description and analysis of a past landscape at a particular time without substantive reference to the periods preceding or succeeding that of immediate interest. Darby (1952) was the first volume of a series of regional historical geographies aimed at reconstructing eleventh-century England based on one data source, the Domesday data. The seventh and final volume appeared in 1977 (Darby 1977). Brown (1943) described the geography of the eastern seaboard of the United States for the year 1810 as it might have been written by a geographer of that time using only pre-1810 materials. In Japan, Senda and Tanioka (1980: 18–19) suggested that

The most popular method in historical geography is the reconstruction of the cross-section of each stage of a series of landscape changes, and this fact seems to have given a special position to the branch of historical geography in Japan. Such isolation of historical geography from the other branches of geography makes it difficult to apply the historical approach to a diachronic analysis.

Although there are similarities between such approaches and a contemporary piece of geographic writing there is one fundamental distinction. Contemporary writing is relevant because of its contemporary character, whereas the creation of a past geography has necessarily to answer the criticism which questions the date selected. Typically, as in the case of the descriptions of England in 1086, the date is determined by the data source as noted above. Where data are available one logical development of the static cross-section is the presentation of some chronological sequence of cross-sections. Early examples include those by Dodge (1938) and Cumberland (1949), the latter going so far as to provide a linking narrative between cross-sections. With such developments the division between studies of the past and studies emphasizing change became less and less clear. Other well-known examples of a form of combined approach are those by Broek (1932) in a study of the Santa Clara Valley of California and Clark (1959) in a study of Prince Edward Island. For Broek (1932) the principal aim was an understanding of landscape change in a region which had experienced several different cultures and economies during a brief 200-year time-span. A first cultural landscape was related to aboriginal occupation, a second to Spanish occupation, a third to pioneer American settlement and a fourth to post-1870 American commerical horticulture. Each of the above periods was divided into two parts, an explanation of appropriate processes and a description of resultant landscapes. Studies of this type were a response to the suggestion that most landscapes remain relatively stable for a given time, followed by rapid and profound change, in turn followed by stability, and so on. Such studies, originally labelled as sequent occupance (Whittlesey 1929), represent a combination of static and process-oriented interests. One trend evident in French historical geography concerns the recognition of the regional character of the *pays*. No such focus has developed in Britain, possibly as a consequence of the dramatic landscape changes imposed by the industrial revolution and related urbanization. Rather, much British work has centred on areas of marginal land, relatively unaffected by eighteenth- and nineteenth-century developments. Darby (1973) provided six cross-sections of England between 1086 and 1900 and also discussions of the periods of intervening change. More recently Dodgshon and Butlin (1978) have provided a historical geography of Britain with chronological divisions as the essential organizing framework.

The theme of past geographies is no longer part of a major methodological squabble. It has emerged and developed as one standard practice for the historical geographer and continues to be exploited at the present. With the resolution, or simple removal, of the methodological issue there is no longer a need to justify such studies *vis-à-vis* alternative approaches; rather such studies are appropriate where required by the research problem or data.

THE STUDY OF CHANGE THROUGH TIME

The second principal concern of the historical geographer focuses on change. Initially unacceptable to some, as indicated above, such an interest has developed as paramount. The eventual dominance of studies focusing on change was, perhaps, inevitable for the exclusion of time was necessarily artificial. Prince (1967: 169) noted that all geography is concerned with change and Baker (1972c: 94) noted that there were more studies emphasizing change than there were cross-sections in British historical geography. The greatest impetus for studies of change was provided by Sauer (1963) with the pioneering statement outlining the basic tenets of landscape geography.

Much emphasis was placed on culture, as an agent of natural landscape change, operating through time to create the cultural landscape. According to Sauer (1963: 343) 'the cultural landscape is fashioned from a natural landscape by a culture group'. This transformation is summarized in Fig. 3.1. Recent

Fig. 3.1   Evolution of the cultural landscape. (Adapted from Sauer 1963: 343)

work by Duncan (1980) clearly exposed this fallacy of viewing culture as an entity above man but this, for our purposes, relatively technical distinction does not invalidate the temporal approach advocated by Sauer. A later article (Sauer 1941) was an explicit protest against what was perceived to be a neglect of historical geography. Emphasis was placed on origins and on processes of change, an emphasis which Harvey (1969) later saw as verging on the genetic fallacy. Again, it is reasonable to ignore the extreme view, that something can only be comprehended by reference to its genesis, and concentrate on the proposed emphasis of studies of changing landscapes. Undoubtedly, the most forceful statement advocating such studies was provided by Clark (1954: 73) with historical geography being defined as, 'the study of the past circumstances of, or of changes in, phenomena of concern to geography'. The emphases of this view are clear; geographical change, time and processes. Thus this approach, most dogmatically argued by Clark (1954), proved to be the dominant view of historical geography for at least two reasons. First, as an approach, a means of analysis, it proved much less restrictive than the somewhat contrived past geography. Second, it is directly concerned with causes or processes, and is, therefore, by definition more oriented towards explanation.

It is important to place the above contributions in perspective. Both Sauer and Clark followed their advocacy of a temporal approach with empirical studies and hence the influence was reinforced. Similar arguments, however, were developed elsewhere. Ogilvie (1952), for example, noted that any causal discussion necessitated a search for origins, that previous evolution was important to existing landscape and that, in regional geography, the historical past merited consideration. In somewhat similar vein Platt (1957: 190) defined geography, not historical geography, as 'the science of regional process patterns of dynamic space relations', a remarkably advanced definition which anticipated many subsequent developments in geography.

According to Planhol (1972) there has always been a close relationship between geography and history in France, and historical geography has not been seen as a separate branch of geography. French geographers have focused on temporal concerns and French historians of the *Annales* school have introduced *géohistoire*. Helmfrid (1972) emphasized the view that historical geography involved a dynamic approach to geographic problems and argued that Scandinavian work was characterized by a large number of local and regional studies. Rather similar comments are appropriate outside of Europe. During the early twentieth century geographers in Japan produced a series of studies which emphasized both change and understanding of the present (Senda and Tanioka 1980: 14–15). Historical geography in Japan has also been strongly influenced by historical writers. In India 'evolution, change, dynamics and variable character have become catchwords in analysing the geography of a region or a place' (Prithvish 1980: 26). Again, prevailing views in Czechoslovakia do not see historical geography as the geography of a past time but rather as a 'synthesis explaining the regularities of the genesis of the contemporary geosystems in all natural and, particularly, socially economic and political associations of the social evolution' (Jeleček 1980: 77).

This second, and generally preferred approach to historical geography, necessarily encompasses a wide variety of methods and techniques from the general form of the vertical theme, both in chronological and retrogressive terms,. through to the process orientation most fully developed within spatial analysis. Within the wide framework of this approach is evident most of the substantial research evident in historical geography.

THE PAST IN THE PRESENT

An approach which can be distinguished from the basic two already noted relates to the assertion that many insights into the character of past landscapes are offered by the present landscape. Here the aim is to utilize the present as a means of understanding the past. The retrogressive method permits the reconstruction of the past from the present by means of proceeding from the relatively well-known present to the less well-known past. An example is the study of field systems by Baker (1966). A principal advocate of this necessity to read history backwards was Bloch of the *Annales* school. Jager (1972) noted that historical geography in Germany used a predominantly retrogressive method.

This approach also includes studies of relict features in the contemporary landscape without any direct concern for the relevant former landscapes. As

Prince (1969: 113) noted, all features in present landscapes are relict features according to one interpretation. Other interpretations are more limited (Prince 1971: 33). For the study of relict features a retrospective approach may be appropriate for it involves studies of the past as a means of elucidating present conditions with the focus being on the present. This method is closely comparable to the German approach to cultural geography which emphasizes genesis and evolution (Jager 1972: 46).

Also included within this theme are matters of conservation and preservation (Lewis 1975; Newcomb 1967; Prince 1982). Changing views of antique landscape features were discussed by Prince (1982) with reference to the English county of Hertfordshire. Stages recognized were a renaissance phase from 1540 to 1680, a phase of romantic antiquity to 1830 and a phase since 1830 which emphasized the past for its own sake. The renaissance phase included country-house development and land reclamation and inspired an interest in local history. The phase of romantic antiquity saw the creation of sham ruins and a variety of building styles. The final phase lead to the desire to protect all relict features.

RELATIONSHIPS TO SPATIAL ANALYSIS

The impact of spatial analytic developments upon the work of the historical geographer has not been especially evident although it was anticipated by several writers. Smith (1965: 139–40) expected an increasing use of statistics and theory, especially in historical urban studies; a tendency for new trends to transgress the boundaries of the many views of historical geography; and an explicit attempt to focus on process as a means of understanding geographical change through time. Prince (1969: 116–17) referred to the use of models in historical geography and, specifically, to the creation of abstract worlds. These ideas were more fully developed in Prince (1971: 44–58) which contained discussions of such spatial analytic procedures as network models, gravity models, simulations and probability models. The movement away from description and towards interpretation is now even evident in regional historical geographies with the subject becoming more general and less particular (Dodgshon and Butlin 1978). Such a trend is in close accord to the *Annales* school of history. Finally, in a review of Australian historical geography, Williams (1970: 412–13) referred to the value of diffusion and simulation studies. The majority of work referred to by such writers was not typically accomplished by geographers known for historical work; rather it was accomplished by geographers who focused on a temporal or historical aspect of work which was essentially rooted elsewhere in the discipline. This is not to imply that such work does not properly belong within a review of historical geography, rather it implies that such work was stimulated from elsewhere in geography and accomplished by workers from elsewhere in geography. Haggett (1965: 60) reviewed diffusion and simulation and concluded that there were 'exciting simulation possibilities of direct interest to historical geographers' in studies of physical barrier effects on settlement spread. Diffusion studies are now commonplace in historical geography and have been particularly evident in agricultural history (Emery 1976; Hellen 1972; Walton 1978) and in economic history (Colman 1968; Pomfret 1976).

In addition to the literature noted there have been two substantive discussions by historical geographers which have centred on the implications of spatial analysis. Cant (1969) produced a provocative essay concerned with the way in which historical geography was to develop in the light of the seemingly dramatic changes in geography. Four basics were established (Cant 1969: 40–1): geography is concerned with both the unique and the general; geography is concerned with a wide range of phenomena and is committed to the principle of multiple causation; order and pattern can be discovered; and, finally, geography is both a science and a social issue. Having established these four points, and added a temporal dimension to those of location and phenomena, Cant (1969: 47–9) asked how historical geographers had coped with this problem. The answer included references to cross-sections, narratives, the employment of a localized area and a limited time-span and the likelihood that research might demonstrate a generality of process. This final theme was developed into a discussion of economic growth models, systems procedures and simulation and Cant (1969: 54) concluded that historical geographers must learn to speak two languages and reconcile two research moralities. It seems appropriate to mention that such a need has not been evident and thus the impact of spatial analysis has not been as dramatic as expected.

A second contribution which attempted to discuss historical geography within a framework prompted by the emergence of a scientific geography during the 1960s was that by Koroscil (1971). This pioneering attempt to incorporate the field within a wider scientific geography pursued the following stages: philosophy, science, philosophy of science, philosophy of natural sciences, philosophy of social sciences, unity of method – natural and social sciences, philosophy and methodology – geography – history – historical geography, historical sources, geographical interpretations of historical sources and research technique problems. Although designed as a teaching course, this framework clearly indicated a direct concern with a sound philosophical and methodological basis for the subject-matter of historical geography. Again, it seems appropriate to mention that courses are rarely structured in this way if, as seems reasonable, journal and textbook literature are any indication. A third study advocating an increased scientific content was that by Hepple (1967: 42) which suggested an integration of model-building and historical geography for future work. Although French (1972: 124) noted that most historical geography in Russia was accomplished by historians, recent initiatives focus directly on the theme of historical changes in spatial organization (Annenkov 1979) which is in close accord with a spatial analytic interpretation.

This section has noted some relatively early statements advocating the employment of methods associated with spatial analysis to the subject-matter of historical geography and has briefly reviewed two explicit studies which attempt to relate the two interests. The overall conclusion is that the relationship is a limited one. One clear indication of this limited effect is that, in 1976, Edwards and Jones (1976: 188–9) found it necessary to re-emphasize the value of quantitative techniques and the value of a theoretical approach.

CHAPTER FOUR

The present status of historical geography

Determining the present character of historical geography is not an easy task. Even a cursory appraisal of the literature indicates a remarkable diversity of approaches and interests, a diversity which appears to have been increasing in recent years with the emergence of several new methodologies and Baker (1979a: 560), in the third of a series of brief reviews, goes so far as to suggest 'a new beginning'. This chapter comprises four sections. First, a brief discussion of the nature of historical geography is presented on the basis of recent developments. Second, developments involving data, theory and quantification are summarized. Third, several alternatives to a positivist emphasis are presented and appraised. The final section presents the view that historical geography may be legitimately interpreted as the evolution of spatial form and includes discussions of process, simulation and counterfactuals.

WHAT IS HISTORICAL GEOGRAPHY?

The character, content and even the validity of historical geography have long been questioned. Zelinsky (1973b) revived the debate concerning the credibility of the field by asserting that there was no logical basis for historical geography and that historical geographers could be better described by other terms. The basic justification for these two claims was that all geography, including historical, is spatial and that the historical geographer did not ask a set of questions distinctive from those of the wider body of researchers. Baker (1974) responded to these assertions by noting that they were not original and were open to logical criticism; Jakle (1974) responded by defining the field as the study of the geographic past, and Moodie, Lehr and Alwin (1974) responded by stating that it was a broadly synthesizing discipline. These somewhat varied reactions confirm the suggestion of Ward (1975a: 82) that there has been little evidence of a new methodology, certainly not of a new and accepted methodology. A more dogmatic claim was made by Dickson (1972). Historical geography was seen as fundamental to the discipline as a whole in that it offered the basis for valid probabilistic explanations. In rather similar vein, Goldenberg (1972: 421) argued that: 'The apparent conflict of views and definitions of the concept of "historical geography" can be resolved only on the condition of recognizing a unified historical geography (both "geographical" and "historical") as an independent scientific discipline located in the transition zone between geography and history.'

Thus, questioning the viability of historical geography as a legitimate area of research is not too difficult a task because of the many and varied interpretations of the field. These various interpretations result from four factors. First, the internal differences within the field itself, for example the alternative views of a study of the past or a study of change. These differences are briefly described in Chapter 3. Second, the very different interpretations of historical geography in different countries. In France, it has not been seen as a separate area of study and has not developed any specific methods, rather it has been an integral component of human geography. The prevalent view in Germany has seen it as closely tied to a wide variety of disciplines and hence an area of interdisciplinary work. An association with agricultural and settlement studies has characterized Scandinavian historical geography. Overall, there is little evidence of any well-accepted interpretation of historical geography, either within or between countries. Third, the influences of other disciplines such as history, economic history, sociology and anthropology and, indeed, physical geography. French (1972: 115) noted that in the USSR historical geography has been seen as one subdivision of physical geography. Figure 4.1 suggests some of the possible impacts of these related disciplines. Fourth, the influences of the

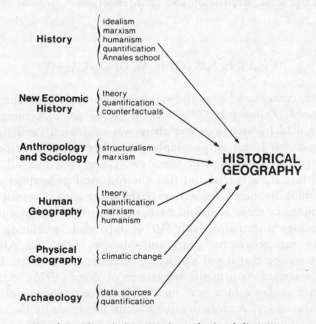

Fig. 4.1 Historical geography and related disciplines

geographic discipline which necessarily encourage divergent views. During the early 1970s, for example, some writers were advocating a scientific approach while others were rejecting theory and quantification. Jones (1974), in a book review, advocated the use of the new geography and of new economic history as a means of achieving explanations. Ward (1975a), on the other hand, was critical of the available theoretical concepts. When it is considered that the early 1970s were also a time of developing non-positivistic methodologies the confused nature of historical geography is all too clear. Of necessity, the question posed in the heading for this section has not been answered. Rather, a foundation has been established for discussions of the present status of historical geography, discussions which serve to emphasize the continuing diversity of the field.

TECHNICAL AND CONCEPTUAL ADVANCES

Data

The historical geographer faces some difficult problems because of the separation of researcher and data, problems which have long been recognized. It is necessary to be aware of the motivation behind past data collection and the best general advice proffered is 'to read as widely as possible about the source to be exploited, concerning the administration and collection of the data and the purpose for which it was intended' (Baker *et al*. 1970: 16). The importance of primary data and related empirical analysis cannot be overemphasized, particularly in British work where one recent book is focused entirely on source material (Morgan 1979). Elsewhere in Europe data have also been instrumental in determining research orientations. With reference to Scandinavia, Helmfrid (1972: 63) noted: 'The most typical feature of historical geographical research is that it has to rely upon historical evidence, either directly or indirectly man-made features of landscape, maps or written sources, more or less randomly preserved and inherited from past generations.' Senda and Tanioka (1980: 19) noted four important Japanese data sources, namely archives and maps, land registers, placenames and statistical data. In India, available literary sources have proved a valuable source of data and stimulated much research (Prithvish 1980: 27). It seems clear that historical geographers generally have typically recognized the overriding importance of data. For American research, however, Ernst and Merrens (1978: 277) noted that the use of primary data was relatively recent despite the earlier recognition by Friis (1975) of the enormous potential of the National Archives in Washington. Somewhat similarly, one major data source for western Canadian work, the records of the Hudson's Bay Company, have been acknowledged as such and utilized only in recent years. Despite some use of these data, Moodie (1977: 273) was able to conclude that 'the full potential of this massive corporate archives for historical geographical research is yet to be realized'.

One recent study which was explicitly concerned with the problems posed by data referred to expansion of the Russian frontier between 1600 and 1800 (Shaw 1976). While it proved relatively straightforward to plot major settlement and economic advances, more detailed matters were necessarily unanswered. The implication of such a state of affairs goes beyond the mere failure to complete the work for 'lack of historical evidence frequently precludes the final acceptance or rejection of a theory or hypothesis apart from the most simplistic' (Shaw 1976: 81).

Few historical geographers have chosen to focus explicitly on data problems. Indeed, as much research has been conditioned by something akin to 'hunt the source', the situation results wherein the data employed can always safely be described as the 'best available' (Harley 1973: 71). Harley (1982) advocated more explicit study of historical evidence and this was a call which seems likely to be respected. Discussions of data have often incorporated reference to the apparent dilemma regarding the use of data and the use of theory. It appears that historical geographers have characteristically found it necessary to emphasize one or the other, but rarely both (Clark 1975b). However correct such a suggestion may be, there are no sound reasons why that state of affairs will remain. Most research involves, at some stage: data from which generalizations may be inferred and used in theory construction; theories from which specific data-oriented hypotheses are derived; and finally, data used to test the generated hypotheses. Emphasizing one at the expense of the other is inappropriate for a complete research analysis although it may well be valid at a given stage of analysis.

In a somewhat similar fashion to historians, historical geographers have often been overly dependent on data sources. The reliance on a single source is less evident today with the increasing influence of the *Annales* school and their focus on a diversity of data. Further, the handling of data is much easier today with the potentially widespread use of computers to perform the functions of data storage and data retrieval. A discussion of historical evidence by Prince (1980: 231) emphasized that the stock of archival material is continually changing, with some material being lost and other material being discovered. British historical geography in particular is replete with studies based on, or dealing directly with, data sources (see, for example, Adrian 1977; Glasscock 1975: Kain 1979).

Theory

Ambivalence is perhaps the best single word to summarize the attitude of historical geographers towards theory construction and the use of theory. At various times and by various writers theory has been regarded as opposed to empirical work, as opposed to description, as opposed to synthesis and as opposed to data-based studies. Following the widespread acceptance, in principle, of theoretical work in geography, historical geographers reacted by disagreeing. A strong argument in favour of theory was presented by Baker *et al*. (1970: 19–22) responding to developments in geography apparently aimed at the creation of dynamic location theories. Such favourable arguments emphasized the use of systems analysis, the advantages of mathematical formulation, the merits of analytical techniques and the pressing need to uncover generalizations about past processes. The need for theory was given strong support by Harvey (1970: 265) with the comment that 'historical geography can only progress through a careful integration of theory and empiricism'. This quote has since been employed by Moodie (1971) and by Edwards and Jones (1976) to support specific arguments, but it is not a statement which has been adhered to by the majority of practitioners. This is not surprising, for the expected upsurge of theoretical work in geography as a whole did not materialize during the 1970s with Harvey's (1969: 486) exhortation to geographers concerning the construction of theory receiving limited response. In this respect historical geographers have fallen behind human geographers. This failure to develop a theoretically oriented subject-matter reflects two factors. First, the very real practical and conceptual difficulties in constructing theories, particularly in a human discipline. Second, the quite separate rejection of many of the basic principles of theory and the related positivist approaches in favour of alternative methodologies. Thus, theory construction has been retarded because it is difficult and because other approaches are available. It has not been totally rejected and, most certainly, has not been proven invalid, rather it has been but little attempted. There has been a tendency for historical geographers to avoid theory *per se* and only to use theory in the analysis of empirical problems (Harley 1973: 72). A review by Wilson (1980: 211) argued that recent developments in theory in human geography have been significant and 'that there is now a very rich basis of ideas in theoretical geography'. Many of these developments stem from other social sciences and also relate to either a mathematical or a marxist viewpoint. Overall, the developments discussed by Wilson (1980) do not appear to reflect the growth which was anticipated in the late 1960s for the historical emphasis within human geography (Harvey 1967: 1969).

The one area in which theory construction has been explicitly criticized is in arguments advocating geographical synthesis (Harris 1971), idealism (Guelke 1971) and structuralism (Gregory 1976). Harris (1971) was an early and strong critic of the notion of geography as a formal deductive science, pointing out that the very act of creating theory violated the content of geography which was seen as a wide variety of phenomena and their interrelationships. Geography was compared to history: 'Both are broad synthesizing fields concerned primarily with the particular' (Harris 1971: 163). Studies of particular issues, for example the twelfth-century spread of European settlement in Europe when treated as but one example of a diffusion process, defeat the logic of a geographical synthesis. These arguments have been expanded and an idealist alternative proposed by Guelke (1974) who argued that theoretical approaches have worked well in the physical sciences but not in the social sciences and history. A major difficulty in historical geography, then, has been the failure to develop laws as a result of theoretical and related empirical analyses. Rather different criticisms of a theoretically oriented historical geography have been proffered by Gregory (1976) and rely on a substantive and critical

41

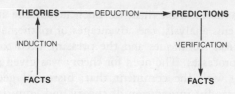

Fig. 4.2   The scientific method. (Adapted from Kemeny 1959: 81)

assessment of positivism as interpreted and exploited by geographers. One alternative proposed, structuralism, is discussed later in this chapter.

A theoretical historical geography has not, then, been without critics. Moodie and Lehr (1976) examined the dangers of a wholesale adoption of a theoretical approach and emphasized that fact and theory are inseparable, a state of affairs with which most would agree but which is not in itself any indictment of theory as a part of historical geography. It is important to place the proposed theoretical component in perspective. Theories do not thrive in isolation, they result from inductive work and, in turn, are subject to verification. Kemeny (1959: 86) provided a useful diagram of the scientific method which indicated the role of theory (see Fig. 4.2). Clearly, theoretical work is both dependent on and generates empirical work. Placed in this perspective it is appropriate to suggest that theoretical work can still contribute significantly to studies in historical geography.

Quantification

Theory and quantification are closely related. It is unfortunate that both human geographers and historical geographers have emphasized the latter at the expense of the former. Harley (1973: 71) perceived a 'hunt the technique' phenomenon in British historical geography at the same time as he also perceived a lack of interest in theory. Certainly there has not been any shortage of statistical studies by historical geographers. Baker *et al.* (1970: 18 – 19) referred to studies using linear regression, variance analysis, numerical taxonomic techniques and various non-parametric procedures. Other historical problems have been studied using graph theory (Carter 1969; Pitts 1965), network analysis (Dicks 1972) and canonical correlation (Leaman and Conkling 1975), to name but three examples. Detailed computer analyses have been accomplished by Hamshere and Blakemore (1976) with reference to English Domesday data and by Overton (1977) with reference to the handling of probate inventory data and by French historians of the *Annales* school (Le Roy Ladurie 1979). Despite the many instances of quantitative work which can be cited it is nevertheless clear that, overall, historical geographers have paid limited attention to such procedures. The reviews edited by Baker (1972a) of developments in nine regions reflect this state of affairs.

At least two quantitative procedures have been introduced into geography in connection with historical issues, namely content analysis and catastrophe theory. Content analysis is an established procedure in social science and has been advocated and employed by Moodie and Catchpole (1975) and by Hayward and Osborne (1973). The latter research studied the effect of the mass migration of 1847 from Britain to Upper Canada, specifically Toronto, and showed that the migration was most clearly seen by the Toronto press as a problem at the local level. Undoubtedly the insights provided using content analysis contributed greatly to the overall understanding of the migration process. One particular advantage claimed for content analysis by Hayward and Osborne (1973: 400) is that research is performed in a relatively objective structure as rules and procedures are established at each step of the analysis. Despite this advantage and the clearly demonstrated value of the procedure, there is no evidence that content analysis is emerging as a major research tool. Certainly it has not been exploited in the manner suggested by Baker (1977: 470) to 'reveal fundamental structures in past societies' either in history or historical geography. At this time content analysis appears to be limited to very specific research issues, although when it has been employed it has proven a penetrating tool. Three general uses are apparent. First, it can be used to describe the content of source materials, even when these materials are disorganized. Second, it can be used for purposes of hypothesis testing. Third, it can be used to generate data which can then be further investigated. A major disadvantage is that, in common with other such procedures, the technique does pose limitations on what can be researched.

Arguments advocating the use of catastrophe theory are also recent following evidence of perceptive studies on, for example, medieval European town growth (Mees 1975) and favorable reviews (Amson 1974). The theme has been especially pursued by Wagstaff (1978a) in an analysis of settlement change in Greece over a period of 1,500 years. This particular work and catastrophe theory in general have been questioned by Baker (1979b). In principle the method is well suited to many issues of change through time as it is concerned with sudden change in otherwise continuous systems or what Berry (1973: 17) called revolutionary as opposed to evolutionary processes. It provides a means of conceptualizing a variety of problems and a means of modelling complex phenomena by virtue of offering a topological method of integrating discontinuities into systems analysis. Given that historical geographers are explicitly concerned with landscapes and changing landscapes the technique is clearly relevant. It is necessary at the outset to be able to model the process being analysed and it is this requirement which may limit further applications.

A further area of potential interest to the historical geographer is that of space–time modelling. Although essentially one aspect of specific quantitative research, these procedures are clearly relevant in historical analyses. Many systems in which non-linear and dynamic behaviour are important require explicit mathematical modelling, with differential equations being appropriate where change is seen to be continuous and difference equations where it is appropriate to regard change as discrete. Among recent literature Bennett and Haining (1976) provided an introduction to space–time modelling concepts, Cliff (1977) provided an appraisal of time-series methods and Bennett (1975) discussed an empirical example. Bennett (1975) was primarily concerned with the spread and growth of population in north-west England between the years 1891 and 1971 by means of relating the population at a given time to that of an earlier time and allowing for births and deaths. Results showed that the evolving spatial forms were dominated by long-term temporal dependencies. Studies of this type have as one goal the building of spatial forecasting and policy models. Although these quantitative advances are not the responsibility of historical geographers they are of direct relevance to the field. Such advances are temporal not only historical, in the sense that predictions may be incorporated as well as analyses of past change.

The close links between the *Annales* school and historical geography might have been expected to prompt some quantitative work as might the new economic history of the United States. However, both of these have been subject to some criticism and neglect. Cobb, a British historian, has been critical of the quantification of the *Annales* school (Prince 1977) and Plumb (1972) has deplored Braudel's use of statistics. Reviews by historical geographers of *Annales* work have been characteristically favourable although the quantitative content is not typically singled out for approval. Nor has *Annales* work resulted in significant advances in French historical geography and, indeed, Planhol (1972: 31) noted that it 'seems to be in large measure a residual discipline', despite the example of the works of Dion. Reviews of American and Canadian work by Clark (1972) and Harris (1967) respectively do not reflect the advances in new economic history which had begun in the late 1950s. Rather it has been characteristic in North American literature to criticize quantitative work (Clark 1972: 136–7). A review of research by Conzen (1980), however, commented favourably on quantitative work and also recognized the paucity of such work.

Other advances

In addition to developments in the areas of data, theory and quantification there are several other trends which merit mention. Glottochronological techniques were discussed by L. J. Wood (1974) using a Kenyan example to identify origins, routes and rates of diffusion. The value of phosphate analysis, the systematic analysis of phosphate rates of soil, was demonstrated by Joachim and Hambloch (1977) in a study of a deserted medieval town. Similarly, the value of remote sensing procedures has been indicated by Newcomb (1970). These and other archaeological techniques are clearly useful where the historical problem is suitable. Indeed there are many close ties between contemporary archaeology and historical geography, ties particularly evident in spatial archaeological research. Techniques developed within the spatial analytic school of geography have been convincingly introduced to archaeology (Hodder and Orton 1976). Work by Danks (1977) on medieval and post-medieval artefact distributions at a regional scale is suggestive of a new area of historical geographic research based on largely unfamiliar data sources. Work on abandoned settlements by Eidt and Woods (1974) and by Eidt (1975) was also strongly supportive of combining geographic and archaeologic approaches.

In common with other aspects of geography there are indications of an increasing awareness of the need to ensure that historical geography becomes more relevant, both environmentally and socially. To what extent such an aim is likely to be fulfilled is difficult to anticipate. By definition the field is less concerned with the present than are other aspects of geography although the possibility of prediction remains (Cliff 1977). Piellusch (1975) outlined the need for an applied historical geography and noted that many contemporary developments have their roots in past decisions. One example of applied work is that by de Vorsey (1973) dealing with Florida's seaward boundary. A directory of applied work is now available (Association of American Geographers 1977). Although substantive studies are limited it is probable that there is to be an increasing emphasis on problem-solving.

One further advance which might be expected to have ties with historical geography is the emergence of time geography. A set of concepts is being developed which aims to make it practicable to incorporate time with space and thus render void the possibly artificial distinction between form and process. Among many recent contributions to this theme are the three edited volumes by Carlstein *et al.* (1978) which include but one contribution from a historical geographer (Prince 1978). A closely related growth of the study of time *per se*, a chronogeographical view (Parkes and Thrift 1980), explicitly omits historical geography. It is not at all certain that the concepts being developed in these two approaches are to have any major influences upon historical geography.

ALTERNATIVES TO POSITIVISM

A disenchantment with positivism and related theoretical and quantitative approaches has already been noted and is evident both within human and historical geography. King (1976: 295) specified two principal difficulties with the geographic use of positivism, namely, the failure to deal with matters of ethics and values and the failure to acknowledge marxist views. Positivism might also be faulted for assuming that the methodology of natural science can be applied to social science, for assuming that the ultimate aim of research is the derivation of laws and theories, and for assuming that the knowledge generated is value free. More developed criticisms were presented by Guelke (1978) relating to both positivism itself and to its employment by geographers, and prompted Guelke (1978: 53) to note: 'The dissatisfaction of many geographers at the level of understanding achieved in the application of statistical techniques and *a priori* models to geographic phenomena has led them to explore alternatives to positivism.'

Perhaps the earliest and most easily accommodated criticism of positivism was quite simply that the theories being developed were not good theories by any criteria and that explanations were not readily forthcoming. Human geographers responded to this criticism by expounding a behavioural approach, based on psychological and sociological concepts, which centred on human perceptions and decision making. However, the work accomplished in this area proved to be very close to earlier positivist work (R. J. Johnston 1979: 121). Subsequent methodological advances have largely rejected such behavioural work and have advocated phenomenological approaches, idealism and structuralism and related marxist approaches. The remainder of this section outlines the various alternatives to positivism, indicating their intellectual heritage and noting available conceptual and empirical contributions.

Perception and behaviour

'Every day all over the world, men are making decisions which lead to transformations of the earth environment. Although the impact of an individual decision may be small, the cumulative effect of all such decisions is enormous, for both the number of people and the technological power at the command of each is greater than ever before and is growing rapidly' (Saarinen 1974: 252). Any cultural landscape is the end-product of a large number of individual decisions, each made under different circumstances and for very different reasons. To gain insight into the complex processes of landscape creation, historical geographers may look at the factors influencing behaviour; in short, they analyze the perceived environment. The importance of subjective views of the environment has been acknowledged for a long time, but it is only since the 1960s that environmental perception has become a major research orientation. Two early statements were provided by Wright (1947) and by Kirk (1951). Wright (1947) discussed the meaning of *terra incognitae* and emphasized that, because knowledge can be inferred from facts, there are no true *terra incognitae* today. Three imaginative processes were introduced, namely promotional, intuitive and aesthetic, and the latter was explained as follows: '. . . a geographer may portray a place or region . . . with aesthetic imagination in selecting and emphasizing aspects of the region that are distinctive or characteristic' (Wright 1947: 6). A third major contribution was the introduction of the term 'geosophy' meaning the study of geographic knowledge: '. . . it covers the geographical ideas, both true and false, of all manner of people . . .' (Wright 1947: 12). Kirk (1951: 159) developed similar arguments and related them directly to historical geography: 'In as much as in historical geography we are concerned with the behavior of human groups in relation to environment it behoves us to reconstruct the environment not only as it was at various dates but as it was observed and thought to be. . .'.

Despite these two pioneering statements and some appropriate empirical work by historical geographers (Brown 1943; Darby 1948) the major thrust of behavioural work occurred in close relation to spatial analysis and tends, accordingly, to have received similar criticisms. Work within historical geography has maintained a relatively straightforward view of perception and behaviour emphasizing images, image-makers, changing environmental perceptions and the creation of distorted perceptions (Cameron 1974; J. A. Johnston 1979; Kelly 1970; Ruggles 1971). Despite the real success of this type of literature, it would be misleading to suggest that a coherent viewpoint has emerged which represents an effective and viable alternative to positivism.

However, it has led to the emergence of several relatively distinct views with a common focus on perception, decision-making and humanism. Much of the impetus has stemmed directly from historical geographers, particularly that relating to idealism. These alternatives are now discussed.

Phenomenological approaches

Phenomenology may be interpreted as a legitimate alternative to positivism which emphasizes that there are relevant non-quantifiable sources and that a subjective viewpoint is quite appropriate to research (Billinge 1977: 66). Whereas positivism insists on a separation of facts and value, no such separation is required by a phenomenological outlook. Initially advocated by Relph (1970) and developed by Mercer and Powell (1972) and Tuan (1974), pheomenology was seen as a humanistic interest focusing on people and their lives with the ultimate aim of arriving at a clearer understanding of these matters. Although this emphasis is most closely related to the humanities, including history, rather than to the social sciences, there is, as yet, little evidence of substantive empirical analyses within historical geography. Work by Powell (1970, 1977) on Australian and American settlement provided the clearest examples of a phenomenological approach.

Phenomenology entered geography as a reaction against the objectivity implied by positivism and the level of abstraction involved in theory construction. Unfortunately it has, to date, failed to develop sufficient advocates for a clear, well-defined, school of thought to have emerged. Given the difficult philosophical underpinnings, and the minimal evidence that the approach is a major advance, the reactions of the majority of historical geographers have proved unfavourable. Guelke (1978: 54), the principal advocate of a non-positivistic historical geography rejected phenomenology: 'It has power to touch our emotions but it does not give us the tools to understand or explain human behavior in an intersubjective or objective way.' Gregory (1978a: 166), another major critic of positivism, was also critical of phenomenology because, 'it ignores the material imperatives and consequences of social actions'. Baker (1978: 497) referred to positivism and phenomenology as extremes. Thus, analysing human behaviour in terms of actual experiences appears unlikely to emerge as other than a peripheral approach for historical geography.

Idealism

Idealism is discussed separately from phenomenology although Billinge (1977: 56) equated the two. Guelke (1978) chose to discuss these approaches separately, as did Hay (1979), despite the common interests of an opposition to positivism and a shared emphasis on humans and subjectivism. The basic position of idealism is relatively well known to historical geographers because of an explicit and established use in history and because of the well-articulated advocacy of Guelke (1971, 1974, 1975, 1976a, 1977, 1978). However well argued, the approach has not been readily accepted by historical geographers.

For example, Gregory (1976) rejected the approach and, in turn, advocated a structuralist view.

Guelke (1974) argued for idealism as follows. A criticism of positivist theory led to the conclusion that a non-theoretical and yet analytical and non-descriptive approach was required. Idealism satisfies these requirements, focusing on the explanation of rational actions by means of discovering the thought behind the action. The evolution of a human landscape is explained in terms of rethinking the thought of those responsible. Guelke (1978: 54) wrote: '. . ., an idealist analysis will focus on the beliefs and ideas behind individual and group actions, . . .'. There is a major distinction between the explanation of human behaviour and other phenomena, a distinction not made by the positivist. There is also a distinction between the emotional identification required by the phenomenologist and the understanding, or *Verstehen*, required by the idealist. Despite the clear and frequent claims in support of idealism there is, again, little evidence of substantive empirical work in this vein. Rather there have appeared a number of serious attacks on idealism which merit comment.   An early critic of idealism was Chappell (1976) who queried the very meaning of idealism and the role to be played by theory. More developed criticisms were made by Watts and Watts (1978) and the notion of a state of theorylessness was rejected. Hufferd (1980) reviewed attitudes towards idealism and offered suggestions designed to advocate the approach. Several additional difficulties need to be noted. First, idealism is centred on rational actions and irrational actions cannot, presumably, be accommodated. Second, the concern is basically with individuals, whereas many geographic problems focus on groups. Third, there is really very little indication as to how thoughts are determined and for many research problems this could be a most difficult task. It appears that, despite persistent and early (Lowther 1959) advocacy, idealism is proving unattractive to historical geographers, both positivist and non-positivist.

Structuralism

The most recent alternative to positivism in historical geography is that of structuralism, initially suggested by Gregory (1976). Rather like phenomenology, the intellectual underpinnings are complex and there is, once again, little evidence as yet of structuralist-oriented empirical work other than brief contributions by Sitwell (1976, 1980). Elsewhere in human geography structuralist thinking is evident in work on urban systems (Harvey 1973) and work on development (Brookfield 1972). Gregory (1976: 295) argued that, for historical geographers, '. . . it is only by relating the way in which individuals constitute and apprehend their phenomenal world to the deeper structures framing their actions and experiences that such experiences can be transcended'. It is this search for structures, including subconscious structures, that renders structuralism clearly distinct from both phenomenology and idealism. For some, structuralism might represent a valid meeting-ground for objective positivism and subjective phenomenology and Baker (1978: 497) wrote: 'A structuralist interpretation of the past which effectively combines these two approaches would, however, seem to be potentially more productive.' The support expressed for structuralism reflects the rather informal, yet highly successful, structural content of some *Annales* work, especially that of Braudel (1972) and Le Roy Ladurie (1974). Their view of structuralism is similar to that of economists and is related to the notion that the visible is often incomprehensible without an exploration of the hidden.

There are parallels between structuralism and systems theory, which Gregory (1976) viewed as the positivistic approach to structures, but which was criticized for the insistence on a spatial element. Structuralism in social science was expounded primarily by Piaget (1971) and by Levi-Strauss (1963) and it is to the latter that geographers have turned. Hay (1979) provided a succinct summary of the approach and emphasized that the transformation of structures was not merely a temporal process, that both major and minor structures can prevail and that structuralism is opposed to simple causation. In essence this approach is concerned with the study of relationships in order to understand the meaning of structures and their transformations. As yet, then, the search for hidden structures and their analysis has not succeeded in becoming a major methodology in historical geography. Rather similarly, the closely related marxist approach evident in urban geography remains a peripheral concern.

Other approaches

A marxist approach has also been advocated in the guise of a marxian humanism and Baker (1979a: 566) wrote: 'Marxian viewpoints might appeal to many historical geographers both because they take seriously the dynamics of historical change and of social groups in conflict and because of their overt concern for social justice.' With respect to the historical geography of France Baker (1980: 76) again proposed a marxian humanist approach. This would involve perceiving geographic evolution as comprising a steadily increasing rationality of both economic and social organization. Once again, such an argument has ties to the *Annales* school, despite their continuing uneasy dialogue with marxism and their all-embracing view of history. Probably the most logical area for such research is an analysis of class struggles. There is an interesting link here with the work of the French historian Halévy (1971). Halévy proposed that one religion, namely Methodism, incorporated attidues to work which the industrial classes adopted in the nineteenth century. These attitudes, specifically that of individual discipline, in turn prevented the growth of revolutionary ideas. A link between catastrophe theory and marxism was noted by Day and Tivers (1979), as both deal with discontinuous change, although the suggested link has been criticized by Wagstaff (1980) on the grounds that marxism contains some basic weaknesses.

Harris (1978) has framed a procedure for explanation within the context of the 'historical mind' and suggested that a good example of such works is Sauer (1966). Unfortunately, most historical geography has failed to achieve such heights and it is not easy to understand how future work might do so. The historical mind needs to be merged in the past, to doubt the existence of general laws, to be aware of the motives behind individual actions, and possibly most crucially, continually to rewrite the past. However well argued, the relevance of this concept is best assessed by the historical geography which results and which successfully combats the criticism of an unsatisfactory subjectivity. In common with related phenomenological and idealist procedures this approach is subject to abuse by researchers who are inadequately prepared for their work, and there is a real possibility that only a very few studies will meet with the sort of widespread acclaim ascribed to the work of Braudel (1972).

An examination of the work of three nineteenth-century geographers, Schouw, Marsh and Reclus, prompted Olwig (1980) to criticize the view of geography as an ahistoric science. Geography was seen as integrating spatial and ecological views by means of historical studies which centre on human and environment relationships and results of the relationships. Although this view is essentially an established part of historical geography it may receive fresh impetus from the discussion provided by Olwig (1980).

THE EVOLUTION OF SPATIAL FORM

It is quite clear that there are varied and partially valid criticisms of spatial analysis, as a representative of positivism, in both human and historical geography. Phenomenology, idealism and structuralism are all opposed to positivism and are at least partly unified by this opposition. Such strong reactions against spatial analysis by historical geographers are somewhat of a surprise, for there has been but little inclination on the part of scholars to immerse themselves in the procedures of theory and quantification. It might be suggested, somewhat cynically, that the criticisms of spatial analysis are exploited and used as advantages of alternative approaches. Perhaps the principal failure of spatial science has been the failure to develop the explanatory theories presumed necessary. One reason for this failure, however, has been the exclusion of a historical component in much spatial work. Those studies in spatial analysis which have utilized time have been relatively successful (Hudson 1969; Levison, Ward and Webb 1973; Webber 1972). Perhaps the most compelling work by a spatial scientist in the area of dynamic model construction is that of Curry (1964, 1966, 1967, 1977) who has developed a series of models relating to a wide variety of empirical issues. Following developing criticisms of spatial analysis for, among other matters, the ahistorical aspect, Amedeo and Golledge (1975) provided a convincing account of temporally oriented theory development which was favourably reviewed by Langton (1977a). Unfortunately, the advocacy of time and space has not proved to be the 'pleasant surprise to many historical geographers' which Langton (1977a: 90) anticipated. Rather than being prepared to consider the merits of a temporally oriented spatial analysis, historical geographers have, characteristically, preferred to remain within mainstream historical geography or to argue for non-positivistic methodologies. This section attempts to redress this imbalance by discussing process and form, simulation and counterfactuals. Analyses which focus on such procedures and which may include a theoretical component and quantitative testing represent an extension of the conventional change-through-time approach which is enriched by the additions. Studies of spatial form evolution are seen as distinct from traditional historical geography because of the inclusion of some or all of the above characteristics. The fundamental addition is that of process–form reasoning which obliges the researcher to analyse explicitly cause-and-effect relationships in a rigorous manner. A plausible method of analysis is outlined in Table 4.1

Table 4.1   Spatial form evolution

Step I.   Definition of research problem.
Step II.   Specification of hypotheses and formulation of the process derived from theory, relevant knowledge of the region, if appropriate, and comparable studies.
Step III. The process is expressed as a set of variables changing through time.
Step IV.   Appropriate desired forms are generated by the process, possibly including counterfactual forms.
Step V.   Real and generated forms are compared, the process model evaluated and revisions made if appropriate. This final step involves the data collection and analysis required to test the process model and also to assess the related hypotheses.

Process and form

The current trend towards the construction of dynamic theories and the adoption of a process–form approach is best represented outside of historical geography although it is evident that historical geographers are in an advantageous position in any attempts at dynamic explanations. Much of the following discussion is, accordingly, closely related to the earlier account of temporal explanations in geography. Recognizing the limitations of static analyses and of inferential procedures, much recent literature has argued that the best approach to explanation is to hypothesize process and then deduce form. Such a procedure is well suited to much of the subject-matter of historical geography. Harvey (1967) advocated such a framework for historical geography and, further, the theme has a sound basis in the change-through-time approach best exemplified by Clark (1954). A persuasive argument was presented by Amedeo and Golledge (1975: 177): 'we expect that the spatial manifestations of processes (i.e. form) will change from one time period to the next and, therefore, the time factor must be explicitly included for any complete modelling of a process and its spatial implications'.

There are, however, a number of problems which may emerge in attempts to apply such procedures. Four specific difficulties are noted. First, and most fundamental, this approach requires awareness of both previous forms, if appropriate, and generating processes. Unfortunately the meaning of process may be unclear and information difficult to attain. Two words often associated with process are 'ongoingness' and 'change' and it may be interpreted as a succession of actions which lead eventually to a result. The problem remains as to the means by which the initial understanding of process is achieved. Three sources are suggested in Chapter 2: available theory, comparable empirical studies and form analysis, although this third source introduces the inference problem.

A second problem recognizes that both process and form are liable to change through time and are scale dependent. A process, as considered here, comprises variables and their interrelationships and these may experience continuous change. Necessarily, an analysis of process requires simplification and generalization in order to accommodate presumed change. Further, there is not likely to be a sound reason to contend that a given form indicates a final response to a suggested process. A form is typically but a stage in an ongoing development and, as noted earlier, ideal states such as that proposed by Thünen for an agricultural landscape, are unlikely. Formulation is further complicated by the realization that processes operate at a variety of scales. A causal process is liable to consist of a mix of local and regional influences. In this respect there is not one clearly defined and unchanging set of variables which may be interpreted as the basis for spatial form evolution. The scale problem also complicates form description, this is clearly acknowledged for point-pattern techniques. Both of the problems noted so far refer to the critical question of achieving a simplied yet appropriate version of the realworld process. Given that a process is not easily observable in the sense that a form may be, if evidence remains, it is clear that process formulation is a principal task in the search for dynamic explanations.

A third problem notes that a given form may result from a variety of different processes. This is, of course, a principal drawback to the procedure of inferring process from form. Deducing form from process minimizes this problem as there is, presumably, a sound theoretical or empirical basis for the use of a particular process.

Fourth, a stochastic process is able to generate more than one outcome. This is critical because it introduces the idea of the real world being but one of many possibilities and one which may, indeed, represent an unlikely outcome. Historical geographers may profitably analyse other, more or less likely, outcomes. Simulation is an appropriate technique for deriving outcomes and for assigning probabilities to the entire range, including that which occurred.

Although several problems are evident they do not represent deterrents to the adoption of a process–form approach. Indeed they raise some intriguing questions concerning spatial form evolution which require consideration and which invite the use of simulation, the adoption of counterfactual arguments and the incorporation of a behavioural approach. Given that spatial form evolution is a legitimate concern of the historical geographer there is a sound basis for adopting a process–form approach. An appropriate and established method for generating forms from hypothesized processes, that is for operationalizing process models, is simulation. A simulation framework in turn easily incorporates counterfactual assertions, the use of which is well established in economic history in particular. Further, the employment of counterfactuals may require the historical geographer to indulge in behavioural analyses. These links between simulation, counterfactuals and behavioural analyses are now developed further.

Simulation

The discussion of simulation presented in Chapter 2 is now further developed and the potential within historical geography is noted. The value of simulation as a technique for operationalizing process models is related primarily to its ability to incorporate the time dimension. Simulation techniques permit the relationships between process and form to be explicitly investigated. Despite these advantages the procedure has been minimally exploited in historical studies (Levison, Ward and Webb 1973; Norton 1976; Widgren 1979; J. D. Wood 1974). According to Baker (1972b: 19) the 'early flush of enthusiasm over the use of Monte Carlo simulation has now moved into a more modest assessment of its utility'. Expressed simply, simulation is a technique which facilitates the generation of forms from hypothesized processes. A process–form methodological framework combined with the use of simulation is one means of increasing knowledge regarding human landscape evolution.

It is recognized that nature shows only one result, but that this result is the historical realization of a process which might have produced alternative results (Gould 1964). This observation is implicit in many simulation analyses of diffusion and the historical significance is noted by Norton (1978). Simulation permits analyses of output variance and affords the opportunity of emphasizing these chance factors. Non-geographic simulations are also typically probabilistic; Harbaugh and Bonham-Carter (1970) favour such an approach in geology because processes incorporate random components. Simulation is a procedure by means of which output may be derived from models which represent the structure of dynamic processes, and one particular simulation is therefore an experiment. The result of the experiment may provide insight concerning the process model and its relation to output, and each experiment may be designed as a means of testing a specific input–output or process–form hypothesis. A process model to be simulated comprises a set of variables with specific values which represent the process and require exogenous inputs, while the resulting output is a new set of values for the appropriate variables which describe the form derived from the hypothesized process (Meier, Newell and Pazer 1969). The precise means of deriving output from input varies, but is usually a Monte Carlo procedure involving the selection of numbers randomly from appropriate probability distributions which represent the variables. By definition a simulation model includes assumptions which are at variance with reality and it is essential that the model should not be as complicated as the overall process. In extreme cases 'Bonini's paradox' may result if the simulation is no easier to understand than is the real process (Dutton and Starbuck 1971). Similarly, it is critical that the probability surfaces employed in a simulation model are not derived from the actual surface of development but are based upon either theoretical statements or surrogate empirical observations.

Two principal advantages of simulation are that it permits the generation of forms from hypothesized processes and that it incorporates time. For processes which operate through time, simulation emerges as a most valuable technique. Analyses can be accomplished under well defined, controlled conditions, and the consequences of various processes investigated and this procedure of sensitivity analysis represents an important means of assessing the significance of individual components of the hypothesized process. Other advantages of a simulation include the following: minimization of mathematical content, imposition of a degree of logical rigour and the possibility of predictive outputs. Detailed statements of particular simulation models are available from several sources (Kibel 1972: 23–48).

A principal drawback to simulation concerns the means by which the output or spatial form are evaluated. Two questions require answering: first, is the model internally correct and, second, does it represent the required process? The first is relatively easily answered by means of trial runs. The second question is more difficult, for most geographic applications require a comparison between simulated and real forms and the means of comparison must vary according to the aspects of the output which are regarded as relevant. If, of course, the model is predictive then evaluation is not feasible. Tests either advocated or employed for comparing simulated and real forms include visual or subjective assessment, non-parametric tests, regression and factor analysis, quadrat counts, nearest neighbour analysis, spectral analysis, canonical correlation and simple correlation. Hanna (1971) suggested evaluating in terms of the amount of information provided about the behavioural processes being simulated. It is commonplace to acknowledge the unsolved problem of evaluation but, significantly, one of the most satisfactory simulation analyses accomplished does not concern itself with the issue and the authors are satisfied to make subjective comparisons between simulated outputs and the outcomes of available theories (Levison, Ward and Webb 1973). These comparisons involve visual appraisal of maps and assessment of simulation results in the light of prevailing ideas concerning the research problem. Given an intimate knowledge of the problem such comparisons are perhaps quite adequate.

As an example of how simulation can be used in conjunction with counterfactuals consider the problem of settlement location decision-making for which an appropriate process model might comprise the following three variables: measures of distance from points of attractiveness such as market centres and entry locations; measures of physical environmental quality relevant to the emerging economic landscape; and measures of institutional control such as the availability and cost of land. Quantification of these variables and assumptions about their interrelationships permit the simulation of forms from the hypothesized process. Simplified processes are liable to produce simplified outcomes. Further, as noted, the outcome of a stochastic simulation is but one of a large number of possible outcomes. Assume an individual may make one of three possible location decisions, namely, A, B or C, and that the decision-maker evaluates these three and anticipates their probable consequences, namely X,

Y or Z. An assessment is made regarding the relative desirability of the perceived consequences and the appropriate decision is made. It is possible that the anticipated results are incorrect to some degree. Hence there are X', Y' and Z' which are the actual outcomes if the appropriate decision is made.

This simple example demonstrates the important point that historical decision-makers consider a variety of possibilities, only one of which becomes the 'past' and, indeed, that this past may depart from that which was anticipated. The outcomes of the remaining possible decisions are the 'might have beens' of historical geography. By amending the formulation of the simulated process, either by attaching different values to variables or by incorporating a stochastic component, it is possible to observe the effects of alternative decisions, the might have beens. Such a procedure requires explicit use of counterfactual assertions and also requires an understanding of the past decision-making environment. This second requirement suggests that historical geographers approach what historians refer to as 'historical understanding'. Simulation, then, facilitates the explanation of human activities for both the real and a variety of possible pasts may be produced. It is because we seek to explain why people act in a particular way that we elect to consider the unrealized possibilities. Both Baker (1976) and Prince (1978) have advocated the use of counterfactuals to extend the limits of inference and to assess the consequences of particular processes.

In addition to enabling a consideration of possible outcomes, the use of simulation, combined with a counterfactual assertion where appropriate, facilitates comparisons between evaluated outcomes and the corresponding actual outcome given the necessary decision is taken. In this sense the accuracy of the evaluated outcomes may be assessed within the limitations of the simplified process framework. Such logic assumes that we are able to achieve a degree of historical understanding, able to observe the real world and able to develop a process model. Comparable procedures were discussed by the historians Todd (1972) and, to a lesser extent, by Porter (1975) and Forrester (1976), and these were noted in Chapter 1.

Counterfactuals

In historical geography, as in history and economic history, the use of counterfactuals is a basic component of a cause-and-effect analysis. The succeeding discussion relies heavily on the earlier account of counterfactuals as used in the new economic history.

Applications in historical geography are limited, a state of affairs which is not surprising given the general lack of interest which historical geographers have also shown for the two related advances in economic history regarding the more rigorous use of statistical and theoretical approaches. The unpopularity of counterfactuals may be attributed to the overall rejection of all three developments. Those statistical and theoretical contributions made by historical geographers resulted largely from the stimulus provided by spatial analysis, a stimulus which did not incorporate explicit uses of counterfactuals despite their incorporation in many simulation models in the form of sensitivity analysis. Explicit counterfactual usages have not played a role in recent human geography, and communications with history and economic history have, apparently, not provided the necessary stimulus. This absence of counterfactual analyses is despite their potentially valuable role in any temporally oriented explanation (Norton 1982a).

One application of the method is now outlined. This application, a descriptive account of the possible consequences of the early seventeenth-century discovery of the mouth of the Hudson by Champlain, suggested several important consequences of such an event and is of the, *if not A, then not B* variety where A did occur and B did occur. The aim is to emphasize the dependence of B on A by showing that without A an alternative outcome would have transpired. This also serves as an example of generated counterfactuals producing counterfactual outcomes quite different to the real.

This example of the early exploration and development of Canada was detailed by Clark (1975a). With reference to the water routes into North America Clark (1975a) was concerned with the consequences of a discovery which, although it did not occur, was a likely outcome of the exploratory process taking place. The discovery is that of the mouth of the Hudson River by Champlain during any one of his three voyages south from Port Royal during the summers of 1604, 1605 and 1606. Referring to the detailed circumstances of these voyages Clark (1975a) showed that a series of misfortunes, such as difficult disease-ridden winters, and delays, such as the late arrival of supply ships from France, prevented Champlain from voyaging sufficiently far south. Given that the discovery of the Hudson by Champlain satisfied the requirement of being a feasible alternative to reality, Clark (1975a) then proceeded to assess the consequences of such a development. Discovery of the mouth of the Hudson would have resulted in exploration to the Hudson–Mohawk confluence, recognition of the importance of that location to command the fur trade and a subsequent commitment to that area rather than to the St Lawrence as occurred in 1608. The argument was developed further and involved suggestions of an alliance between the French and the Five Nations, a stronger French core area as a result of a better environment for the seigneurial system and a more attractive area for settlers, and a more secure development in the Upper Mississippi. Such a French empire may have been indestructible. The significant changes to the historical process resulting from the counterfactual are intriguing, but one cautionary note is evident for, as North (1977: 190) noted, the value of a counterfactual declines as the potential side-effects of the variable change increase.

Although of considerable potential value in historical geography the issue of counterfactuals needs to be approached with caution. When it is asserted that *if A, then B* in the knowledge that A did not occur, then it is evident that certain conditions need to be satisfied. First, the occurrence of A needs to have been either a feasible alternative to reality or an alternative which, although unlikely, leads to interesting conclusions regarding the process as a whole. The incorporation of an unlikely event may increase understanding of those variables which did operate. Second, if we suppose A to have occurred then it may be appropriate to consider what events might have led to this occurrence. It may be the case that the occurrence of A implies real changes in the overall process which, in turn, lead to the negation of *if A, then B*.

Further uses of counterfactuals by historical geographers may profitably focus on the following three applications. First, to test hypotheses which associate an event, A, which we know did not occur, to a consequence, B. Such usage is appropriate where the counterfactual event or decision was a feasible or interesting alternative to the actual and where there is sound theoretical or empirical support for the subsequent occurrence of B. Second, counterfactuals may be used to determine whether or not an actual outcome would have occurred without a specified assumed cause. In this second usage the sensitivity of result, B, to event, A, is being tested. It may be that the result occurs regardless of the assumed cause. This is a principal use of the procedure by economic historians. In the first use above we are testing the hypothesis that *if A, then B* in the knowledge that A did not occur. In the second use above we are testing the hypothesis that *if not A, then B* in the knowledge that A did occur. In both of these cases the likelihood of a given form being generated by more than one process is being investigated. A third use the counterfactual approach might consider is the decision-making process. Analysis may show that particular results stem from different decisions and that the evaluated outcomes of the decision-makers appear to be at variance with what would have occurred. For the historical geographer a principal advantage of the explicit incorporation of counterfactuals into analyses is that it offers one means of achieving a combination of the frequently diverse approaches of the positivist and the behaviouralist. In answer to the criticism that the possible worlds resulting from counterfactuals are spurious entities, Climo and Howells (1976) observed that conventional historical worlds are also possible in that they are typically derived from limited empirical data. Further, they represent an interpretation of that data. The distinction between such worlds and counterfactually derived worlds is a matter of degree not principle.

In conclusion, the counterfactual methods are sufficiently well established in both history and economic history to merit further consideration by the historically inclined geographer. There are procedures which permit the detailed investigation of process and which focus on the relationship between cause and effect in such a way as to provide information regarding the validity of supposed cause-and-effect relationships. Given the strong methodological and empirical support from related disciplines it is appropriate to advocate the increased use of counterfactual procedures and to anticipate useful contributions to the historical geography literature. Any procedure requires careful consideration before it is presumed to be of no value and ignored, particularly a procedure regarding which Clark (1975a: 19) noted: 'To those contemptuous of, or simply uninterested in counterfactual models, and perhaps dubious of their value in stimulation of ideas and challenge to timeworn historiographic wisdom, . . .' Clark (1975a: 19) also recommended relevant reading utilizing the procedure.

Summary remarks regarding process and form

One empirical application of the process–form methodology was accomplished by Norton (1976). This study was concerned with the analysis of agricultural settlement forms in southern Ontario between 1782 and 1851. Two aims were achieved: first, the isolation of variables relevant to a settler's decision to locate and, second, the production of forms for the years between 1782 and 1851. Data were available for both 1782 and 1851 so that these forms were known. Data for the intervening years were both limited and of dubious quality. Considerations of available pertinent literature and of the settlement history of the region suggested several principal variables: namely, availability of agricultural lots, distance from entry points, land quality for agriculture and potential in relation to market centres. These four variables were incorporated into a probabilistic model of the settlement process which was operationalized by means of simulation at the township scale of analysis. On the basis of the variables, attractiveness values were calculated for each township and interpreted as the probability of receiving a settler. Forms were generated for 1851 and for the years between 1782 and 1851 and then compared to available real-world data by means of visual map analysis and correlation analysis. Results showed the four variables to be relevant and allowed exponent values to be calculated. The following ranking emerged: entry points, land quality, lot availability and potential. Such an analysis involved the creation of theoretical worlds of the past and involved a counterfactual analysis.

The specific question posed and approached by means of a counterfactual concerned the effects of land surveying on the spread of settlement. The area analysed was surveyed into agricultural lots between 1782 and 1851 and the process of surveying was concentrated in specific areas at specific times. The earliest surveyed townships were located in the immediate vicinity of Loyalist entry points, particularly east and west of Kingston. During the 1790s surveying took place along the shores of Lake Ontario and Lake Erie and in the area between the Ottawa and St Lawrence rivers. Nineteenth-century surveying continued the tendency to survey townships contiguous to already surveyed townships and along lines of transportation. Accordingly, the distribution of surveyed townships reflected both distance and environmental variables. Settlement outside of the surveyed area was technically illegal, although there is much evidence to suggest that squatting was prevalent. Available data relating to settlement forms are indicative of a close relationship between the progress of surveying and the spread of settlement through time. Results of the analysis designed to simulate settlement forms from 1791 to 1851 suggested a close relationship between surveying and settlement. These results prompted the use of a counterfactual such that a simulation was performed with all townships being available at all times, rather than utilizing the real constraint imposed by the presence of unsurveyed townships. The consequences of the counterfactual were interesting. The resultant 1851 form differed only in detail from that derived without the counterfactual, thus suggesting that land surveying was not a decisive factor for the 1851 form. For forms prior to 1851, however, the counterfactual results varied notably from those of the real world and from the simulation incorporating a surveying constraint. Thus, the process of land survey was unimportant to the eventual 1851 form but exerted an influence on earlier forms, particularly through to 1831. These conclusions were the result of a counterfactual analysis designed to query the significance of survey as a causal factor of settlement form.

This example of a counterfactual application is of the *if not A, then B* variety where A did occur and B is the actual outcome. The aim was to query a supposed relationship between A and B by removing A and speculating as to the consequences. Such an approach conforms to the basic technique in economic history with a possible cause-and-effect relationship being questioned (Norton 1978).

Despite the attention paid to emerging anti-positivistic approaches the crucial question raised in this chapter concerns the question of whether social sciences, including historical geography, can be studied by the same methods as apply to the natural sciences. The view taken here is in accord with that of Kemeny (1959: 247): '. . . in principle there is no difficulty in applying the scientific method to the social sciences, but in practice we run up against severe difficulties'. Difficulties include verifying predictions, deducing consequences of laws and formulating theories, and it is for these three reasons that the social sciences as a whole have developed more slowly than the physical sciences. This difference in stage of development is clearly exemplified by comparing the laws of physical science and those of social science. A physical science law has a precise mathematical statement, is unambiguous and has been repeatedly verified. A social science law is usually stated in ambiguous language, includes qualifications and has known exceptions. The crucial point, however, is that these differences reflect the stage of development and not any absolute differences.

One recent empirical analysis in historical geography which is explicitly framed in scientific terms is that by Langton (1979). Two causal models are applied although precise mathematical rigour is not feasible. Langton (1979: 31) realistically noted that: 'Those who lament, from the sidelines, about the lack of firm and definitive causal analysis in historical geography, of explanations of the geographical past and the way that it changed are crying for the moon.' This recognition does not, however, detract from the usefulness of a theoretical approach about which Langton (1979: 32) noted that it offered a more varied set of interests 'concerning the geographic patterns and processes of the industrial revolution, and therefore about one aspect of its dynamics, than would the bill of fare presented by historical geography's stereotype'. There is reason to suggest that a concerted interest in causal analysis and developing theory construction is one way leading to a more mature and successful historical geography. Unfortunately, it is a harsh reality that patience is necessary. The physical sciences developed at a time of minimal appreciation of the potential of science and hence it was acceptable initially to construct laws relating to trivial matters. Today, with the power of science so evident, the social sciences are impatient and are trying to either develop sophisticated explanations or are rejecting the procedures of science altogether. The intermediate approach, however slow it may be, is perhaps more appropriate and it is such an approach, involving the derivation and testing of simple laws that is advocated here within the frameworks offered by process–form analyses, by simulation and by counterfactuals. The remaining chapters focus on historical geographic literature which appears to meet this criterion of approaching a scientific methodology in order to demonstrate both the value of such a methodology and the variety of studies available. It is hoped that the succeeding discussions might generate continued work based on scientific lines and that such work will not decline simply because many existing advances might prove unsatisfactory. As Kemeny (1959: 256) noted: 'Without these false beginnings we would never find a fruitful approach.'

It appears that historical geography, interpreted as the evolution of spatial form, can readily incorporate several useful and related procedures. A process –form methodological framework has strong support in human geography and may be operationalized by means of simulation. Counterfactual arguments may be included and these shed light on both the complexities of the process–form relationship and the decision-making behaviour of individuals. The suggested emphasis is closely aligned to: (a) developments in history and the new economic history, particularly with reference to counterfactual arguments; (b) developments in human geography which argue for temporal explanations; (c) a traditional view of historical geography as the study of change. Process analysis and spatial form evolution is thus noted as one valid research theme for historical geography to be used where the nature of the problem is amenable to such an approach. Acceptance of the proposed emphasis does not imply rejection of alternative methodologies, for the analysis of process is but one valid theme. Although one aim of this chapter has clearly been to articulate and advocate a process-oriented methodology, it is not being suggested that this is either the only or even the paramount approach. Perhaps the variety of approaches which can be successfully exploited by the historical geographer is best exemplified by the work of Le Roy Ladurie (1979), of which Stevenson (1981: 197) noted: 'Despite the fulsome use made of computer processing and interdisciplinary gleanings from hard and soft science, Le Roy Ladurie convincingly reveals in these essays that the most powerful tool at the disposal of the student of the past is a sympathetic yet controlled imagination.' It is, however, suggested that historical geographers rethink their apparent rejection of a process approach in the light of the strong support from history, new economic history and human geography. Process analysis may be regarded as one extension of spatial analytic thinking and – notwithstanding the recent statement by Baker (1979a: 562) to the effect that historical geographers are concerned less with 'time and space and more properly with period and place' – such a development appears to have much to offer the historical geographer.

CONCLUSIONS

The following conclusions are evident from the discussions contained within this chapter.

1. A meaningful and acceptable definition of historical geography is neither available nor desirable. Historical geography is a set of approaches and not a subdiscipline.

2. Many interpretations are evident because of internal differences, differences between countries, and because of the influences of several other areas of knowledge including human geography.

3. Three principal technical and conceptual advances have been evident in recent years, namely involving data, theory and quantitative approaches. Neither theoretical nor quantitative interests have emerged as of paramount importance and, indeed, there are presently signs of disenchantment with these procedures.

4. Both content analysis and catastrophe theory have been introduced to human geography via historical problems.

5. Space–time modelling interests may contribute directly to historical research.

6. Various objections to a positivist approach have contributed notably to the advocacy of some behavioural analyses, phenomenological studies, an idealist approach, structuralism and marxian humanism. The influences of other disciplines are especially evident in these developments. With the exception of behavioural analyses there is as yet only limited evidence of successful applications of these proposals.

7. One approach to historical geography which is a variant of the traditional change-through-time approach appears not to have been fully developed. This involves explicit cause-and-effect analyses relating process and form and possibly incorporating simulation and counterfactuals.

8. Although various difficulties are noted the process–form approach appears as one legitimate method.

CHAPTER FIVE

Regional, cultural and perception analyses

REGIONAL HISTORICAL GEOGRAPHY

The regional paradigm has dominated geography throughout much of the twentieth century and has continued to be a significant component of historical work after a relative demise elsewhere in geography. Practitioners with historical interests have maintained a regional concern for at least three reasons, despite the rejection of such interests by Hartshorne (1959). First, the descriptive tendencies have proved attractive. Second, the region has served both the interests of those concerned to delimit formal and functional areas and those concerned to reconstruct past areas and study the evolution of areas. For the regional geographer proper the region is used as the essential purpose of the analysis, while for the historical geographer it is used as a convenient means of limiting the areal extent of the study. Third, both interests view geography as being concerned primarily with synthesis, the integration of facts leading to the best possible description. The continuing regional concern in historical geography is not, then, a maintenance of traditional regional geography. Rather the regional emphasis is to be viewed as the geographic equivalent of the historical period, a framework within which study is conducted and not an end in itself. A working definition of historical regional geography involves an areal delimitation, an emphasis on description and a concern with the total landscape. This somewhat all-embracing definition necessarily includes much of the existing literature and comprises both static and dynamic analyses.

Rather more precise definitions, or rather proposals, are available. According to Guelke (1977: 5), 'the adoption of a Collingwoodian or idealist approach would open up new possibilities for regional geography'. In addition to focusing on human and environment relations such an approach would acknowledge, and analyse, historical evolution. This proposal is an explicit suggestion of a formalized historical regional geography. Necessarily, however, it is likely to suffer from many of the same problems experienced by the more generalized idealist position. A second proposal was made by Gregory (1978c: 171) with the assertion that geographers 'need to know about the constitution of regional social formations, of regional articulations and regional transformations'. The means of accomplishing these tasks is uncertain beyond the recognition that spatial and social structures are closely related.

One difficulty in much of the existing literature results from the oft-made assumption that contemporary regions had an identity in past times. Everitt (1977) focused on this issue and noted that historical regions vary spatially through time and also vary according to whether emphasis is placed on regional landscapes or regional societies. Further complications relate to the likelihood, clearly demonstrated for specific areas of England, of important differences within small areas. A crucial fact, essential for any full understanding of the historical development of England, is stated by Everitt (1977: 19): 'until recently England has never been a monolithic community but an incomplete amalgam of differing but related societies, of differing but related *pays*'.

There have also been questions asked concerning the overall validity of the regional concept and these are especially relevant for the historically inclined researcher. Perhaps the most substantive criticisms came from Kimble (1951) who defined regions in Europe as the result of earlier self-sufficient feudal areas. This contention necessarily leads to the conclusion that regions cannot exist outside of those larger areas which have experienced such histories. Minshull (1967: 85–92) assessed this argument in detail and showed that the limitation results from a very personal definition of regions. Certainly the majority of geographers, regardless of their commitment to regional geography, would be unlikely to accept a special concept which excluded physical factors, required formal and functional unity, specified that the region was both self-evident and unchanging and which involved coincident boundaries for all relevant factors. There remains a continuing interest in regions and regionalization, an interest which chooses to ignore the long and somewhat sterile debates on the regional approach but rather focuses on evolution. For the United States Zelinsky (1973a: 118–19) suggested and justified a set of regions as one part of a larger appraisal of the cultural landscape. Somewhat similarly, Meinig (1978: 1191) considered the study of the 'sequence of territorial formation from points to nuclei to regions' to be an important research goal.

There is little doubt that historical geographers continue to be interested and actively involved in a form, or in various forms, of regional geography. Necessarily, these are not the static versions of regional geography but rather are a distinctly historical set of interests where a prime concern is the evolution of regions. The interest is in origins and development and not in regions *per se*. The regional approach or, more correctly, an interest in regions, remains at the heart of much work and the following section briefly reviews some of the characteristic approaches and reviews selected studies in regional historical geography.

Regional historical descriptions and analyses

The somewhat imprecise definition being employed allows for discussion of a wide range of literature, much of which might be regarded as cultural regional geography. Cultural geographers typically acknowledged the importance of regions and related this concept to those of landscape and culture history (Wagner and Mikesell 1962: 5–19) and, more recently, to the concept of community (Wagner 1975: 8–9). Probably the greatest impact on this matter has come from Sauer and the related 'Berkeley school' of thought. In 1925 Sauer (1963: 343) argued that: 'The cultural landscape is fashioned from a natural landscape by a culture group. Culture is the agent, the natural area is the medium, the cultural landscape is the result.' Historical geography could then be seen as being concerned with cultural landscape change and with reconstruction of the past. The links between the historical and the cultural are exceedingly close. According to Leighly (1979: 8) the exemplar of such work was a study of the Santa Clara Valley by Broek (1932) which reconstructed past landscapes, described change and observed the past in the present. In such work the regional content was limited to the necessary delimitation of a research area.

More recent work by Meinig has proved to be focused much more explicitly on regions and their evolution, with detailed studies of the Mormon region, the American west, American south-west, Texas, Great Columbia Plain and South Australia. For that most distinctive of American religious regions, the Mormon region, Meinig (1965) developed the concepts of core, domain and sphere. Core was defined as the central focus of the region, domain as the area in which the culture was dominant and sphere as the area of peripheral acculturation. Precise recognition of the spatial extent of these three was permitted by an account of the evolution of the region. A second example of the work of Meinig concerned the Texas region (Meinig 1969). This was regarded as a culture, as a region and, indeed, as an empire with a strong self-image of distinctiveness. Again, the approach was evolutionary and for this specific case four stages were recognized: implantation, reflecting Spanish and Mexican influences; assertion, including the periods of republic and early statehood; expansion, being the period after the Civil War; and, finally, elaboration, involving twentieth-century developments. Within the Texas cultural region nine lesser regions were located.

The above studies of Meinig represent a well-articulated concern with both evolution and region delimitation. These two are viewed not as separate considerations but as closely related aspects of the human geography of an area. Nor has this work been isolated, for other studies reflect similar concerns, for example that by Nostrand (1970) on the Hispanic-American region which delimited the region on the basis of both contemporary and historical considerations.

The majority of other regional historical geographies are less conceptual and less analytical than those of Meinig, rather they represent examples of historical descriptions, although admittedly there is considerable variation. The remainder of this section considers a variety of such studies and attempts to identify certain trends. Table 5.1 lists the twenty-seven texts considered and includes comments on the region analysed, the period of analysis, the major data sources employed, the apparent influences of other disciplines and the approaches employed.

Of the twenty-seven, five were published during the 1960s and the remainder during the 1970s, indicating a deliberate bias to relatively recent work. The scale of analysis varies markedly from such large areas as Canada and Europe to relatively local studies of, for example, the Bay Islands off Honduras and the Musconetcong Valley of New Jersey. Although region delimitation was often discussed and occasionally, as in the case of the Balkans, proved somewhat arbitrary, delimitation *per se* was not an issue. Nor was it deemed necessary in most cases to divide the region into smaller units on the basis of any coherent criteria. Rather the use of a region was merely a convenient device to facilitate analysis. It is clear that the regional historical geography being discussed is quite apart from the traditional regional approach in this respect.

A considerably greater deviation from regional geography proper is evident from a consideration of the time-spans employed in the twenty-seven texts, for only two of these do not embrace a lengthy period. The study by Bowen (1978) of the Willamette Valley, Oregon, focused on the decade of the 1840s and was not explicitly concerned with the evolution of the landscape in other than an initial discussion. This concern with a limited time-span, effectively a static or cross-sectional approach, reflected the aim of the work which was the mapping and interpretation of one data source, the 1850 census. Despite the relatively brief time period this work succeeded in providing discussions of relevant processes, particularly as they operated during the 1840s. A second work which focused on a relatively brief period is that by Merrens (1964) which concentrated on a twenty-five-year span from 1750 to 1775. Again, such a focus did not prevent substantive consideration of evolutionary developments. The remaining twenty-five texts embrace a variety of periods. Prehistoric or aboriginal times represent the starting time for thirteen of the texts although the discussions of such remote periods are typically brief and may rely heavily on archaeological research (Carter 1977; Clout 1977; C. T. Smith 1967). Only seven of the texts effectively continue discussion to embrace contemporary landscapes. It appears that historical geographers are somewhat reticent about involvement in recent issues. Christopher (1976: 13) concluded his discussion of southern Africa in 1960 on the grounds that: 'The main outlines of southern Africa had then emerged, yet the latest rapid transformation, the "wind of change" associated with the breaking of political ties with Europe in the 1960s had not yet had a great impact.' A characteristic terminal date appears to be the end of the nineteenth century with six texts concluding their discussions *c.* 1900, another in 1867 and another in 1939. There is a clear emphasis, in terms of content, on the eighteenth and nineteenth centuries in those texts dealing with areas outside of Europe and which experienced immigration largely from Europe. Several such studies begin at the time of initial European exploration and development as in Canada (*c.* 1500), Southern Africa (1500 or 1652) and South Australia (1836).

Overall, it appears that delimiting meaningful periods has proven to be even more difficult than delimiting meaningful regions. For the latter, political units proved a convenient device in almost all cases. For the former relatively arbitrary decisions prevailed when the discussion terminated prior to the pres-

Table 5.1 Some major features of selected historical regional studies

Text	Region	Period of study	Data sources	Other disciplines	Principal approaches
Bowen (1978)	Willamette Valley, Oregon	1840s	1850 census	—	Past landscape reconstruction, much use of maps
Carter (1977)	The Balkans	Prehistory to present	Varied, archaeological, archival, fieldwork	Archaeology	Regional and local studies, emphasis on processes and change
Christopher (1976)	Southern Africa	1652 to 1960	Fieldwork and archival	Economic history	Landscape transformation through agency of European settlement
Clout (1977)	France	Prehistory to 1900	Varied, archaeological, archival fieldwork	Archaeology, history	Varied, thematic treatment, rural and cultural emphasis
Darby (1973)	England	c. 450 to 1900	Archival	History	Combined narratives and cross-sections
Davidson (1974)	Bay Islands, Honduras	Aboriginal times to present	Archival and fieldwork	Anthropology	Landscape history (Sauer), effects of cultural groups and related processes
Dicken and Dicken (1979)	Oregon	Aboriginal times to present, especially after 1840	Archival and fieldwork	—	Landscape change, primarily related to post-aboriginal occupation
Dickson (1969)	Ghana	Prehistory to 1939	Archival	—	Evolution of cultural and economic landscape, cross-sections and narratives
Dodgshon and Butlin (1978)	England and Wales	Prehistory to 1900	Archival and secondary sources	—	Both syntheses and thematic studies, focus on process and interpretation
Gerhard (1972)	New Spain	1519 to 1821	Archival	History	A regional listing of descriptive source material, some data synthesis
Harris and Warkentin (1974)	Canada	c. 1500 to 1867	Secondary sources	Social and economic history	Chronological discussions of social and economic change in six regions
Head (1976)	Newfoundland	1675–1820	Archival and fieldwork	History	Combined narratives and cross-sections
Jeans (1972)	New South Wales	Aboriginal times to 1901	Archival and secondary sources	Economic history	Economic change, concern with changing regional patterns

Source	Area	Period	Sources	Discipline	Approach
Jones (1977)	Finland	Prehistory to present	Archival	Physical geography	Human response to the physical land uplift
Lambert (1971)	The Netherlands	Prehistory to present	Archival	History and economic history	Humans as agents of landscape change, landscape evolution
Merrens (1964)	North Carolina	c. 1750 to 1775	Archival and secondary sources	Economic history	Analysis of changing geographies and forces contributing to change
Millman (1975)	Scotland	Prehistory to present	Secondary sources	History	Chronological analysis of landscape change
Patten (1979)	England	c. 1500 to c. 1800	Archival and secondary sources	Economic history	Varied, both static analyses and studies of change
Pawson (1979)	Britain	1700 to 1801	Secondary sources	Economic history	Economic change
Perry (1975)	Britain	1800 to 1900	Secondary sources	Economic history	Economic change
Pollock and Agnew (1963)	South Africa	c. 1400 to 1910	Secondary sources	History	Geography used to give depth and fullness to historical events
Pounds (1973)	Europe	450 BC to AD 1330	Secondary sources	Economic history, history	Five cross-sectional accounts at 'peak' periods
Pounds (1979)	Europe	1500 to 1840	Archival and secondary sources	Economic history, history	Combined narratives and cross-sections
Smith (1967)	Western Europe	Prehistory to 1800	Secondary sources	Archaeology, economic history	Emphasis on periods and process of geographical change
Wacker (1968)	Musconetcong Valley, New Jersey	Aboriginal times to c. 1800	Archival and secondary sources	—	Landscape history (Sauer), humans as agents of landscape change
Wacker (1975)	New Jersey	Aboriginal times to 1820	Archival and secondary sources	Anthropology	Landscape history (Sauer), humans as agents of landscape change
Williams (1974)	South Australia	1836 to present	Archival and secondary sources	History	Processes of landscape creation and change

ent. For Canada, Harris and Warkentin (1974) concluded in 1867 which, while it does represent a key political date, is arguably not especially meaningful in geographic terms as it does not, for example, permit discussion of the mass migrations to the prairies which may be seen as largely responsible for the present prairie landscape. In the British context the end of a century has been an attractive concluding date. Both Darby (1973) and Dodgshon and Butlin (1978) terminated extended studies in 1900 while Patten (1979) analysed the years 1500 to 1800, Pawson (1979) the years 1700 to 1801 and Perry (1975) the years 1800 to 1900. Only Millman (1975) continued the study of Scotland through to the present.

The majority of the twenty-seven texts being considered were intended as overall regional accounts and were not the product of principally primary research. Accordingly the major data sources employed are a wide variety of secondary sources, and most of the texts chose not to include elaborate discussions of data. Given the oft-assumed dependence of historical work on data sources this state of affairs is a little surprising. One text, that by Gerhard (1972), stands somewhat apart in that it comprises a regional listing of data sources and is, perhaps, not a regional historical geography in the more accepted sense of that phrase. Substantive discussions of data are evident in Bowen (1978) and Merrens (1964).

Table 5.1 includes a reference to 'other disciplines'. This is a rather crude attempt to indicate the general orientation of the work. For eleven of the texts an association to conventional economic history is apparent. This is particularly evident in Pawson (1979), Perry (1975) and Pounds (1973, 1979). Pawson (1979: 11) explicitly hoped 'that this book will also be of use to economic historians' and Pounds (1979: xvi) observed that the study of Europe from 1500 to 1840 'must look remarkably like economic history'. A strong historical orientation is present in nine of the texts and especially in Head (1976) and Pollock and Agnew (1963). Although Head (1976) asked different questions to those asked by historians the answers were sought largely from historical data. For Pollock and Agnew (1963: ix) 'geography is called upon to give depth and fulness to historical events'. Archaeology, anthropology, social history and physical geography are also listed in Table 5.1, but are of lesser significance.

The final column of Table 5.1 is a presumptuous attempt to summarize the principal approaches utilized. Diversity is to be expected and diversity is discovered. Most significantly the majority of texts do not overly concern themselves with methodology and are not conveniently categorized. Cross-sections were employed by Pounds (1973) at what were perceived to be key periods of time, and combinations of cross-sections and narratives were used by Darby (1973), Head (1976) and Pounds (1979). The majority of other studies were concerned, one way or another, with landscape change through time and several studies adopted the emphasis advocated by Sauer (1963). Davidson (1974) studied the effects of a series of cultural groups while Wacker (1968, 1975) focused on humans as agents of landscape change. A state of 'organized chaos' is perhaps the aptest way to summarize the principal approaches. There is, all too clearly, not just one approach to regional studies. Overall the texts considered do not exhibit significant theoretical or statistical content. Clear exceptions to this generalization include parts of Carter (1977) dealing with prehistoric Greece and seventeenth-century settlements in the south-central Peloponnese, and parts of Dodgshon and Butlin (1978) dealing with prehistory, Roman times, industry and towns from 1500 to 1730 and agriculture from 1730 to 1900. Nor is there substantial evidence of emerging non-positivistic emphases in the regional literature appraised, although a discussion of the process of industrial change in Dodgshon and Butlin (1978) stands as one example.

Historical geographers have been involved in regional studies throughout the current century, an interest which shows no signs of diminishing. Regional historical geography continues as a principal concern and the need for further detailed analyses of regional landscape evolution remains. For many parts of the world useful historical geographies remain to be written.

HISTORICAL CULTURAL ANALYSES

The links between historical and cultural work have been especially close since the emergence of the Berkeley or landscape school in the 1920s. This section first considers the meaning of culture with particular interest in the super-organic interpretation. A second concern relates to the issues of culture contact, transfer and acculturation. The final emphases involve discussions of landscape evolution where the principal concerns are the effects of cultural groups, the emergence of related landscapes and the possible recognition of regions.

Culture and cultural geography

In an introductory text Spencer and Thomas (1973: 6) offered the following statement regarding culture: 'Culture is the sum total of human learned behaviour and ways of doing things. Culture is invented, carried on and slowly modified by people living and working in groups as each group occupies a particular region of the earth and develops its own special and distinctive system of culture.' Jordan and Rowntree (1979: 5) offered a shorter definition: 'We can say that culture is a total way of life held in common by a group of people.' The general notion of culture as *genre de vie* or 'way of life' is frequently emphasized by geographers. The primary concern of cultural geography is the relationship between humans and environments and Sauer (1963: 343) wrote: 'Culture is the agent, the natural area is the medium, the cultural landscape the result.' According to Duncan (1980) such a view reflected one specific interpretation of culture which emerged as paramount in anthropology in the early twentieth century, namely, the concept of the superorganic. Initially developed by Kroeber and Lowie this concept argued that culture was to be seen as an entity above man and that landscapes and landscape change were best explained via culture. This cultural determinism approach has been readily and essentially uncritically incorporated into cultural geography from the 1920s onwards and

69

received especially clear expression in the historical analysis of American regions by Zelinsky (1973a).

The meaning of the superorganic and acceptance of this concept by cultural geographers is clearly of importance in the present context. As a concept, the superorganic is but one of several concerning culture and has largely been rejected by anthropologists since the 1950s. Perhaps the strongest supportive statements in recent times come from White (1959: 12): 'In the man-culture situation, therefore, we may consider man the biological factor to be a constant; culture the variable.' Kniffen (1954: 222) had earlier written:

Three factors produce the data with which cultural geography is concerned: man the animal, the physical earth, and culture. For the cultural geographer man is largely a constant factor in time and space; the physical earth is constant in time but a variable in space; culture is a variable in both time and space. Culture is then the great variable factor that may reflect earth qualities and affects the patterns of earth occupance.

Both of the above quotes separate humans and culture, one of four superorganic assumptions (Duncan, 1980: 187–95). The remaining three assumptions relate to the notions that cultures have typical values and norms, that any given culture is homogeneous and that individuals accept cultural values via conditioning. Undoubtedly the superorganic thesis and the four related assumptions have exerted a marked influence on cultural geography, but there are several signs that such a state of affairs no longer prevails. In 1968 Kniffen (1968: v) removed the earlier distinction between humans and culture and wrote: 'Although man has been here only a relatively short time, he is a powerful force for change. He gains power through sheer numbers and an awesome growth of technical capacity.' More general challenges to the cultural–determinist stance are incorporated in many perception-based studies, in ecological approaches and in humanistic concerns. This latter concern was reviewed by Cosgrove (1978) and a linking of humanist cultural and marxian social approaches advocated. A cultural–determinist stance was explicitly rejected by Newton and Pulliam-Di Napoli (1977: 362) in a discussion of log houses in the southern United States, for they 'called into serious question the basic assumption that "culture determines" the form of houses'. This present discussion of culture and cultural geography is important because it emphasizes the acceptance by many writers of an essentially unproven and unsatisfactory approach. Necessarily, the following discussions of empirical work are more easily understood with the methodological background at hand.

Contact, transfer and acculturation

The movement of culture groups from a home environment to a new environment results in landscape change in the new area. These changes result from at least two factors. First, it may be the case that characteristics of the home culture are transferred from one environment to another both during and after the physical movement of people. This is certainly a major factor in most movements out from Europe to the expanding colonies of the seventeenth century onwards. Second, contact with cultures in or adjacent to the new environment is likely to result in the acceptance of previously unknown culture traits which affect landscape evolution. Again, this is typically the case in any culture contact situation.

A principal determinant of the relative importance of these two factors is, of course, the similarity between the two environments, with similar locales encouraging the migration and continued acceptance of traditional traits. A second determinant is the technological difference between the cultures. In situations where there is a significant technological discrepancy the prospects of the higher, usually incoming, technological groups are greatly enhanced. Mannion (1974) conducted a detailed analysis of the modification of traditional Irish traits in three parts of eastern Canada settled by groups of Irish during the nineteenth century. Focusing specifically on aspects of the material folk culture and settlement morphology Mannion (1974) was able to conclude that the movement to Canada involved a rapid loss of culture traits. The rate of loss, however, varied markedly from place to place. As might be anticipated, the greater the tendency to transfer traditional traits the less likely was the group to borrow from other groups contacted. Mannion (1974) noted that the extent of transfer and durability of transferred traits was greatest in the Avalon Peninsula of Newfoundland and least in the Peterborough area of southern Ontario. Cultural borrowing, on the other hand, was most evident in Peterborough and least evident for the Avalon Peninsula immigrants. The third area analysed, the Miramichi River area of New Brunswick, represented the middle ground in both cases.

For the historical geographer these issues of culture transfer from one environment to another and the consequences of culture contact, whether it be between immigrant groups or between an immigrant group and an aboriginal population, have proved intriguing. A consideration of transfer and contact helps shed light on the processes of both culture and landscape change. According to Fried (1962: 316) there are three possible consequences of a contact situation involving groups with differing levels of technology. The first is complete annihilation of the aboriginal group as a result of the spread of disease and conflict. The second is a gradual process of transformation by which the aboriginal group adjusts to a cultural level which permits the two groups to coexist. The third possibility involves incorporation of the aboriginal group into the way of life of the incoming population with relatively little loss of numbers. One study which has focused explicitly on these questions of acculturation following contact concerned the spatial reorganization of the Haida population of the Queen Charlotte Islands, British Columbia (Henderson 1978). For the Haida the results of contact, beginning in 1774, involved rapid depopulation, village abandonment and an erosion of the annual cycle of subsistence activities. Contact between 1774 and the 1830s was primarily related to fur-trade activities. Renewed contact occurred in the 1850s related to a brief mineral rush, and was followed in turn by a series of missionary contacts after 1876. Rapid depopulation as a result of disease, especially smallpox, and migration resulted in a decline from at least 10,000 in 1774 to 593 in 1895, and village abandonment occurred with a 1774 count of 34 villages being reduced to 2 in 1900 (Henderson 1978: 6). Details of the effect of contact on the annual cycle are more complex. The early fur-trade activities caused nominal change, even when some farming practices were introduced, and the later and determined efforts of missionaries to encourage a sedentary life-style were likewise largely unsuccessful with only 18 acres of cultivated land by 1919. The annual cycle of activities is still evident although the specific activities changed to include, for example, a fish-oil industry and commercial logging. Thus contact, for the Haida, involved an acceptance of permanent settlements and of village fusion and a retention of the annual cycle. Henderson (1978: 19) argued that the former were accepted because they 'functioned to meet the immediate needs of Haida society' while the latter was retained because change 'would have caused change throughout the entire cultural system'. Historical analyses of culture change stemming from contact situations appear to be a highly relevant contribution to an understanding of the processes causing change in various contexts and at various scales.

One factor in determining the character of contact refers to the possibly differing attitudes towards land tenure (Fried 1962: 315). This issue was considered in detail by Hornbeck (1979) in an analysis of the patenting of private land in California following United States' acquisition in 1848. Individuals claiming ownership under Mexican title were confronted by American settlers who ignored any prior claims and proceeded to squat. An Act of 1851 attempted to resolve the land conflicts, but failed to achieve this objective for some thirty years. Certainly land, and attitudes towards land, have often proved to be a major conflict issue between groups, and Hornbeck (1979: 448) concluded that research should focus on 'understanding and coping with the larger differences of resource interpretation and use'. More general studies of contact have tended to be ordered over longer periods of time and have provided overviews of cultural change. McKee (1971), for example, analysed the Choctaw group of the southern United States and emphasized the character of the group both before and during a series of contacts with Spanish, French, English, Americans and missionaries. Overall the Choctaw adopted new traits rapidly, especially those relating to agriculture and education. The major change, however, was the removal of many Choctaw from Mississippi to Oklahoma in the 1830s. Questions of contact remain relevant in many parts of the contemporary world and historical geographers may play a vital role in resolving misunderstandings and improving relationships between groups.

The evolution of cultural regions

The evolution of cultural regions has received relatively little attention by historical geographers. For North America the most provocative writings have been those of Meinig (1972, for example) and Zelinsky (1973a). Only three of the regional texts considered emphasized cultural landscapes (Davidson 1974; Wacker 1968; Wacker 1975). For the larger area of the American west Meinig (1972) delimited regions and proposed four stages of cultural develop-

Stage

selected <u>transplant</u> from one or more source regions; never a complete cross-section of the older society; experimental adaptation of imported cultural traits to new environment.

I

<u>regional culture</u>; new amalgam of people, forming cohesive society, adjusting to insularity and new environment; high potential for cultural lag and divergence.

II

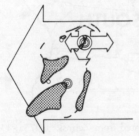

strong <u>impact of national culture</u>; nationwide communications, marketing networks, and control of facilities diffuse national culture through central place network. Only subcultures with tenacious social patterns (religion, language, race) can persist as distinct.

III

<u>dissolution of historic regional culture</u>; all areas directly exposed to national culture; emergence of ethnic mosaic and new innovative centres; new consciousness of local environmental and cultural values.

IV

Fig. 5.1 Cultural region evolution. (After Meinig 1972: 163)

ment (see Fig. 5.1). The first stage, transplant, involved a selected and experimental adjustment to the new environment; the second stage, regional culture, involved the development of a cohesive society; the third stage, impact of national culture, reflected the influences of communication and marketing; the fourth stage, dissolution of historic regional culture, allowed for a new awareness of regional values. The four stages were suggested with reference to six regions of the American west. The distinction between the first two stages and the later two is especially important, for the onset of stage 3 'marks the end of insularity and a sharp increase in the power of forces working toward national cultural uniformity' (Meinig 1972: 179). For North America, then, it appears that cultural regions have developed, but are perhaps losing some of their distinctiveness only some 150 years after their genesis. Suggestions such as this require further elaboration, in North America and elsewhere.

A regionalization of the United States has been achieved which placed great reliance on the doctrine of first effective settlement: 'Whenever an empty territory undergoes settlement, or an earlier population is dislodged by invaders, the specific characteristics of the first group able to effect a viable, self-perpetuating society are of crucial significance for the later social and cultural geography of the area, no matter how tiny the initial band of settlers may have been.' (Zelinsky 1973a: 13). The outcome of such an approach is shown in Fig. 5.2 which recognizes five regions in the United States, namely New England, the midland, the south, the middle west and the west, with the final

Fig. 5.2   Cultural regions of the United States. (Adapted from Zelinsky 1973a: 118)

region including some 50 per cent of the total area. These five are European not aboriginal in origin and are closely related in that the first three Atlantic regions are responsible for the emergence of the middle west and west. The idea that the first effective settlement essentially determined subsequent cultural regions is an intriguing one and an application to Canada facilitates recognition of five regions. The maritime area experienced a series of early penetrations and settlement following the Cabot voyage of 1497 and the interest in fishing shown by several European nations. Early settlement involved both French, in the Acadian coastal areas of Nova Scotia and New Brunswick, and English in Newfoundland. Despite the ethnic diversity there were some evident common factors. Primarily, this region was one of difficulty and the historical record shows that Europeans had to struggle to establish themselves. Further, no one period of settlement was crucial to subsequent cultural evolution in any specific area. Newfoundland became increasingly British while the other Atlantic provinces received a significant population input at the time of American Independence in the form of Loyalist settlers.

Throughout this area population growth and cultural landscape evolution were gradual. The Lower St Lawrence comprises a second region with a clear determining criterion, namely French settlement, initiated in the early seventeenth century by Champlain following the sixteenth-century explorations of Cartier. A distinctive cultural landscape emerged and was little altered by the French defeat in North America of 1763. Despite the demands of an English-speaking continent this region remains an area of French culture today. The region of southern Ontario, a third area, was not settled initially from Britain but rather from the United States by Loyalists. Prior to these Loyalist movements the area was largely unsettled despite some 150 years of European activity in eastern North America.

Surveys and settlement began in earnest in the 1780s, in 1791 the political separation of regions 2 and 3 occurred, and in 1792 the basic survey system for the area settled through to the mid-nineteenth century was established. Before 1812 most of the immigrants originated from the United States and subsequently from the British Isles. The French and Catholic area of Quebec received relatively few nineteenth-century immigrants while British and Protestant southern Ontario received large numbers, especially during the 1840s. The fourth region demarcated comprises the prairies, an area which experienced much exploration and fur-trade activity but which, with the exception of the Red River settlement, received few settlers and related development before the 1870s, some 100 years after the onset of settlement in southern Ontario. Late nineteenth- and early twentieth-century in-movement largely comprised people from Ontario and from continental Europe with a series of religious groups, such as Mennonites and Dukhobors, receiving special privileges. Today the prairies remain largely agricultural and have a wide variety of ethnic groups. The fifth and final region comprises Vancouver Island and the mainland, a region which received a high proportion of British settlers initially, followed by significant numbers of Asiatics. The city of Vancouver grew notably in 1886 following the decision to terminate the transcontinental railway at that location. Although this discussion has not resulted in a clear relationship between first effective settlement and the emergence of cultural regions, an overall correspondence is evident with a particularly clear distinction between southern Quebec and southern Ontario. The proposed regionalization also leaves most of Canada unclassified, an inevitable consequence of the low population density and lack of widespread development. It appears that the concept of first effective settlement has some merit in both Canada and the United States.

A significant development was achieved by Mitchell (1978) in a discussion of early American cultural regions. Three processes were seen to be at work: duplication of culture traits from an earlier area, deviation from earlier traits related to local factors and fusion of traits from two or more source areas. The process of fusion was shown to be the most important prior to 1820.

The use of models and concepts of cultural landscape evolution has not been restricted to North America. For north-east Wales Pryce (1975) used the concepts of core, domain and sphere in an investigation of regional evolution between 1750 and 1851. Two major language regions were demarcated on the basis of church records, a predominantly Welsh area and a bilingual or English area. For north-east Wales industrialization processes encouraged growth of a bilingual zone or domain by 1851, an area which has now disappeared with the continuing pressures of English-language expansion. This suggestion that a domain appeared partly in response to processes of migration and economic growth and subsequently decayed as these processes intensified is an intriguing addition to the established concepts.

The mapping of past cultural regions may be achieved by reference to specific culture traits. Ennals (1972), for example, classified and mapped six principal barn types in nineteenth-century southern Ontario, an exercise which permitted comments on origins, diffusion and resultant regional landscapes. Log houses in Canada provided a forum which Wonders (1979) used to discuss regional variations in the diffusion of techniques. A distinctive agricultural trait of the mountain west of the United States, the hay derrick, was used by Francaviglia (1978) to discuss the evolution of the Mormon region, while Carney (1974) related the twentieth-century emergence of a country-music-listening region by considering the spread and growth of appropriate radio stations.

The cultural landscape

Interest in the evolution of distinctive cultural landscapes is often associated with specific ethnic groups, although some of the stereotypic ethnicity and economy ties have been questioned by Lemon (1972). For parts of nineteenth-century Texas Jordan (1966: 193) concluded that the agricultural landscapes of German settlement involved greater intensity, productivity and locational stability. Four classes of agricultural trait, based on the relative success of transfer, were noted and the fate of specific traits attributed to physical, cultural and economic variables. The differences between German and other settlers is less evident today as a result of common commercial interests. The emergence and subsequent disappearance of a distinctive landscape possibly reflects the initial importance of established cultural variables and the later importance of economic variables. If this suggestion is at all appropriate then it might be instructive to consider an area with a diverse ethnic population and a relatively low level of commercialization. Gerlach (1976) analysed the Ozark region of Missouri by mapping past and present ethnic groups, assessing the degree of cultural continuity and comparing ethnic to other settlers. Although a tendency towards homogeneity is evident it is not fully developed and there are distinctive German, Amish and Mennonite landscapes. Distinctions relate to settlement patterns, architecture of both home and church, farming equipment, agricultural practices, placenames and locational stability. Gerlach (1976: 177) discussed reasons for the emergence and retention of ethnic landscapes and concluded that the Ozarks are not an ethnic melting-pot. This example appears to support the suggestion that loss of traditional traits is at least partly a function of commercial demands.

An analysis of three immigrant ethnic groups in central Kansas demonstrated the way in which ethnic territories were established and maintained (McQuillan 1978a). By the early twentieth century the French Canadian was most Americanized, followed by Swedes and finally Mennonites, with assimilation being influenced by the length of residence in North America and the maintenance of ties with home areas. More general discussions which focus less explicitly on ethnic issues, for example the analysis of the Musconetcong Valley by Wacker (1968), nevertheless placed much emphasis on the varying cultural backgrounds of settlers and their resultant perception and use of the land. Aboriginal occupation affected subsequent European and American landscapes, with cleared areas being attractive to incoming settlers and established routeways being adopted. English settlers arrived first and were followed by Dutch and German groups and the contemporary landscape 'reflects a continuity from the eighteenth-century pioneer period to the present' (Wacker 1968: 151). In addition to the ethnic imprints Wacker (1968) also outlined the interrelated evolutions of the cultural and economic landscapes with discussions of agriculture, transport, early industry and nucleated settlement. In a wider analysis of New Jersey Wacker (1975) emphasized the consequences of proximity to other settled areas, of political history in general and of institutional controls over such matters as landholding and settlement. Again the effects of initial settlement were seen as instrumental to subsequent landscapes.

The discussion so far has identified a number of empirical regularities. First, it appears that the doctrine of first effective settlement is relevant for region delimitation and for analyses of evolution in that current landscapes may reflect the early periods. Second, for North America the relevant settlement is typically not aboriginal and a similar comment is appropriate for most colonial and former colonial areas. The possible exception of areas of Africa, especially South Africa, is to be discussed. Third, recognition of a different cultural landscape often results from consideration of minority ethnic groups, with ethnicity being defined in terms of language, religion or national origin. Fourth, the degree to which early cultural landscapes are retained is a function of, especially, the degree of commercialization and the ties which hold the groups together, with religious ties often proving most significant. Fifth, for areas of European settlement it seems fair to generalize that a rapid initial regionalization is gradually eroded as a result of increased mobility, the effects of national cultures and economic requirements. Finally, a variety of concepts appear to have some empirical support, including those of core, domain and sphere, of the four chronological stages suggested for the American west and of first effective settlement. The combination of conceptual and detailed empirical analysis bodes well for further research.

These discussions have emphasized the North American scene. This is not to suggest that such analyses are inappropriate for, say, Europe, but is rather a reflection of current literature and of the emphasis with which this book is concerned. Relevant work is abundant in France with a traditional interest in local landscapes, and, to a lesser extent, in Britain. An account of vernacular housing in Britain discussed the evolution of styles and related development to two cultural regions, essentially the south-east and the north (Aalen 1973). Another quite different example is that of South Africa. The contemporary cultural landscape of this region, including those areas which are currently in the process of becoming independent, is a mosaic of primarily European and primarily African, aboriginal, regions. Since the first Dutch settlement in 1652 an overriding institutional control has been the maintenance of European rule and of related physical separation. Full separation has proven impractical both because of the economic dependence of Europeans on Africans and because of the size of the African population in relation to the assigned land. Despite some variations the policy has essentially focused on separation and has now developed a related set of regulations (Christopher 1982). The outcome is a most distinctive cultural landscape. Rural areas under European ownership include both conventional farming elements and areas of radically different African labourer settlement. Rural areas assigned to Africans are typically over-populated and over-utilized. The urban landscape comprises European areas, Indian areas, Coloured areas and African areas, each of which is typically separate in spatial terms and distinctive in terms of quality of life. The South African example is suggestive of a developing cultural landscape, the future of which is to be determined by political events in much the same way that the current landscape is a response to political decisions. The present situation reflects a culture contact and conflict history which has developed without either annihilation or integration of the aboriginals and the result is distinctive.

One final area of concern which relates to both region and landscape evolution relates to the process of diffusion. Following Sauer (1963) there has been a major interest in culture trait diffusion and Kniffen (1951b: 114) noted: 'Knowledge of the origin and diffusion of the covered bridge contributes to an understanding of cultural differentiation.' Recent discussions include those of Leighly (1978) dealing with placenames and their out-movement from colonial New England and Crowley (1978) which is one example of ethnic group diffusion, in this instance Old Order Amish, and their European and American movements. Overall, such studies have been little influenced by the developments in diffusion studies evident in the 1960s and the emphasis is on empirical description and interpretation. One very different analysis is that by Kirk (1975) which investigated the role of India in the spread of cultures during three periods after approximately 1500 BC.

A concluding comment

Historical cultural geography is a broad area and precise delimitation is both difficult and undesirable. The above classification into the meaning of culture, culture contact and evolution does leave much unsaid. Some additional concerns are now briefly noted. The debate over culture excluded the issue of cultural evolution, long a major concern in anthropology. Newson (1976: 254) summarized established anthropological ideas and argued that, once certain problems were overcome, 'the concept of cultural evolution promises to constitute a valuable mode of explanation in the analysis of cultures and cultural change and since the presence of a culture implies an area, this applies to spatial patterns too'. Newson (1976: 255) further argued that historical geographers have neglected the culture contact process and the impact of colonialism as factors relevant to culture change, and urged researchers to test ideas such as the law of cultural dominance which proposes that the most effective culture, in terms of energy exploitation, overcomes less effective cultures. These are intriguing suggestions which relate closely to many of the earlier discussions. It seems reasonable to anticipate a continued response to these pleas and to the earlier and not dissimilar comments of Kay (1971) which advocated technology as one major variable influencing development.

PERCEPTION ANALYSES

'It is impossible to achieve a comprehensive understanding of the evolution of settlement and the transformation of regional landscapes over large areas of the globe without careful examination of the central processes of image, which in the context of human geography may be loosely described as the subjective, socially based processes of environmental appraisal' (Powell 1977: 25).

Many historical geographers appear to agree, for there is a large and growing literature which is concerned with perception and related behaviour, a relationship which is well established in human geography. Fielding (1974: 281) wrote: 'Behaviour is affected by the way each person perceives situations and remembers them; the way each learns and thinks about alternative courses of actions, and decides to act.' The creation of a human landscape may be seen, then, as the product of trial and error. Two implications of such a learning process were noted by Fielding (1974: 286). First, there is stimulus-response with the response being premeditated. A clear instance of the application of such logic is environmentalism where tradition, culture and the free will of humans are ignored. Second, there is stimulus-meditated-response where the stimulus is perceived and considered before a response is made. The appropriate learning process for landscape development is the second version.

Any human landscape is the end-product of a large number of individual decisions, each made under different circumstances and often for very different reasons. Landscape creation is hardly a straightforward affair. To gain insight, historical geographers look at the factors influencing behaviour; in short they analyse the perceived environment. A basic assumption is that behaviour and decision-making are based on individual or group perceptions of the real world. These perceptions are often called 'images'. The importance of subjective views of the environment has been acknowledged for a long time, but it is only since the 1960s that environmental perception has become a major research orientation. In many respects this belated research effort is surprising given the authoritative voices advocating a form of perception analysis: in 1850 Von

Humboldt stated, '. . . in order to comprehend nature in all its vast sublimity, it would be necessary to present it under a twofold aspect, first objectively, as an actual phenomenon, and next subjectively, as it is reflected in the feelings of mankind' (quoted in Saarinen 1974: 255–6). An early and definitive statement was that of Wright (1947) which included a definition of geography as the study of geographical knowledge. Specific ties with historical work were noted by Kirk (1951) who argued for the use of the behavioural environment in historical geography.

Overall, any view of the world is always a partial view and often is imperfect. Delusion and error are quite normal. Each image of the world is a result of personal experience, learning, imagination and memory. It is not difficult to appreciate that the discovery of past or present perceptions is a major task. Indeed, it is such a major task that researchers often recourse to inferring perception from behaviour. In other words behaviour, effects, are observed and perceptions, causes, are assumed. Any form of inference is of course a dangerous route to new knowledge for it is usually difficult to be certain that the inferred cause is the true cause. An alternative approach to analysing is the approach in which behaviour is deduced from assumptions about perception. Such deductive logic is a more reliable procedure, but it does presuppose that information about the perceived landscape is either available or can reasonably be assumed.

Closely related to the theme of perception is a discussion of the stochastic or chance factor. Given that the contemporary landscape is a result of a myriad of individual decisions it is apparent that the details of a landscape are extremely sensitive to such decisions, and many of these decisions may be a matter of chance. This idea can be developed further with the recognition that uncertainty is a basic fact of life for both individuals and cultures. Curry (1966) observed that this uncertainty must be manifested in the human landscape. The implication of this second point in particular is that it is very difficult to reconstruct images on the basis of behaviour. A real landscape is the realization of a process of development which might just as easily have been responsible for other landscapes. Different specifics of development, by chance, lead to different, at least in detail, landscapes.

The remainder of this section reviews and discusses a variety of literature and ideas which are divided into seven, somewhat overlapping, themes. The themes are as follows: exploratory images, especially in the Great Plains; New World expansion and the related removal of aboriginals; image-makers and their biases; agricultural and settlement images; group perceptions, especially of religious and ethnic groups; image distortion; and, finally, some summary comments.

Exploratory images

It is reasonable to suggest that perceptions of unknown or little-known landscapes have been less in accord with reality than have perceptions of relatively known landscapes. The processes of exploration and related mapping abound with uncertainty and many decisions regarding movement must have been subject to chance influences, as was the case in the explorations of Champlain discussed in Chapter 4. A particularly vivid example of the discrepancy between image and reality in the exploratory process is that of the Canadian west in the mid-eighteenth century (Ruggles 1971). Although much was known by this time there remained a great deal to surmise and contemporary maps provide evidence of such speculation with cartographers offering a 'conspicuous amalgam of supposition and reality' (Ruggles 1971: 239). Typically, these maps included what was thought to be there and, most crucially, what was hoped for. For western Canada this latter category included a large inlet of the Pacific, the 'Sea of the West', a series of water routes from the Great Lakes to the west and only a minor mountain barrier. Although short-lived, such imagined landscapes played an important role in the eighteenth-century geography of the region. A second example of images substantially different from reality and, indeed, highly variable from one to another, is provided by early-nineteenth-century Oregon. Dicken and Dicken (1979: 1) noted that images 'depended on the point of view, as well as on the sources of information', and as a result the initial maps were based on knowledge gained by sailors and fur traders and on the imagination of the cartographer.

Perhaps the most discussed example of exploratory images is that of the Great Plains of the United States and their Canadian counterpart. On maps through to the 1870s the notion of a 'Great American Desert' was perpetuated and it is likely that such an image exerted a significant effect on western expansion. The plains of the United States were acquired in 1803 and, despite earlier French and Spanish explorations, American knowledge was limited. A series of expeditions appears to have prompted the desert concept, especially those of Lewis and Clark in 1806, Pike in 1806 and Long in 1820. Further, both Pike and Long predicted that the desert would restrict settlement. It is generally argued that this image persisted until perhaps 1875 and was ultimately changed as a result of railway expansion and settlement. According to Bowden (1969), however, the notion of a desert was not as widespread as some have suggested, with no real negative image being communicated to potential settlers.

Discussion of the Great Plains has not focused entirely on the desert concept. Allen (1975) observed that incorrect arrangements of rivers confused the early American knowledge of the area. At the beginning of the nineteenth century the Missouri was seen as a possible North-west Passage, or route to India, by the then President Thomas Jefferson. This image prompted official support of the Lewis and Clark expedition, 'one of the world's greatest exploratory ventures' (Allen 1975: 111). In a very similar vein a series of efforts designed to locate a North-west Passage above Canada proved to be grounded in incorrect images: 'The whole enterprise was founded on a misapprehension, a geographical fiction, a fairy tale, springing out of the kind of stories sailors tell to amaze landsmen, or delude other sailors, to which were soon added the inferences, speculations and downright inventions that scholars manufacture to amaze themselves' (Thomson 1975: 1). Inevitably, pre-exploratory and exploratory images are liable to be least in accord with reality.

Frontier movement

Early images of the North American interior are but one example of perceived landscapes which influenced the behaviour of explorers, entrepreneurs and possibly settlers.. Frontier movement throughout the new areas of settlement reflected the available land appraisals and pressures from the source areas. An early attempt to relate perception and the frontier was made by Heathcote (1965) in an exemplary study of interior New South Wales and Queensland. Heathcote (1965) distinguished between popular and official ideas about the area, assessed the process of exploration and provided a discussion of settlement and development from first occupation in 1836 to mid-twentieth century. The importance of varied and often incorrect images is evident from the trial-and-error character of the pioneering phase.

The relevance of various pressures from the source areas is clear in the South African case. Friction between Dutch settlers and an English administration was one reason for the spectacular inland movements of the Boer population away from the established Cape area. In the United States the notion of manifest destiny and the Monroe Doctrine of 1823 were important pressures, and the frontier movement was being continually justified in terms of a right to occupy the empty west and the notion of natural growth. Wishart (1979) noted that the impact of frontier spread on the Pawnee groups of Nebraska and Kansas included attempts to convert the aboriginals to American ways and that the ever-decreasing land available to them prompted a migration aimed at maintaining a traditional life-style. The American perception of an appropriate aboriginal life-style was a poor match of the corresponding aboriginal goal. One especially clear example of the forces at work behind frontier expansion and of related culture conflict is provided by Jackson (1966) as one part of a discussion of the 1874 Custer expedition to the Black Hills of South Dakota. This area remained *terra incognita* in 1874. For the army it was seen as an area containing hostile Sioux populations, while for settlers to the east the area was assumed on the basis of limited knowledge to be a valuable source of gold. A Black Hills Exploring and Mining Association was formed in 1861, but before any exploration occurred a treaty of 1868 reserved a large area west of the Missouri, including the Black Hills, to the Sioux. The pressure of westward movement was lessened briefly, but arguments for American involvement soon returned and Jackson (1966: 9) quoted a Dakota judge in 1872: 'There are other sources of wealth in the Black Hills besides the gold. We want the lumber to build our cities and towns. . . .' The Custer expedition of 1874 was an army endeavour aimed at reconnoitring an area sheltering hostile Sioux but, to civilians, Custer was going to discover gold. Indeed, Custer was accompanied by private miners and the hoped-for gold was discovered. The response was inevitable. Miners moved into the Hills, army efforts to enforce the 1868 treaty were of limited success and a new treaty was signed opening the Hills to American settlement. Jackson (1966: 120) summarized these developments as follows: 'The American people had put the Hills on their list many years before, neatly ticketing it as land the Indians did not need.' This example emphasizes the importance of the very different aboriginal and American perceptions of an area and the forces at work behind the American perception.

Image-makers

Although the details of image creation varied from place to place and time to time there have been attempts to generalize the appropriate image-makers (Merrens 1969). In the South African context Christopher (1973) argued that the image-maker was crucial and five classes, following Merrens (1969), were recognized: promoters, officials, settlers, travellers and natural historians. Promoters were prolific writers but with little first-hand knowledge and their accounts, which reflected their interests, were typically exaggerations. For pre-settlement New Zealand J. A. Johnston (1979) showed, by means of an evaluation assertive analysis, that the view being promoted of New Zealand soils was exceptionally favourable. Official literature was much more variable than that of the promoters, but did include some objective accounts. For interior eastern Australia Heathcote (1965: 61) noted that official attitudes changed through time partly in response to actual settler experience. Settler literature is necessarily biased reflecting, as it does, the views of only the more literate pioneers. Initially such literature was optimistic, as in New Zealand (J. A. Johnston 1979) where settlers might not wish to admit defeat after a costly migration, but gradually it became more realistic. Accounts by travellers were typically of limited value, but some offered realistic accounts of difficulties and of settler achievement. A major study of the Ohio Valley focused exclusively on the impressions of travellers and noted utilitarian, romantic, picturesque and ecological approaches to landscape (Jakle 1977). Finally, the work of natural historians was of limited relevance to image creation as there were few comments on human landscapes.

Merrens (1979) developed the image-making concept further by providing a selection of contemporary colonial accounts of one area, South Carolina. The accounts include, for example, initial views by settlers from specific source areas. The overall result is a picture of the area as it was perceived by a number of relevant individuals and it is clear that many different perceptions prevailed.

It is evident that early appraisals of a landscape were typically widely divergent. A clear instance of differing interpretations was provided by Peters (1972) with reference to open oak woodlands in a part of Michigan. Early surveyors regarded these openings as infertile and unsuitable for settlement, only to be followed by settlers who viewed the openings much more highly. The different interpretations were explained in terms of the source areas of the assessors, with those who evaluated the areas poorly being from the Ohio Valley and those with favourable appraisals being from western New York. Another example is that of colonial Port Royal in South Carolina which was also evaluated differently by different groups (Kovacik and Rowland 1973). The early seafaring image was favourable because of strategic factors and the availability of timber and fish. The early settler image included travel difficulties, isolation, lack of security and lack of a commercially developed hinterland.

Images in frontier areas

Much has already been said concerning the images created and held for areas of new settlement. The following discussion emphasizes the crucial importance of prevailing perceptions for economic development in general.

According to Bowen (1978: 95), 'the weight of Oregon's pioneer literature argues convincingly that a search for good health brought many, if not most, settlers west' and thus encouraged development. Early appraisals of the Sacramento Valley for agricultural purposes, however, delayed growth for the cultivation possibilities were thought to be limited (Thompson 1975). Several of the early negative appraisals of the valley resulted from equating trees with fertility. Precisely this procedure was employed by settlers in southern Ontario when land was being chosen for wheat cultivation (Kelly 1970). Indeed, for southern Ontario farmers a variety of guidebooks were available which ranked soil according to vegetation and according to the ease of clearing and cultivation. It is uncertain as to how correct such assessments were and as to the influence they exerted. An analysis of settlement location decisions in Texas concluded that pioneers favoured having both forest and grassland and did not avoid grassland as is often assumed (Jordan 1975).

Settlement and development of the southern prairie region of Canada were affected by the mid-nineteenth-century surveys of Palliser which resulted in the notion of an infertile area. According to Jankunis (1977) these perceptions resulted from the area being assessed by humid forest standards. One result of these early impressions was, possibly, a delay in settlement, and when settlement did take place after 1905 many technological developments and adaptations were necessary. For the Peace River area of northern Alberta and British Columbia, which was first settled after 1910, there were highly variable initial appraisals and eventual settlement is difficult to explain. Unlike much North American expansion, settlement preceded the railway and Tracie (1973: 121) was uncertain as to whether 'settlement was *pushed* into the Peace or was *attracted* to the Peace'. Overall it appears that 'the individual settler or speculator was a law unto himself in regard to the selection of land' (Tyman 1973: 89). All settlers received considerable and conflicting advice and ultimate decisions were a response to advice, background and need.

The core area concept was applied by Quastler (1978) to emphasize major changes in images of Californian agriculture between 1800 and 1890. The changes resulted from writers focusing on different locations at different times in response to other economic developments. This example, and others, indicate a steadily increasing correspondence of image and reality through time as experience develops. Such a statement applies in the perception of port sites on the Cape coast of South Africa. Conflicting early-nineteenth-century reports included recognition of twenty-four landing places which met specific environmental criteria (Clark 1977). Eventually, however, port site selection was in close accord to physical realities.

A discussion of environmental perception in frontier areas clearly has enormous implications. There was often a difference between image and reality, images changed through time, at any one time there were several different images and images affected behaviour. It is hardly surprising that perception is a fundamental component of many analyses of landscape change.

Group perceptions

So far in these discussions there has not been any explicit distinction between individuals and groups. Such a distinction is often not needed, but there are some instances where a group perception is fundamental. Usually this applies when a religious or ethnic group occupies a landscape and has some distinctive and effective institutional structure. Perhaps the best American example of such a group image was that held by the Mormons of the Great Salt Lake area. According to Jackson (1978) a Mormon perception was formulated prior to settlement and influenced the direction of settlement spread for over three decades. A key feature of their image was that the area north of Salt Lake was unsuitable for crops, hence expansion was southwards into a relatively difficult environment. To encourage movement the Mormon leaders found it necessary to claim that the Salt Lake area was no better than land to the south, a claim which contradicted their early views and which resulted in some marginal agricultural settlement. A rather different example of Mormon spread concerned movement into the Greybull Valley of Wyoming where Mormon migration decisions were made 'on the basis of information furnished to them by horse thieves, casual travellers and back country stockmen' (Bowen 1976: 48). Specific location decisions reflected the assumption that the best soils supported the tallest sagebrush. Such decisions were not a result of central Mormon influence.

Powell (1977: 152–69) provided a discussion of the perceptions and related behaviour of Utopian and millennial groups in the United States, Australia and New Zealand and noted the distinctive resulting landscapes. However, distinctive landscapes did not result only from well-organized groups. For one part of Texas Jordan (1980) noted that German settlers had retained characteristic landscape features, including church towers. Somewhat similarly Ostergren (1980) analysed Swedish settlement patterns in one part of South Dakota, a pattern which reflected community organization. Any discussion of group experiences in areas of new settlement tends to reflect the consequences of individuals adhering to a group perception, a group perception which may essentially result from one leader's assessment and aspirations.

Image distortion

The likelihood of substantially incorrect images prevailing during the years of exploration and of first settlement has already been recognized. However, it is also likely that images, incorrect or otherwise, were distorted in the process of communication. A vivid example of such distortion was offered by Cameron (1974) with reference to the Swan River colony of Western Australia. Information on the area was gleaned from a voyage by Stirling in 1827 and a report produced which was made public only in an edited version written by Barrow, an authority on the southern hemisphere, and published in the *Quarterly Review* in 1829. The report by Barrow was then used for an article in the *Mirror* and another in the *New Monthly Magazine*, both in 1829. The distortions of Stirling's original report proved remarkable. For example, the area suited for cultivation was estimated at 100 square miles by Stirling, 8,600 by the *Quarterly Review* and the *Mirror* and 22,000 by the *New Monthly Magazine* (Cameron 1974: 66).

Information available to potential settlers is always distorted and research needs to focus explicitly on the degree of distortion and how distortion came about. Perceptions depend upon points of view as well as upon information, a position made abundantly clear by Dicken and Dicken (1979: 8) referring to one pro-Oregon United States senator who suggested that a canal be built to that new territory.

Summary comments

Perception literature in historical geography is now commonplace and there is every reason to anticipate both further studies in similar vein and a continuing sophistication and expansion of interest. Clark (1975c: xiii) outlined a number of models of image-making and noted that the number of different perceptions of a given area was often large. In addition to offering a valuable corrective to many regional analyses a perception approach also invites a humanistic emphasis. A further area of study in which perception promises to play a key role is that of past landscape preservation (Lowenthal 1979). Our understanding of both past and present will continue to be enhanced by studies utilizing perception-based approaches.

CHAPTER SIX

Exploration, immigration and the frontier

Accounts of the emergence of human landscapes in areas of new settlement characteristically proceed by first examining the details of exploration, contacts with existing aboriginal groups, immigration trends and the related evolution of a frontier economy and society. It is unusual for a specific analysis to concern itself with the broader issue of European expansion as a whole. This attempt to focus on these issues uses a diverse body of research literature relating primarily to the United States, Canada, South Africa, Australia and New Zealand. The chapter is divided into four sections dealing with exploration and the role of aboriginals, immigration processes and trends, the frontier scene and, finally, a consideration of relevant processes. The magnitude of European overseas movement is remarkable. The demographic invasion of the temperate zones has increased the European percentage of the total population from 18 in 1650 to over 30 in 1900 in association with an increased life-span and a high birthrate. The available literature is, inevitably perhaps, largely framed in terms of a western capitalistic mentality and has accordingly been subject to some criticism. The process of European overseas expansion is regarded by Blaut (1970: 65) as imperialism or 'white exploitation of the non-white world, a plague that began some 500 years ago on the West African coast and spread across the globe'. Although such comments relate essentially to a Third World context, today there is a clear application to historical studies which focus on European expansion. This view has argued that western models of thought govern all aspects of analysis into current Third World problems and past problems of any area being settled, and that such models may be highly inappropriate for they often 'convey the root belief in an ineffable European spirit, a sui generis cause of European evolution and expansion' (Blaut 1970: 73). Such a view is exemplified by the following statement: 'European civilisation arose and flowered, until in the end it covered the face of the earth' (Bloch, quoted by Blaut 1970: 73). Four assumptions characterize this approach: first, that Europe can be regarded as an entity; second, that European developments were internally generated; third, that cultures outside of Europe were primitive when first contacted; and fourth, that European expansion was also internally generated. Certainly, the literature utilized in this chapter requires appraisal in the light of this potential criticism.

EXPLORATION

The literature of historical geography includes many examples of writings which focus explicitly on exploration (for example, Crone 1962; Gilbert 1966). Unfortunately the majority of such work does not attempt either to place specific explorations in any general context or to relate exploration to subsequent developments. The topic has been pursued largely *per se* without any substantial discussion of related issues. Further, most studies have not exploited recent, largely post-1960, advances in human geography. Such a state of affairs is hardly surprising, but it has meant that exploration has not typically been included as a substantial component of wider evolutionary discussions. There are indications, however, that historical geographers are revising their approach. The incorporation of behavioural concepts into research has led to assessments of exploratory images (Dicken and Dicken 1979) and to attempts to conceptualize the exploratory process (Allen 1972; Overton 1981).

With particular reference to the Lewis and Clark expedition of 1804–06, Allen (1972) analysed the relationship between geographical knowledge and exploration as measured by the accuracy of regional knowledge. Allen (1972: 14–17) argued that such knowledge was based on both accepted geographical reality and perceptions. Exploratory behaviour is likely to be successful when an explorer can correctly distinguish between actual and perceived knowledge, as was the case with Lewis and Clark. Somewhat similarly Ruggles (1971) focused on a series of inaccurate cartographic images of the Canadian west and their relationships to exploration. The discussion of exploration needs, however, to go beyond considerations of images, correct or otherwise. Taking cues from contemporary geography, from history and from economic history Overton (1981: 56) developed a conceptual framework of the exploratory process on the grounds that: 'Patterns should be recognized and explained and greater emphasis should be placed on the causes and effects of exploration.' The framework involved six factors: a demand consideration; the choice of area; the exploration itself; the resulting reports; evaluation of reports by decision-makers; and subsequent development. Most writing on exploration has, of course, focused on the journey itself although some work has emphasized the reports and their evaluation (Cameron 1974; J. A. Johnston 1979). The framework was the basis for a study of the Nelson Colony of New Zealand between 1841 and 1865 and facilitated the conclusion that exploration was neither a random nor an even process through time. Explanation of the temporal pattern relied upon the three economic motives of land shortage, a need for new routes and a search for mineral resources. Use of such a framework, possibly amended for specific areas, is likely to enhance understanding of both the exploratory process itself and the association between the process and the subsequent economic developments.

The role of aboriginals

The significance of native populations for both exploration and, indeed, for subsequent landscape change has been little studied. The in-movement of Europeans has typically been seen as a major cultural break, a revolutionary change, rather than as one part of an ongoing process. Recent literature, however, has emphasized the aboriginal groups as explorers and the incoming European groups as being much dependent on existing regional knowledge. Further, the aboriginal groups were effective settlers with the European contribution being imposed upon existing land use (Reynolds 1980).

One important role played by aboriginals related to their employment as advisers and guides for explorers. For Australia Reynolds (1980: 214–17) referred to their value as experts in bushcraft, as providers of locational information and as diplomats when contiguous groups were contacted. Following exploration the first settlers could also learn a great deal from the existing inhabitants. The Australian example is probably characteristic. The early *coureurs de bois* in Canada relied heavily on Indian knowledge of the environment to survive and made considerable use of Indian cultural traits, especially the birch-bark canoe. For the fur trade of the northern Great Plains Wishart (1976: 319) noted that the Indians' role permeated the entire process. Indeed, Indians typically represented the edge of the fur-trade system, playing an active exploratory role. A comparable example is that of the Canadian fur trade through until the twentieth century and Usher (1975) related the western Canadian Arctic fur trade to the expansion of Inuit groups. Thus, in addition to providing detailed and locally accurate environmental data, the aboriginals also provided needed technology and involved themselves in both exploration and early economic growth. The importance of the aboriginal contribution was closely related to the quality of the environment with difficult locations demanding much dependence. Reynolds (1980: 222) noted that exploration in arid Australia occasionally involved pressuring natives to provide needed information, especially the whereabouts of water.

European penetration of new lands was not a penetration of unoccupied or untouched environments. The frequent conflict situations which developed are a clear indication of the widespread distribution of natives and of their attachment to and exploitation of particular areas, and North American literature frequently emphasizes the process of land surrender (for example, Raby 1973). Thus, aboriginal populations were utilized where and when necessary and removed where and when necessary. They played key roles in most explorations and in some economic developments, especially fur-trade activities in North America, but experienced conflict and pressure when their exploitation of the land was not compatible with that of the European newcomers, as was largely the case in South Africa.

THE PROCESS OF MIGRATION

There is an abundance of literature, both conceptual and empirical, relating to the causes, details and consequences of migration. This section considers, first, migration as it relates to distance and economic factors, second, the New World migration and third, restrictive immigration policies.

Distance and economic factors

The basic premise that distance is one of the principal determinants of spatial patterns is widely accepted (Watson 1955), but merely to recognize that distance is important is not adequate. It is necessary to ascertain what form of distance is appropriate and it is necessary to examine the nature of the relationship between distance and the volume of movement. The impact of distance may be in terms of the physical distance, the perceived distance, the cost of travel or the time involved in travel. For example, in early-nineteenth-century Ontario distance was a reflection of transport costs, time of travel and effort expended, with settler migrations aiming to minimize all three, each of which may increase with distance. The problem is further complicated because in making a migration and location decision the individual is not actually moving, for decisions were normally made in a major centre prior to any move. Further, an individual may be only slightly concerned about the cost, time or effort of the original move; the principal concern may be the distance between the selected location and a market and distributing centre, with prospective farmers anticipating frequent trips for the purpose of buying and selling. In such a situation the crucial interpretation of distance is likely to be that of the effort expended, for cost of travel increases only slightly with increasing distance and the time taken is probably directly related to distance. Given the assumption that the volume of migration decreases with increasing distance between source and destination it is necessary to identify relationships between migration and distance which indicate the friction of distance.

'Mathematical distance decay functions are convenient formalizations to reflect real behaviour of perception and response to distance (Morrill and Kelley 1970: 297). Unfortunately, most such functions are descriptive not explanatory, they are able to describe a relationship but not to isolate cause and effect. Essentially this limitation results from the fact that they reflect the effects of a variety of factors, all of which are associated with distance. Morrill (1963, 1965a) discussed a variety of functions with the intention of fitting these to observed data such that the most appropriate were discovered. It was emphasized that, 'it is futile to seek one simple function that will always relate distance to migration since the underlying logical conditions or circumstances of nature constantly vary for different kinds of movement' (Morrill 1963: 76). A function and specific parameters which might successfully indicate the friction of distance on migration in 1840 Ontario might be a poor description for 1840 Cape Province. In general, simple inverse linear relationships are unrealistic and some form of negative exponential relationship is favoured such as a logarithmic, log-normal, exponential or gamma function.

The role of the economic motive was emphasized by Isaac (1947) and Porter (1956) with most long-distance migrations being economically oriented. Much of the migration from Europe to the New World was a movement of people with little to lose. Descriptions of the conditions of Irish and Scottish peasants illustrate the suffering experienced by many (Woodham-Smith 1963). Given sufficiently poor home conditions, migration anywhere might appear desirable, and hence the pull exerted by the New World need only to have been its availability.

Many of the above comments have relied implicitly on the seminal work of Ravenstein which was summarized and reviewed by Grigg (1977). Two of the laws, restated by Grigg (1977: 42–3), refer to the effect of distance, with the majority of migrants moving short distances, and to economic causes as being paramount. Most subsequent work has demonstrated the validity of both of these laws.

Much of the recent work on migration in a historical context has treated migration as a behavioural process, emphasizing perception of environments, information-gathering, search procedures and decision-making. Roseman (1971) noted that it was necessary to identify the decision-making unit, to acknowledge the two-step, first general then specific, location decision-making, and to research thoroughly the process of information gathering. The following discussion of New World migration applies and reinforces these and other ideas by reference to a series of conceptual and empirical analyses.

Migration to the New World

Migrations have origins, obstacles and destinations. Discussions of origins have often focused on the causes of movement, causes which are subject to continual change. One analysis of Scottish data for the period 1760–90 revealed that 'economic, political and technological forces came into play at varying times and at differing intensities during the critical period' (Adams 1976: 4) Between 1760 and 1775 the agricultural changes occurring in Scotland provided an economic incentive to migrate; between 1775 and 1783 substantial military movement took place, and, from 1783 to 1790 migration was lessened as industry began to offer a legitimate alternative to movement. In arriving at these generalizations Adams (1976) acknowledged several data limitations, a point which was also made by Handcock (1976, 1977) with reference to British migration to Newfoundland. For Newfoundland the eighteenth- and nine-teenth-century situations are confused by the considerable presence of temporary migrants. Two major source areas were defined, namely south-east Ireland and south-west England, and the relationship between prior trading routes and subsequent migration streams generally confirmed (Handcock 1977: 44). A final example of this type of work was provided by Cameron (1972) with reference to Scottish emigration to Ontario during the first half of the nineteenth century. Five types of obstacles were defined (Cameron 1972: 404): distance, associated cost and the availability of transportation; a set of political barriers; the problems of organizing such a basic move; the tendency to personal inertia and, finally, the availability of information.

Studies of migration have typically focused on home conditions, on the mechanics of movement and on the qualities of the receiving environments.

Despite much work there remains only a limited comprehension of the causes of migration beyond simplistic push-and-pull logic. Attention needs to be focused on the source areas and on their social and economic character as it affected migrants and others. Recognition that some leave while others, similarly affected, elect to remain prompts analysis at the individual behavioural level. In some cases the decision to migrate represented a deviation from normal behaviour, in other instances it was a normal route to follow. Detailed analyses of source areas might reveal much about the emigration process. Somewhat similarly, analyses of individual moves increase our understanding of the choice of new location. Cameron (1972), for example, emphasized the importance of available knowledge and especially the sometimes crucial role played by friends and relatives. The related question of the place of birth of migrants was considered by Walker (1975: 59) with the aim being to 'devise a measure which will indicate a concentration of settlers with a common area of birth which would likely be greater than that produced by a random combination of migrants in a settlement region'. Such a measure was used to analyse one California county between 1860 and 1880, and it was shown that most settler groups had a low clustering propensity and that clusters tended to weaken as rural districts declined. Certainly this measure might be applied to areas, such as southern Manitoba, where it is possible that the location of friends and relatives was a key location consideration.

A somewhat different approach to the causes of movement and to the choice of a new location has been evident in economic history. Dunlevy and Gemery (1976) analysed data relating to the intended destination of Scandinavian migrants for 1897–98 using a series of multiple regression models. Independent variables related to the per capita income of particular states, the number of people with jobs in particular states, the population density of particular states, the distance from the entry point of New York to the principal city of the state, a measure of climate and a measure of regional location. Both *per capita* income and the number employed emerged as positive and significant variables. Distance, however, seemed unrelated to settlement intentions. A second set of results distinguished between four groups of Scandinavians and offered support for the hypothesis that family and friends were an important consideration such that 'Scandinavian settlers were strongly attracted by the presence of their countrymen who had earlier settled in the United States' (Dunlevy and Gemery 1976: 150). This study and others (Vedder and Galloway 1972) suggested the paramount importance, at a group level of aggregation and at a regional scale, of economic causes as opposed to measures of distance. Further work by Dunlevy (1980) focused on both intended one-year and the actual lifetime settlement patterns. Migrants were shown to be more dispersed over their lifetimes than their original intentions suggested. With regard to distance, Dunlevy (1980: 89) found no evidence that the most recent immigrants moved furthest west, rather they initially settled at ports of entry and only gradually moved west. This state of affairs is intriguingly similar to the observation of Ravenstein (Grigg 1977) that migrants move step by step and is also in accord with established thinking in economic history (Williamson 1974: 223).

The above discussion has employed only a small portion of the available studies of migration which refer explicitly to the overseas movement involved in New World migration. Several foci are evident. First, there continues to be a growing concern with the causes of movement and causes are characteristically classified as economic and distance. Second, there is an increasing concern with the specifics of the process, details of home environments, of the available information and of the mechanics and cost of movement. Third, detailed studies have exploited behavioural procedures aimed at clarifying such issues as search, uncertainty and decision-making. Fourth, a significant positivistic emphasis is evident in the work of both historical geographers (for example, Handcock 1976, 1977) and in that of economic historians (Dunlevy and Gemery 1976; Dunlevy 1980). A final emphasis, explicitly evident in economic history although only implicitly used by historical geographers, relates to the use of counterfactuals. Williamson (1974: 247) considered the question of immigration and economic growth and concluded that 'immigration to America in the late nineteenth century was not significantly influenced by either the frontier or indigenous demographic forces'. Analyses of historical migrations are of course but one component of a major field of research, and the historical researcher has a wide body of literature which can be exploited.

It is generally accepted that New World migration was a multi-stage process with internal movements succeeding the overseas trip (Williamson 1974: 223). For Iowa, between 1840 and 1910, Conzen (1974) noted that settlement was mainly by native-born Americans and also by direct and indirect European immigration. Migration was both westward, local and regional, and urban oriented. Similar results are evident for the late-nineteenth-century Dakotas (Hudson, 1973, 1976). Discussion of internal and especially frontier movements has prompted speculation concerning the character of the movements as either a response to economic stimuli or as a way of life. A penetrating analysis of the emergence of North American communities emphasized that mobility was a major concern in any explanation (Sutter 1973). For South African settlers there is little doubt that life at the Cape was unsatisfactory c. 1800, for the policy was to regard Cape Town as a supply base and actively discourage a developing economy. In migration terms this represented a push to settlers. Inland movement was also caused by the prevailing law of inheritance, namely equal division among sons. It might be argued that the movement from one land to another and any movement within the new land are very different phenomena. Even where both sets of causes are economic in character they are liable to be different in detail.

Restrictive immigration

The movement of populations to a new land was not a simple process. In some cases the movement was forced, as with some early Australian immigrants; in other cases it was a desperate response to severe economic hardship, as with many European migrants in the 1840s; for others it was a carefully made and rationalized decision aimed at improving economic circumstances, as with some ventures in nineteenth-century Ontario such as that by John Langton in 1833 who 'decided to try his hand at farming in the colony, in preference to what might be a long and unrenumerative period as a junior barrister in England' (Langton 1950: ii), and for yet others it was a movement aimed at escaping persecution in the homeland, as with Dukhobor moves to the Canadian prairies in the 1890s. The classifications are numerous and in some respects not especially useful although they do suggest one thing, namely that the New World was available to all. Unfortunately such was not the case, and restrictive immigration policies evolved in Australia, New Zealand, South Africa, Canada and the United States. London (1970) argued that policies such as that of 'White Australia' resulted from feelings of European, especially British, superiority and were explicitly racist in character. This issue has been further developed by Huttenback (1976) although the work fails to explain why racism emerged in particular places at particular times (Monk 1978: 194). Overall, discriminatory immigration policies emerged in the late nineteenth century and continued through as late as the mid-twentieth century. Indeed, such policies are an integral part of contemporary South African attitudes.

The emergence of Australian restrictions stems from the early in movement of Chinese labourers followed by increasing immigration to work in the goldmines. A Victoria Bill in 1855 established restrictive legislation and was followed by similar Bills in other states. By 1901 restriction was extended to all coloured peoples by requiring immigrant literacy in a European language. For New Zealand, Roy (1970: 16) noted four factors explaining the evolution of restrictive practices. First, there was a fear of cheap labour causing incomes to drop; second, fears of competition in the retail business; third, many politicians were explicitly racist; and fourth, the British stereotype was quite simply seen to be desirable. Chinese immigration commenced in the 1860s, often from Australia, and the result of subsequent concern and prejudice was a restrictive Immigration Act in 1881. In 1899 this Act was superseded by one which included the education requirement already noted for Australia. Policies were amended throughout the succeeding years. British Columbia evolved somewhat similar tactics. Initially, Chinese immigrants were welcome as cheap labour, but discriminatory practices began in 1885 with the introduction of a head tax for incoming Chinese. This tax amount was steadily increased until, in 1923, an Act was passed which effectively prevented all Chinese immigration. The Act was repealed in 1947. Similar tactics were employed with reference to both Japanese and East Indians (Lai 1979).

The patterns throughout are depressingly familiar. Restrictive immigration policies typically applied to persons of Asiatic origin and the rationale included explicitly racist assertions and concerns about the economic welfare of existing settlers. Any study of immigration might profitably study those who came, those who elected not to come and those offered no choice. Explanations of movement ought not to exclude institutional controls restricting the source areas.

THE FRONTIER

Historians and historical geographers have developed and exploited the idea of the frontier considerably since it was first introduced by Turner in 1893 (Savage and Thompson 1979: 3). Movements to frontiers and frontier life in general have been analysed, not only in the United States but also in Canada, South America, Australia, New Zealand, Asia and Europe. The notion of the frontier has been very attractive and yet the term remains imprecise today. This section first considers the concept of the frontier and this is followed by a discussion of selected frontier studies. Explicit analyses of frontier agriculture, frontier settlement, urban frontiers and social aspects are reserved for later chapters.

Frontier concepts

One explanation for the attraction of frontier research suggested that the frontier has proven, 'a rich source of metaphorical and mythological inspiration' with recent work having extended the frontier concept to include an urban night frontier and a ghetto frontier (Livingstone and Harrison 1980: 128). Such extensions of the concept are not surprising given the many and varied interpretations which have been evident. Originally the frontier concept was utilized only by historians, and the work by Bowman (1931) on the geography of pioneer zones was detached from the main stream of historical research. It was only during the 1960s that geography began explicitly to apply the Turnerian frontier concept. Turner applied the concept to American history and argued that the combination of expanding frontier and disappearing wilderness was crucial in influencing both American history and American character. Turner (1961. 30) wrote:

'American development has exhibited not merely advance along a single line, but a return to primitive conditions on a continually advancing frontier line, and a new development for that area. American social development has been continually beginning over again on the frontier.... In this advance the frontier is the outer edge of the wave – the meeting point between savagery and civilisation.'

The development of interest in frontier work has been chronologically detailed by Savage and Thompson (1979). Within history the early ideas of Turner have been especially elaborated by Webb (1964) who regarded the American experience as but a small part of a much wider European expansion, and by Billington (1966) who effectively redefined the frontier in terms of a population–resource relationship. Probably the first important geographical contribution to refer directly to Turner was a comparative study of Canadian, Australian and South African experiences (Mikesell 1960). Since 1960 the geographical contribution has been appreciable and has resulted in some intriguing interpretations.

The lack of a precise definition has been criticized by Guelke (1979) for allowing two different phenomena to be subsumed under the heading of frontier work, namely new land settlement and the interaction between Europeans and aboriginals. The latter was favoured and the frontier period was argued to begin with initial European settlement and to end with the effective removal of aboriginals as competitors for land (Guelke 1979: 1). Such a definition clearly allows for both very short and very long frontier periods, indeed it might be argued that frontiers in North America and South Africa are not yet closed as there continue to be land conflicts which are unresolved. Guelke (1979: 8) also chose to define the closing of the frontier as being typically related to the beginnings of commerical development which facilitated recognition of an essentially subsistence-oriented economy. The impact of the frontier was greatest, therefore, in areas of relatively slow economic growth, such as South Africa, and the impact was least over large parts of the United States. These conclusions are open to some criticism as they are so dependent on the definition of the frontier as essentially excluding commercial developments, a definition which is somewhat unusual.

In addition to involving economic, social and political ideas (Whebell 1979) the concept of the frontier has direct spatial implications. Eigenheer (1973–74) referred to four such aspects. First, the frontier can be interpreted as a series of regions of differing economic character. Although largely discredited today the interpretation is an intriguing one. Second, the frontier can be seen as a cultural hearth for such ideas as American democracy and for a creative realism, and as an innovation centre for mining and other technology. A third interpretation views the frontier as a region, in the formal geographic sense of the term, which is continually moving. A final spatial interpretation concerns the closing of the frontier which effectively makes free land unavailable and thus affects human use of the earth.

The frontier is both a complex and a confused concept. Although it has been used extensively it has not been possible, and it is probably not desirable, to achieve an unambiguous and acceptable definition. In the context of emerging landscape the frontier is best seen as the outer limit of new, usually European, settlement. It typically succeeds exploration and immigration and is the scene of initial economic and social growth. In addition the related culture contact is of interest.

Frontier studies

Empirical analyses of the frontier are diverse in character – as might be expected from tests of an ambiguous concept. Three variables are evident in most frontier studies: time, location and population (Hudson 1977), and frontier studies thus have a framework for definition. Within this framework four useful sets of ideas are evident: namely length of residence concepts, migration field concepts, land-use competition concepts and innovation diffusion concepts. Each of these four was outlined by Hudson (1977) and advocated as an area of potential analysis. Unfortunately the reality of empirical frontier research is not quite so straightforward or limited. Certainly both types of migration studies are evident in both economic history and historical geography, land-use studies comprise a significant component of frontier work and diffusion concepts are also evident. Much research, however, is not easily classified for researchers have focused on a diverse set of topics, areas and times. This section attempts to reflect that diversity and is organized regionally, dealing first with the United States followed by Canada, Australia, South Africa, Europe, Asia and South America.

Technically, hypotheses which have been empirically derived in a given area are only legitimately tested using other areas and hence other data. Such restriction has not deterred United States research and rightly so for two reasons. First, Turnerian frontier hypotheses were not derived from the United States as a whole but from specific regions and, further, were not totally empirical in character being at least partly intuitive. Second, Turnerian hypotheses are not the only topics investigated. Turner may have originated frontier work, but not all work can be simply traced back to these early ideas.

One specific area of concern for United States research has been prompted by the traditional measure of the frontier as being the outer edge of an area with a population density of two or more per square mile. This one measure has been regarded as inadequate and Hart (1974: 74) suggested four population-density frontiers: 'Two persons per square mile marked the outer limits of any occupance, six marked the limits of settlement, eighteen the limits of agriculture, and forty-five the limits of urbanisation.' These figures are, of course, considered appropriate for the area analysed, in this case the American midwest. Analysis revealed a straightforward growth model, with rapid early growth in the course of one generation followed by stability or some decline. The size of the rural population is related to farm size and size of farm families. Such ideas require further elaboration and testing. Studies of population dynamics have usually noted the need for a continually expanding frontier to absorb both immigrants and local increases (Ironside *et al*. 1974: 262). A related set of ideas has focused on the retreat of frontiers which resulted usually from expansion into marginal areas. United States mining frontiers represent one example. Economic growth has been a second major area of concern in the United States, with agricultural and industrial growth being evident in studies by Kay (1979), Lewis (1979a) and Wills (1979). Related work has attempted to explain frontier movement in terms of such factors as railroads (Davis 1974) although the lesson from economic history suggested caution was necessary in analysing such relationships. Social issues have been detailed by Bartlett (1974) in a work which largely failed to utilize the contributions of historical geographers. Investigations of the ethnic composition of the American south-west have noted the early rise of prejudicial attitudes towards minority groups, in this case people of Spanish origin (Bailey and Haulman 1977).

Frontier studies in Canada demonstrate an even broader concern for, in addition to historical work, there has been work focusing on contemporary northern frontiers. A classic historical work on the Canadian frontier is that by Eccles (1969). For Canada before 1760 four types of frontier were evident, namely commercial, religious, settlement and military, and these together 'embraced the entire area, not merely the outer fringes of the territory in North America controlled by France' (Eccles 1969: 2). This assertion implies that the early Canadian frontier was quite different to that further south where the frontier was indeed the advancing edge of settlement. A similar assertion might be appropriate for the pre-1800 South African frontier, another area where the level of immigration was inadequate to generate a genuine moving settlement edge. Later Canadian frontiers, from perhaps 1776 onwards, conform more closely to the perceived American norm, being regions distant from food supplies, with little communication with any core area and with low population densities. In many instances it had been necessary to offer incentives in order to encourage growth, as in Ontario with free land until 1826 and free land again after 1868 in the more isolated areas. On the western Canadian frontier railway subsidies were offered to stimulate development, but quite often such incentives were not adequate to result in the hoped-for growth: 'Even a large scale immigration campaign and the completion of the transcontinental railway in 1885 did not produce a rapid extension of the agricultural frontier' (Ironside et al. 1974: 5). The contemporary Canadian frontier is penalized in physical, economic and social terms and is available at a time when large-scale immigration is no longer possible. Thus contemporary frontier development is heavily dependent on government support.

The issue of governmental support is evident elsewhere. A detailed discussion of the wheat frontier in south-eastern Australia argued that, 'having begun by building railways to serve existing settlers, the states found themselves building railways to attract new settlement' (Andrews 1966: 61). The Australian frontier has been used as a testing-ground for Turnerian concepts and the hypotheses found to be inappropriate. The frontier of 1829 involved a sheep frontier, a cattle frontier and a mixed farming frontier, each physically and socially distinct such that any transformations caused by the frontier necessarily varied from place to place (Perry 1963: 123). In the South African context Christopher (1976: 245–50) applied Turnerian ideas and observed some similarities, but concluded that land tenure was a major deviating factor. It is not only the character of the frontier and its spatial movement which is questioned but also the causes of expansion. The inland expansion of settlers from Cape Town was prompted by problems of local food supply, but continued regardless of market demand (Guelke 1976b). Such a conclusion is at variance with many explanations of frontier expansion which relate movement to explicit demand factors. Ironside et al. (1974: 2), for example, noted that frontier movement responded to market conditions. Three factors have been suggested as influencing European settlement advance in northern Australia, namely, distance, the seasonal climate and ignorance (Bauer 1963) with the distance factor being especially elaborated by Blainey (1966).

Frontier analyses have not by any means been limited to the major areas of European overseas expansion. In Finland, c. 1800, little incentive was offered to pioneers, a situation which is reversed today (Mead 1959: 147–8). The contemporary Finnish frontier is unstable, experiencing periodic advances and retreats. A European example with some similarity to New World examples is evident for western Europe between 800 and 1500. Lewis (1958) argued that this area expanded until about 1250 and then gradually expansion became difficult as new land was scarce. The result of a closing frontier was mounting tensions and eventually disease and war.

Changing attitudes towards frontier regions are evident in two studies focusing on China. Samuels (1971) noted changes with reference to the nineteenth-century north-west frontier area, while Eckstein *et al.* (1974) focused on Manchuria after 1860 and emphasized the various policies designed to restrict population expansion and yet defend the frontier region at the same time. A more general frontier analysis is available for Latin America, an area which shares the historical experience of the United States and elsewhere in terms of European conquest, and the history of Latin America involves constant frontier development (Hennessy 1978). Although closely tied to Turnerian concepts, this study demonstrated the diversity of Latin American frontiers and noted the diverse societies generated by the frontiers. In terms of settlement much of Latin America continues to be frontier in character.

The discussions presented above indicate the wide range of frontier studies in terms of the areas researched, the time periods and the aspects of the frontier analysed. Comparative studies play a major role, as evidenced by the continuing publication, from 1975 onwards, of the newsletter *Comparative Frontier Studies*. Attempts to test the ideas evolved by Turner have also been especially evident. The concept of a frontier is clearly a difficult one and there is considerable variation in frontier studies for this reason alone. But there are also common denominators, usually isolation, limited development, limited communications and few people. The remainder of this chapter attempts a synthesis of the frontier concept. Hopefully, what follows helps place the varied examples introduced so far into perspective and, more crucially, provides a sound basis for the discussions of settlement and economic growth which follow.

SOME SUGGESTED PROCESSES

Ecological imperialism

The process of migration overseas involved much more than just humans. According to Crosby (1978) the overwhelming success of Europeans in the temperate latitudes was but one part of a demographic and ecological take-over which also involved domesticated animals, pathogens and weeds. The success of European overseas migration can be explained in these terms rather than in terms of technological superiority. This point is argued by Crosby (1978) in a comparison of temperate and tropical areas. The European success in temperate areas is unquestionable with 90 per cent of the Canadian and American populations together being European, for Argentina and Uruguay together the figure is 95 per cent, 98 per cent in Australia and 90 per cent in New Zealand. The only two nations in a temperate area, outside of Asia, without European majorities are Chile and South Africa. European failure to take over the tropics was related to disease problems and the failure of their crops and animals. European failure in South Africa, in demographic terms, resulted partly from the fact of the Bantu having a higher reproduction rate. Overall, Crosby (1978) has made a major contribution to our understanding of overseas movement by relating human expansion to the spread of other elements.

A world systems view

A brief comment on the process of frontier settlement which was very much dependent on spatial analytic thinking (Norton 1977a) prompted a contribution which rejected evolutionist and diffusionist thinking (Osborne and Rogerson 1978). The alternative advocated involved a world system perspective, a perspective which was subsequently elaborated by Crush (1980). The spatial view was criticized on three major grounds. First, the notion of stages involves a deterministic and unilinear logic. While this comment is true it does not of itself represent a valid criticism as the evolutionary sequence may still represent a set of useful generalizations. Second, issues of economic change are interpreted with the interests and values of only the settlers in mind. This is certainly a correct criticism and relates back to the ideas expressed by Blaut (1970) and referred to at the commencement of this chapter. The third criticism points to the failure of much spatial research to recognize and discuss the variety of social class involved in settlement. The proposed world systems view would correct these deficiencies and focus on the incorporation of a frontier area into a capitalistic world system. One feature suggested as characterizing European involvement overseas was the control by outside interests of the major frontier resources. A world systems viewpoint argues that the process of development is in actuality only a transition from undevelopment to underdevelopment. Historical geographers have not as yet exploited this viewpoint for empirical analysis.

Regions of recent settlement

The above term has been used to refer to those areas which developed during the late nineteenth and early twentieth centuries (Nurkse 1961). According to Fogarty (1981: 412) these areas developed 'through massive transfers of European people, capital and technology in response to the growth of international market opportunities'. Growth of these areas was especially rapid even by frontier standards and requires some consideration. Three types of recent settlement regions may be recognized: first, where these regions are effectively countries, as is the case with Australia and New Zealand; second, where such regions are the majority of a country, for example Canada; and third, where such areas represent intrusions into already established political and economic frameworks

100

as has occurred in Brazil and Argentina (Fogarty 1981: 420–1). Such a classification recognizes that the frontier areas stimulated growth in established areas with the Canadian west between 1890 and 1930, for example, encouraging development in the older eastern regions as well as experiencing an economic boom itself.

Economic growth

Economic growth in frontier areas is dependent on several factors: on the success of ecological imperialism, on our interpretation of economic growth and on the details of time and place. Probably the crucial input is an immigrating population responding to some set of push-and-pull factors. Despite the continued and significant successes of Canadian frontiers, however, frontier arguments have played a secondary role to an explanation of growth which argues that urban centres dominate development. Such a metropolitan view has been especially argued by Careless (1954: 20) who wrote, 'The functioning of metropolitanism may do more to explain the course of Canadian history than concepts of frontierism borrowed from the United States and set forth before the significance of the modern metropolis was clear'. This interpretation is intriguing because it downplays the role of the frontier in the national economy. Hennessy (1978: 141) contended that it is appropriate to Latin America in general, as is the staple theory of economic growth – a theory which explains national development in terms of the export of staple products from the frontier. With reference to Manchuria, frontier economic growth has been analysed in terms of the staple export theory (Eckstein *et al.* 1974). From 1860 to 1900 the economic growth of Manchuria was characterized by rapid settlement, increase of land under cultivation and the export of soybeans and related products through newly opened ports. The sequence of growth outlined for Manchuria in relation to the stage-oriented staple theory is similar to that of both Canada and Australia as well as such older settled areas as Sweden and Denmark. Overall the assumption of universality implicit in such theory appears to have some validity, although such inferences may be misleading when the processes are being discussed and may lead to a 'historically naive and methodologically questionable comparative history' (Mathias 1974: 267).

The Turnerian frontier

Much has been noted already concerning the significance of Turner's ideas for both America and elsewhere and the consensus is divided. The early ideas continue to be developed and used as a basis for intellectual stimulation in a variety of disciplines, including geography (Hudson 1977). The concept of the frontier, especially its Turnerian aspects, has been used for African studies by Deveneaux (1978: 84) who concluded: 'Theories dealing with contemporary aspects of African society must be anchored in the frontier concept.' However, such generalizations tend to neglect one reality of frontier experience, namely that the detailed frontier experience varied markedly between and within regions. Some frontiers involved major pastoral undertakings as in many grass-land areas, others involved the spread of the family farm. For Australia, the relative prevalence of sheep-farming has been related to government policy which failed to implement homestead legislation because of links with British woollen interests (Hennessy 1978: 145). Detailed studies by Perry (1963) and by Christopher (1976) have been inclined to reject Turnerian logic as a general explanation. Lattimore (1962: 25) generalized on the basis of wide and varied research when he noted: 'For both old and new frontiers, however, a general rule can be stated: any and every kind of society creates its own kind of frontier.'

CHAPTER SEVEN

Rural and urban settlement evolution

Evolution of rural and urban settlement is one component of the emergence of the human landscape. Geographers, including those concerned with historical issues, have characteristically regarded rural and urban settlements as separate in order to facilitate research. Although often unavoidable such procedures are unfortunate, and this chapter includes attempts to view the two as parts of one larger process. Even more desirable would be a parallel consideration of agriculture and related developments, but such a discussion is probably more easily framed in a specific empirical context. Realistically, both available concepts and analyses encourage separate discussions of the various components of economic growth. Such a breakdown was apparent even in the sophisticated analysis of the late-nineteenth-century economy of the United States by Williamson (1974), an economic historian.

The ideas discussed in this chapter are contained within seven sections. The primary concern is to establish the availability of both rural and urban theories which focus on settlement evolution, to discuss their content and to summarize their apparent validity. The first section does not therefore include any substantive comments on central place theory which is essentially static in character and which has not been explicitly developed by historical geographers or others engaged in historical problems. There is a somewhat arbitrary distinction between the first and second sections with the second focusing on what are regarded as conceptual formulations. To a certain extent the distinction is one of nomenclature with the material in the first section being characteristically regarded as theory, whether or not it satisfies any rigorous deductive reasoning, and the subsequent material assuming the character of attempts at generalization. Characteristically, material in the second section avoids the narrow perspective which is largely imposed in attempts at theory construction and allows for some discussions beyond issues of settlement in isolation, including economic growth in general. It seems probable that the conceptual matter might lead to valuable theory in due course. For purposes of convenience the first section is divided into rural and urban emphases, and the second section into rural and urban emphases and contributions from economic history.

The third section introduces empirical work which relies largely on quantitative analyses for purposes of description or explanation. Techniques such as nearest-neighbour analysis and trend surface analysis are included and some assessment of the ideas presented in the first two sections is achieved. Land policy and the likely consequences for settlement are the concern of the fourth section. This variable, which is included in process discussions, continues to be a popular topic in historical research and is often regarded as a key determinant of settlement forms. Examples in this section relate to areas of European overseas expansion.

The next two sections are discussions and elaborations of a wide variety of empirical literature focusing first on the New World, second on Britain and third on Europe and a variety of other areas. Although the material is quite varied the principal concern in all cases is the continued testing and assessment of the theories and conceptualization introduced in the first two sections. A brief concluding section follows.

The approach in this chapter utilizes process and form concepts, and the material discussed is necessarily selected with such an approach in mind. Despite this chosen emphasis the chapter does attempt to reflect historical geographic approaches generally. Material on rural settlement types is briefly noted while the discussion of the historical geography of urban places is contained in Chapter 9.

SETTLEMENT THEORY

Rural emphases

Probably the most basic distinction drawn in rural settlement is that between dispersed and agglomerated forms. Attempts at explanation usually invoked physical, agricultural and social variables with the greatest emphasis on land quality, relief, vegetation and the availability of water (Stone 1965).Hence, such works suggested several variables which might be relevant in theory construction.

At present theoretical thrusts in rural settlement remain limited despite impressive contributions from Bylund (1960, 1972), Hudson (1969) and Sarly (1972). Olsson (1968: 116) noted that, 'the theory of colonization and spread of colonization has not yet been developed to the extent that a set of axioms and theorems can be derived from it'. Deterministic formulations for rural settlement advance into hitherto unsettled territory have been developed by Bylund in a series of papers. The suggested models have been based upon three principal factors: distance from the parent settlement; relative land attractiveness on the basis of soil, climate and minerals; and the out-movement of offspring. Bylund (1960) assigned attraction values on the basis of empirical work in Sweden and proceeded to construct six models, two of which represented wave settlement and the other four more gradual and complex settlement by offspring. The models, then, were simplified descriptions of settlement expan-

104

sion, and visual comparison with maps of actual expansion in a part of Sweden indicated that the model outputs replicated the essential features of real-world settlement. Two variables emerged as important, namely physical factors and distance from point of origin. These concepts were employed by Wood (1966) and developed as a probabilistic model in a study of one area of Ontario. Simulation of settlement forms suggested that distance from entry point, distance from line of access and the ease and cost of land clearing were important variables. The specific conclusions arrived at by Bylund (1960) related to an area with little immigration and with expansion resulting from natural increase, but appear to be applicable in a different context. In a later paper Bylund (1972) noted that, again under circumstances of no immigration, a generation effect was adequate to explain periodic variations in colonization activity and it was not necessary to have recourse to economic factors as an explanation.

An alternative approach to rural settlement theory was presented by Hudson (1969). This work is deductively argued and is based on central place theory, diffusion concepts, ecological distribution theory and the somewhat broad viewpoint of morphological laws. Three stages for the evolution of rural settlement were proposed: colonization, spread and competition. Colonization is the stage during which settlement enters into a hitherto unoccupied area. Spread is simultaneous and is the subsequent filling-up of the habitat by the offspring of colonizers and their offspring; this is the stage considered in the models developed by Bylund. Competition is the final stage when nucleated settlements compete for hinterlands and a central place network results. For each of the three processes there is a corresponding characteristic spatial pattern. For colonization, the pattern is one of concentric rings; for spread, nebula-like with several distinct clusters; and for competition, a regular lattice as in central place theory. The spatial hypotheses were evaluated by means of applying appropriate probability models to Iowa data. The first stage was not tested while the other two were partially confirmed. Undoubtedly this theory represented a major advance in the conceptualization of rural settlement and provided an especially clear process and form argument.

For Ontario in the first half of the nineteenth century a principal determinant of increasing density was not spread but rather continuing colonization, or continuing movement from outside the area. A simulation of the rural settlement of the area showed a series of cores succeeded by movement throughout the area (Norton 1976: 285). It seems likely that this disagreement with the hypotheses furnished by the theory was a result of institutional restrictions which compelled settlement initially to develop in specific areas later to emerge as cores. Specific criticism of the theory focused on this issue of governmental control and Grossman (1971a) contended that the theory did not furnish any general laws and that such biologically derived principles were not applicable to patterns of human mobility. The alternative proposed was that settlement forms were largely dependent on cultural factors, which vary from place to place, and not on some constant human behaviour. These criticisms were based on investigations of an African society in Nigeria where forms were conditioned by centralized controls.

Several of the concepts employed by Hudson (1969) have been further developed by Green (1979) in a substantial contribution which sees settlement as but one part of the expansion of a cultural systems habitat. A model was developed which predicted that frontier settlement would occur where expansion was possible and that location decisions would minimize distance. These and other hypotheses were tested for an area of Finland and for Ontario and largely confirmed.

The theoretical discussions of Hudson (1969) do not explicitly consider particular variables influencing settlement decisions, although it is evident that the wave notion proposed for the colonization stage is related to distance from entry points. A similar comment is appropriate for the third major contribution to rural settlement theory by Sarly (1972), a theory which was deductively organized with a set of initial assumptions, resultant relations specified, exogeneous variables acknowledged and finally the theory constructed. Comparisons between this theory and the ideas already discussed are not possible because of their differing objectives. Sarly (1972: 95–6) succeeded in specifying areas with low rates of settlement expansion on the one hand and areas with high rates on the other. Given the formal character of this work, and the related empirical test of a contemporary static form, the work has not received a favourable response from historical geographers although it is able in principle to specify areas of potential growth and could be used for post-dictive purposes.

A final issue in this section on rural settlement theory concerns the contribution of behavioural arguments. Curry (1964: 145–6) noted that, 'men, motivated by various ideas, act so that from the point of view of the locational structure as a whole their actions appear as random'. Subsequent behavioural work has focused on rural residential moves and hypothesized that spatial variation in location is a function of individual behavior (Bohland 1972). An empirical analysis of Georgia data confirmed the hypothesis and showed behaviour differences between single-dwelling residents and those in large clusters. Relevant variables related to accessibility, the aesthetics of site, topographic perception and social interaction. A major advantage evident in this approach is the association of behaviour with form rather than any inference of behaviour from forms.

Urban emphases

Despite the apparent diversity of theory for the evolution of rural settlement the conclusion offered by Olsson (1968: 117) still seems appropriate: 'the existing theory of settlement diffusion is inconclusive and the specific models which can be derived from it are essentially descriptive'. For theories of urban system evolution the situation is even less satisfactory. Despite the diverse set of ideas associated with central place there are few dynamic central place contributions, and those which are available have not been exploited by historical geographers (Janelle 1968; White 1974, 1977). Rather similarly, work on periodic markets has not received significant attention (Gaede 1973; Yeung 1974). Theoretical work comparable to that available for rural settlement is not available and the majority of conceptually oriented literature is much less rigorous and is included in the next section. Three theoretically oriented arguments are introduced at this stage.

According to central place arguments the evolution of an urban system is the outcome of endogenic or internal factors. Such evolution would involve town growth from certain locations with early advantages which then compete for retail markets until a network of centres is established. This is in accord with the third phase of Hudson's (1969) rural settlement theory. An alternative proposed to central place logic has been suggested as an explanation of network evolution by Vance (1970). This alternative proposal argues that the initial urban growth of a major centre is based upon exogenic factors such as long-distance trade and not upon purely internal demands. The distinction between these two concepts is important both in terms of explaining the growth of towns and in more general economic terms. Exogenic factors are more likely to have an impact on links between areas. Somewhat unfortunately the exogenic approach, typically known as the mercantile model, is essentially based upon the wholesaling function and thus its value is limited. The applicability of the mercantile model has been confirmed by Sargent (1975) in a study of Arizona towns, found inadequate by Earle (1977) for early colonial towns in North America and essentially rejected by Meyer (1980) in a broad context. It is interesting to note the links between the mercantile approach to town growth and the staple export approach to economic growth.

A third theoretical contribution has been provided by Pred (1966, 1973, 1977, 1980) on the basis of considerable empirical work in the United States. The relevance of the rank size rule, which states that the population of a given city tends to be equal to the population of the largest city divided by the rank of the given city, was confirmed. Also, the rigidity of central place approaches was found lacking because of processes affecting the movement of information. Sommer (1975: 317) contended that this work 'merits further testing in other urban systems because it does have the appearance of a promising modification of existing theory in the direction of "reality"'.

CONCEPTUAL CONTRIBUTIONS TO SETTLEMENT EVOLUTION

As already noted, the distinction between this and the previous section is somewhat arbitrary. The purpose of this section is to attempt a consideration of settlement processes, of variables and of variable change through time. The ideas are conceptual in character, but have not typically been taken to the point of explicit theory construction. This is hardly surprising, perhaps, given the reluctance of historically oriented researchers to indulge in such activities, but it is unfortunate. Unfortunate in the sense that most of the conceptual material is directly reliant upon empirical case studies and the result is an almost embarrassing variety of conceptual formulations. Although dealing with similar issues the proposed processes vary notably according to the perspective taken and the empirical stimulation. These comments are not intended as criticisms – indeed the quantity and quality of the recent conceptual work is an excellent advance – but rather as cautionary observations. The contemporary historical geographer interested in settlement evolution can turn to a voluminous litera- ture for support. Available concepts are primarily concerned with urban processes although rural, urban, industrial, communication and regional development matters have often been related. Regionally, the emphasis is on New World settlement and much of the work also represents a contribution to frontier research (see Chapter 6).

Rural emphases

The expansion of populations through time prompted Taylor (1973) to differ- entiate three areas: a core area which effectively acts as an entry point and growth centre; the intervening space beyond the core which was initially fron- tier but is subsequently either stable or declining; and the frontier which is a growth area at the edge of the expanding area. There are similarities between this classification and that of core, domain and sphere (Meinig 1965).

For southern Ontario between 1782 and 1851 Norton (1976) contended that four specific variables effectively comprised a settlement process and that loca- tion decision-making could thus be explained. The first variable was a measure of available land based upon the size of standard agricultural holdings. Entry points provided a second variable with distance friction operating to encourage settlement close to such locations. The significance of entry points was assumed to decline after 1821. Replacing entry points as a part of the process from 1822 to 1851 was a measure of potential in terms of distance to market centres. The final variable was a measure of land quality, the assumption being that the better land was first settled. These four variables were combined into one pro- cess formulation and used to simulate forms for the years between 1782 and 1851. Correlation analysis confirmed that the simulated forms were comparable to available real-world forms and Norton (1976: 287) concluded that: 'Further analyses of this type might contribute to the formation of theory.' This type of contribution is relatively close to the theory construction advocated in Chap- ter 4 with a process being derived from available conceptual and empirical work, that process being used to generate forms and, finally, the validity of the process being assessed by a comparison of generated and real forms.

As already noted, most process-oriented work has focused on settlement in general, thus avoiding the inevitably artificial separation of settlement into rural and urban. With reference to both rural and urban settlement Webber (1972) devised a process from the following assumptions: the region analysed is part of a larger area; is experiencing settlement spread and growth; land quality is fairly uniform; farmers are commercially oriented; rural growth is affected by advancing technology which limits demand for labour; finally, towns grow to serve local rural needs. Hypotheses were derived and then tested for Iowa between 1840 and 1960 and not rejected. The hypotheses asserted that rural population was a specific function of time and that the ratio of the number of towns, less one, to the rural population was a linear and increasing function of time. The fact that the hypotheses could not be rejected increased confidence in the assumptions.

Urban emphases

The evolution of urban systems is a concern of both historical and urban geographers, but particularly of the former. Warnes (1977) noted that a series of contributions from urban researchers were somewhat atypical of contemporary work. Recent research by historically inclined geographers and by economic historians, on the other hand, appears to be very much mainstream work. Much of the relevant discussion is closely tied to the issues of frontier character and frontier movement discussed earlier and relates primarily to industrial cities of the nineteenth century onwards. Earlier urban networks have received relatively scant attention, although Rozman (1978) has identified seven stages of pre-modern development and their related network characteristics. The seven stages are as follows. First, a pre-urban stage with settlements being unspecialized. Second, the beginning of urban development with cities being isolated from one another and having weak links with rural areas. Third, evidence of an administrative hierarchy emerged. Fourth, high levels of centralization based on administration prevailed. Fifth, commercial centralization emerged and additional periodic markets were characteristic. Sixth, increased commercial interests resulted in the presence of five or six levels of urban places. Seventh, and finally, seven levels of urban places prevailed and a national marketing system was evident. These stages are summarized in Table 7.1.

Table 7.1 Seven stages of pre-modern urban development

Stage	Number of levels	Characteristic
1	0	Pre-urban
2	1	Tribute city
3	2	State city
4	2, 3 or 4	Imperial city
5	4 or 5	Standard marketing
6	5 or 6	Intermediate marketing
7	7	National marketing

(Adapted from Rozman 1978: 79)

The emergence of each stage was discussed for five areas. For England, the second stage evolved in the second century BC, stage 3 was omitted, stage 4 evolved in the first century AD, stage 5 in the tenth century, stage 6 in the twelfth century and stage 7 in the sixteenth and seventeenth centuries. As the stages progress it is likely that the percentage urban of any given society does not decrease, that rural settlement stages might also be evident and that urban land use changes. Although such work is extremely broad, it has suggested a typical sequence which is likely to foster further comparative analyses.

109

The issue of urban evolution has often been framed in the broader context of frontier developments. According to conventional frontier concepts urban centres succeeded earlier settlement and economic activity. Such a view has been supported by Elazar (1970) with the recognition of, first, a land frontier, second, an urban industrial frontier and third, a metropolitan frontier. This three-stage sequence was reinforced by an analysis of the American prairie region and of thirteen urban areas in particular. Probably the most comprehensive and influential expression of an urban frontier was offered by Wade (1959: 1) who argued: 'The towns were the spearheads of the frontier. Planted far in advance of the line of settlement, they held the West for the approaching population.' Such a view was echoed by Lewis (1972: 325): 'Frontier settlement without a town at the forefront was simply unthinkable for most Americans.' To resolve the question as to whether towns were a part of the frontier or succeeded the agricultural frontier, Nelson (1974) mapped frontier areas and urban centres for the period 1626–1790, and then for ten-year periods to 1859. Altogether this involved the founding of 168 centres. Only a small number were beyond the frontier at their time of origin and, interestingly, the five towns considered by Wade (1959) were included in this category. The majority of towns were founded during the initial agricultural frontier phases and thus were a part of the American frontier experience. A third category of towns was founded well behind the frontier, often in response to new technology. Nelson (1974: 23) concluded: 'city founding in America seems to be synchronous with the first wave of agricultural settlement, a typical activity of the "pioneer farmer" stage of the American frontier'. A more limited analysis of Oregon towns had anticipated this conclusion (E. G. Smith 1967). Again, a series of maps suggested that town founding either preceded or coincided with agricultural beginnings. These issues have been taken further by Reps (1979) who, on the basis of overwhelming empirical work, argued that towns preceded and stimulated agricultural developments.

Such analyses are suggestive of the beginnings of process formulations given the recognition of a temporal sequence of developments. Subsequent work has continued to investigate stages and, more crucially, to relate urban growth to other economic issues and to isolate relevant variables. The technological variable has been employed to identify stages as follows (Borchert 1967: 307): sail-wagon, 1790–1830; iron horse, 1830–70; steel rail, 1870–1920; and auto–air amenity, 1920 onwards.

The need to study urban systems in genetic terms relates to both their structure and functioning. An analysis of bank correspondent activity showed that central place concepts were generally inappropriate for the nineteenth-century United States and verified aspects of the mercantile model (Conzen 1977). The mercantile model was used as a basis for substantial conceptual work by Muller (1976, 1977) with empirical support from the Ohio Valley. As already noted the mercantile formulation argues that long-distance trade was the first stimulus for frontier urbanism and that permanent points of entry were established early. Conceptual elaboration by Muller (1976, 1977) involved recognition of three periods of regional development with the distinctions being based on export production and circulation, especially the staple export theory arguments. A major contribution offered by this sequence is the recognition of the varied and changing implications of location through time. The three periods are as follows.

1. *Pioneer periphery*. This initial development involves the location of permanent settlements and the beginnings of agriculture. Commercial agriculture is limited as a trial-and-error process is in effect, and the characteristic isolation limits exports. Population densities are low as are regional incomes and consumption. For many authors this is the typical frontier stage although the inclusion of urban centres has not always been acknowledged.
2. *Specialized periphery*. Dominant urban centres emerge in accord with mercantile model arguments at points of regional contact. Commercial agriculture and specialization emerge with the spread and growth of rural populations. The significance of specific urban locations may change notably with regional expansion.
3. *Transitional periphery*. In this third stage the region is fully linked to national networks, agriculture is both commercial and diversified and manufacturing industry assumes a major role. Developments at this time are instrumental in determining the spatial pattern of urban centres with continuing export of staples encouraging a continuation of the initial system, whereas the emergence of manufacturing might prompt a revised pattern.

These three stages were empirically verified for the Ohio Valley (Muller 1976). This conceptualization emphasized that a sorting procedure for towns was operating after the frontier phase with early site advantages being subject to change, especially with changes in transportation. For southern Ontario an empirical analysis of urban system growth from 1851 onwards recognized a rapid growth phase from 1851 to 1881, a phase of little growth but marked concentration to 1931 and a final phase of renewed growth and decreased growth-rate differentials (Marshall and Smith 1978). Russwurm and Thakur (1981) analysed an area of Ontario from 1871 onwards in terms of hierarchical and functional stability and change and delimited distinct temporal phases with particular spatial characteristics.

The scale of analysis has been shifted from the regional to the national by Meyer (1980) and specific characteristics of control of exchange were used to establish a model of urban systems in the context of a spatially increasing economic area. 'As successive frontiers are settled, two features will affect the location of metropolises and transport nodes: the density of producers (consumers) will decline from earlier to later settled areas, and a new region will be linked to an older settled region from the side facing the latter (Meyer 1980: 132).

Although the mercantile model and subsequent conceptualizations appear highly relevant to the nineteenth-century United States they appear less appropriate for an earlier period and for other areas of European overseas expansion. The first English towns of North America require an alternative explanation according to Earle (1977), an explanation which invoked ideas of monopoly colonization. The logic was as follows: 'Each colony having a presettlement boundary will contain one chief port, located centrally on the coastal boundary, provided that a commodious harbor for seventeenth-century maritime vessels exists in the vicinity' (Earle 1977: 181). This model offers good explanations. Subsequent urban growth is influenced by both stage theory arguments and by the crucial first years of immigrant in-movement, with the latter being direct to the more prosperous areas. This combined monopolist–migration formulation might also apply to nineteenth-century areas of imperial colonization and to the post-1700 American experience.

The Australian urban experience has also attracted attention and, indeed, has given rise to alternative conceptualizations. Rowland (1977) emphasized capital city dominance, the physical environment and the role of distance among other factors and was able to delimit three stages. During the first stage ports emerged because of import–export demands. The second stage involved industrial activity in the existing centres and the third involved the increasing importance of cities as markets for their own products. This conceptualization explains the system in terms of initial port locations which are subsequently reinforced, and aspects of the approach are supported by Cloher (1979) in a formulation applied to the State of Victoria. Cloher (1979: 288) argued against the use of models which concentrated on one variable on the grounds that only partial explanations resulted: 'Explanations better able to comprehend the complexity of the process would involve conceptualizing the relevant variables in a state of interaction – a mode of explanation which defines what is commonly known as the systems approach.' The resulting process accommodates three stages. The establishment of port towns serving small hinterlands occurred first in response to export requirements. The early rise of towns was a result of economic, demographic, technological and political variables. The second stage involved the rapid growth of scattered inland towns as a response especially to the discovery of gold. Thus a specific economic event disturbed what might otherwise have been an orderly expansion of centres. The final stage was one of major metropolitan growth accompanied by a reduced number of new towns and a decline in growth of most smaller centres. Cloher (1979: 313) contended that the development of the urban system in Victoria deviated from most conceptual statements including mercantile ideas and those based on centre–periphery arguments. The evolutionary sequence proposed for Victoria is not necessarily applicable elsewhere, but it does serve to emphasize that caution is necessary prior to the application of models generated for other regions.

Centre–periphery concepts have been used to explain the evolution of towns in a third region, that of South Africa, with the central argument for this region being that, 'the effective distribution of political and economic power has determined the spatial organization of the South African urban system' (Fair and Browett 1979: 261). This South African analysis proceeded through three stages of evolution. First, the early immigrant–aboriginal conflict period; second, the British–Afrikaner conflicts over the mineral discoveries beginning in 1867 and, third, the conflict between a White ruling group and a subordinate Black population since c. 1910. Empirical analysis demonstrated that early frontier expansion did not demand contact with the initial coastal centres and that by 1870 no core region was evident because of the failure of one political unit to emerge. Population growth through to 1910 was concentrated in mining centres and ports, and a division between a rural Afrikaner and an urbanized British group had emerged. From 1910 onwards a primary characteristic has been the enforced separation of White and Black and the associated creation of Black towns adjacent to White towns. South Africa clearly represents a variation on developments elsewhere with possibly a greater than usual role played by political factors. Nevertheless there are similarities to the Australian example in terms of the early location of ports and the subsequent impact of mineral discoveries. Fair and Browett (1979: 291) characterized the South African example as involving the development of some groups and the underdevelopment of other groups and saw parallels elsewhere in Africa.

Urban analyses in economic history

This section only reflects some aspects of the contributions of economic historians and identifies certain characteristic approaches. Quantitative analyses of concepts dominate and studies are typically focused on a specific region. Taylor (1967: 310) considered American urban growth prior to 1840 and recognized major eastern ports, smaller eastern ports, eastern interior cities and western cities. Detailed analysis showed that the major ports grew at the expense of the smaller, while the two categories of inland towns grew as the frontier moved. An explanation of the city-forming process was attempted by Williamson and Swanson (1966) with respect to the American north-east from 1820 to 1870 while Higgs (1969) analysed midwestern cities from 1870 to 1900. The latter analysis contradicted some ideas regarding the close relationships between urban growth and industrialization, regarding the benefits of increased nodality and regarding the appropriateness of central place concepts. More recent work by Williamson (1974) viewed urban growth as but one component of economic progress in general and argued that urban growth in the American midwest was limited by railroad factors; such was not the case for the growth of eastern cities.

The process formulations appraised in this section on both rural and urban issues permit two basic conclusions. First, the amount and sophistication of such research has increased markedly in recent years. Second, despite the first comment, historical geographers remain confronted with a diverse set of ideas, both empirical and conceptual. Numerous valid generalizations have been made and can be exploited within the constraints imposed by specific regions, but the goal of a single acceptable set of concepts appears as elusive as ever.

QUANTITATIVE APPROACHES TO SETTLEMENT EVOLUTION

This section reviews and appraises three quite different quantitative approaches which have been exploited in settlement analyses. The first, point-pattern analysis, is an approach which provides a precise description of a set of points, but requires that any relevant processes be inferred from the form description. The second, trend surface analysis, is able to smooth a continuous surface and to distinguish between regional and local trends. The third, simulation analysis, is a means by which hypothetical spatial forms may be generated from assumed processes and is one explicit means of accomplishing a process and form analysis.

Point-pattern analysis

Nearest-neighbour analysis indicates the degree to which an observed distribution of points, for example urban settlements, deviates from a random distribution. The size of the study area is especially crucial to the calculations in that the more extensive the area taken around a given distribution the more clustered the form appears. A second difficulty arises when forms are characterized by a repeated close spacing of two or more points; again, an artificially clustered description can result. Difficulties of this type encouraged Dawson (1975: 45) to assert that geographers could be 'indulging in a landscape lottery' when using nearest-neighbour analysis. Probably the crucial issue is not a technical one but rather the difficulty of inferring process from form, for the technique cannot identify the process unambiguously. Random forms might be an outcome of a combination of competitive and clustering processes. Random descriptions may also occur if a clustered form is being transformed through time to a regular form, or vice versa. Further, a clustered form might emerge from any one of a variety of processes encouraging clustering. Clearly, the interpretation of results is dependent on prior conceptual and empirical regional knowledge. Ideally, the technique can be employed to test hypotheses of randomness, clustering or regularity thus negating the need for subsequent inference.

A second procedure for point-pattern analysis involves quadrat techniques which can be used to compare the number of points which occur within various sub-areas with the number that would be expected if the point form was random. Quadrat analysis is typically extended by comparing observed frequencies to theoretical probability distributions which generate clustered, random and regular forms. Again, there are technical difficulties including issues of quadrat size, grid orientation and size of research area.

For the Cape Province from 1806 to 1970 a series of seven sets of nearest-neighbour results were calculated by Norton (1979) in an attempt to describe the evolution of the urban settlement point form. A trend from early clustered forms to later random forms was evident and prompted some assertions regarding relevant processes. Initial clustering was related to the small area available, the lack of pressure on resources and the limited communications. Later dispersion of urban centres was a response to the decreasing relevance of these factors. Distance and environment were invoked as explanatory variables. Both nearest-neighbour and quadrat techniques were utilized in a study of the Cape Province urban system of 1911 and 1970 (Norton and Cook 1976). Again, this exercise in comparative statics showed that the 1911 form was relatively clustered while the 1970 form was less clustered. Use of both procedures on the identical data sets increased confidence in the results obtained and again permitted process discussion. Both procedures of point-form analysis were also employed in a study of dispersed rural settlement in the American midwest (Birch 1967). The value of such techniques can be debated for two fundamental reasons. First, because of the inference issue, the difficulty of comprehending cause from effect, and second, because, despite a series of interesting applications, it can be argued that there has been a general failure further to encourage theory construction. More sophisticated methods are available, but have not as yet been seriously exploited by historical geographers for dynamic analyses (Curry 1977).

Trend-surface analysis

The need to ensure that applications of trend-surface analysis be based on theoretical arguments has often been asserted (Norcliffe 1969) and the method is more of a hypothesis-testing procedure than are the point-form methods. For Cape Province Norton and Smit (1977: 45) hypothesized that the rural population density surface comprised both regional and local components, that distance to two entry points comprised the regional component and environmental quality was local in impact. Accordingly, cubic order trend surfaces were calculated for 1865, 1891, 1921, 1951 and 1970 (Fig. 7.1). The trend surfaces indicated two regional directions of density decline, both being related to the entry points and urban centres of Cape Town and Port Elizabeth. The circularity of the isolines also indicated that the surfaces are related to distance from the coastline and from the Orange River and to the environmentally unattractive interior. The proposed hypotheses were confirmed and the regional influences of environment also noted. Clarke (1972) reported the results of trend-surface analysis of southern Ontario rural settlement in 1851 and achieved an improved description. Somewhat similarly, Florin (1977) mapped trend surfaces for date of settlement in Pennsylvania and noted the high degree of regularity in settlement spread. In all of the three examples noted the technique has facilitated conclusions concerning both form and process. The method seems especially appropriate for analysing changing forms.

Simulation analyses

Of the quantitative procedures considered here there is no doubt that simulation analyses are the most explicitly oriented to hypothesis testing. Following an innovative application to the evolution of Swedish urban settlement by Morrill (1965a) simulation has received varied and valid use. The Swedish analysis generated 'the complex phenomenon of urban development involving as it does locations of economic activities of all types, of towns and settlements and of the movement of persons' by means of developing a model based on central place, industrial and transport concepts (Morrill 1965a: 184). The

115

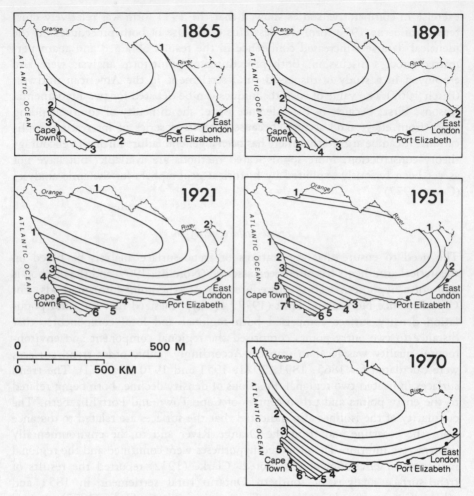

Fig. 7.1   Cubic trend surfaces, European rural population density per square mile, Cape Province, South Africa. (Adapted from Norton and Smit 1977: 44–48)

simulation analysis of southern Ontario rural settlement by Norton (1976) was noted in Chapter 4. This application succeeded in constructing abstract worlds, generated as the outcome of a formulated process, which bore an adequate resemblance to available known forms. The evolution of rural settlement to 1851 showed that availability of surveyed land influenced initial settlement, that cores developed early and that dispersal throughout the areas occurred while the cores continued to grow. A principal achievement of the southern Ontario work was also to generate forms for times when data were unavailable. A more comprehensive simulation was accomplished by Levison, Ward and Webb (1973) for Polynesian migration and settlement. This analysis involved construction of a random sample of the set of all possible voyages given the conditions defined; overall more than 100,000 voyages were simulated. The breadth of such work is remarkable and the results argued that consciously planned and not simply accidental drift voyages were necessary to explain Polynesian settlement.

Summary

This section has appraised but three useful quantitative procedures which appear especially well suited to historical research. Other procedures are relevant but are less frequently used. One emerging but controversial mathematical technique in geography is that of catastrophe theory which has been used to explain changes in the evolution of settlement patterns (Wagstaff 1978a). This approach is quite different to those discussed in the earlier conceptual section. Catastrophe theory hypothesizes sudden cataclysmic changes as a result of slowly developing processes. For a peninsular region of southern Greece a major discontinuity of the settlement system was observed at some time between the sixth and fifteenth centuries and the gradual deterioration of the quality of agricultural land was a possible cause. Conventional point-pattern procedures were not appropriate tools as they assume continuous change. Catastrophe theory, however, has 'the ability to model a discontinuity within a structurally stable dynamical system' (Wagstaff 1978a: 173). It is this ability which might encourage applications in historical geography. Despite the name, this approach is not a theoretical development but is rather the application of a specific model to settlement issues, albeit a model with theoretical underpinnings although not explicitly related to settlement.

LAND POLICY AND SETTLEMENT

The term 'land policy' covers a multitude of variables relating to the manner in which land is subdivided, the availability of land for settlement, the prevalence of speculation, the cost of land and the mechanics of land granting. The impact of land policy on settlement depends on what is being investigated, whether it is date of settlement, spatial forms or the visible landscape.

Land subdivision

'For an understanding of various settlement patterns we must include the great influence of the law' (Johnson 1974: 12). Land subdivision can be classified as irregular or regular, with the former being characteristic for most areas over long periods and the latter being more typical in areas of European overseas expansion. European studies have focused on field systems and such processes as enclosure, whereas New World studies have largely emphasized the impact on the timing and mechanics of first settlement.

For southern Ontario the process of land subdivision is depicted in Fig. 7.2. The first areas surveyed were adjacent to existing military posts and to the

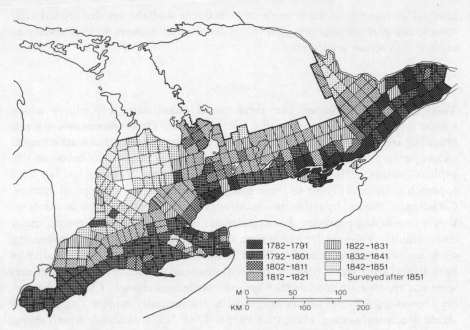

Legend:
- 1782–1791
- 1792–1801
- 1802–1811
- 1812–1821
- 1822–1831
- 1832–1841
- 1842–1851
- Surveyed after 1851

M 0   50   100
KM 0   100   200

Fig. 7.2 Dates of township survey, southern Ontario. (After Norton 1975: 148)

United States. Subsequent surveying spread north and west such that the entire area was surveyed between 1782 and 1851. Because settlement was illegal on other than surveyed land it can be argued that the pattern of surveying was a principal determinant of settlement. Application of a simple counterfactual, however, showed that, although the evolution of the settlement form varied, the 1851 outcome was essentially the same with or without surveying (Norton 1978). This contention certainly merits investigation elsewhere.

The relative consequences of an irregular and a regular survey have been considered by Thrower (1966) with reference to two areas of Ohio. Effects on administration, property areas, field units and transportation varied according to the survey. The prevalent regular survey involved survey prior to settlement, survey lines in cardinal directions, and townships of 6 miles square, sections of 1 square mile with quarter sections being the common size of grant. Manitoba was a second area with two systems of survey. The first, a river long-lot system, was based on that used in Lower Canada and was available to settlers in the Red River area until 1884 (Richtik 1975: 613). The second began in 1869 and was essentially that practised in the United States. For Texas, Jordan (1977b) described four types of survey, namely irregular, rigid rectangular, irregular rectangular and long lots. Each of the four had a distinct distribution, reflected cultural factors and contributed notably to the visible human landscape. It is evident that, in areas where survey essentially preceded settlement or where a major policy change occurred, the resultant landscape reflects land policies.

118

South Africa experienced two very different influences on land policy, the British imperial system and the Cape Dutch system. According to Christopher (1971: 2): 'The two had varying effects upon settlement, and were applied to very different areas for different periods of time'. The British policy, formed in 1832, copied many of the American features but was not conceived with the particular South African, Natal and Cape Province, environment in mind. The Cape Dutch system gradually evolved after first settlement in 1652 and informally recognized a farm as the area within one half-hour's casual riding time of the house. Application of the British policy to Cape Province was unsuccessful because of a shortage of land, and was especially unsuited to the Natal environment with spatially limited agricultural areas.

Land policies and the subdivision which they implied were typically intended to encourage agricultural settlement. In New South Wales in 1861 the Robertson Land Acts were designed 'to encourage the creation of small freehold farms' (Robinson 1974: 17) and were at least partially successful. A series of Australian Acts during the nineteenth century were designed to cope with the difficulties faced by pastoralists in the arid interior (Heathcote 1972). In both Quebec and Ontario the late nineteenth century was characterized by settlement expansion into areas of difficult environment, and land policies, in terms of size of unit and cost especially, needed to reflect these difficulties. Studies by Osborne (1977), Wall (1977) and Parson (1977) emphasized the generous but perhaps misguided policies which encouraged settlement in marginal areas.

Land speculation

Land speculators were characteristic in areas of new settlement, not only when land was scarce but often from the very beginnings of settlement. In southern Ontario middlemen and favoured individuals received large grants in the early years of settlement such that by 1806 individuals averaged 7,100 acres (Norton 1975: 149). By the 1840s most of the desirable land in southern Ontario was alienated and it is clear that speculation, especially close to urban centres, was widespread. A major impact of speculation was to delay settlement. Clarke (1975) investigated the land speculation in the western area of southern Ontario accomplished by government officials and showed that 27 per cent of patented land between 1788 and 1813 went to speculators. The land speculated was readily accessible, but there appeared to have been little appraisal of agricultural potential. For the United States Holtgrieve (1976) observed continuous conflicts between settlers and speculators and suggested widespread effects on various aspects of the economic and cultural landscapes.

Land alienation

This term refers to the manner by which governments disposed of land. Again, the mechanics of this process can have implications for settlement. For southern Ontario the policies of creating reserves for both Crown and clergy had adverse effects on settlement. Similarly the policy, prior to 1826, of a system of free land grants appeared to have adverse affects on settlement largely because of administrative inefficiencies. For an area of Queensland Camm (1967) showed that a series of Land Acts between 1894 and 1917 affected the transition from pastoral to agricultural land use and hence the visible landscape. A crucial issue relates to the fact that, at any given time, some lands were unavailable. This point was investigated by Rice (1978a) for an area of Minnesota and it was noted that a policy of free land encouraged settlement. A solution to land unavailability which was commonly practised was squatting. Although often a serious problem in legal terms, squatters could serve the very useful function of pioneering new areas, as in southern Ontario (Norton 1975: 149). For Victoria, Powell (1969) showed that squatters comprised an important part of the economic landscape.

NEW WORLD SETTLEMENT

The remainder of this chapter attempts a review of New World settlement, British settlement and relevant analyses of other areas. Necessarily these sections each lack a central focus, other than that of settlement, but they do exclude work on theory, process or on land policy. Reviews of this type are necessary both to identify the variety of interests demonstrated by historical geographers and to specify key or emerging themes. A threefold spatial distinction is imposed because it provides a logical and meaningful method of classification. In all three sections the issues discussed are those raised in empirical analyses.

Perhaps the major consideration in much of the literature has been that of settlement spread for, as Williams (1975: 61) noted for Australia, 'history during the bulk of the nineteenth century was largely the history of the successful and satisfactory disposal of a vast and unknown domain'. In many areas that settlement spread has been characterized by a process of intensification, the creation of more and smaller holdings. This theme has been well documented for parts of South Africa by Christopher (1970) as well as by Williams (1975) for Australia. In both cases closer settlement replaced an earlier pastoral land use. For North America this sequence has been less evident. Both Australia and South Africa were more influenced by events, policies and attitudes in Britain, and to a lesser extent the United States, and the history of settlement reflects these influences. A second aspect of settlement spread has involved attempts to map spread. One innovative application involved the location of post offices as a surrogate of settlement in Montana (Alwin 1974). Such a device does not restrict mapping to census years and appears appropriate for regional analyses. Figure 7.3 shows the movement of settlement in Montana between 1865 and 1900.

A second area of research has focused on the variables influencing settlement. Norton (1976) argued that distance to entry points, distance to urban centres and land quality, three variables implied by theory, were crucial in southern

120

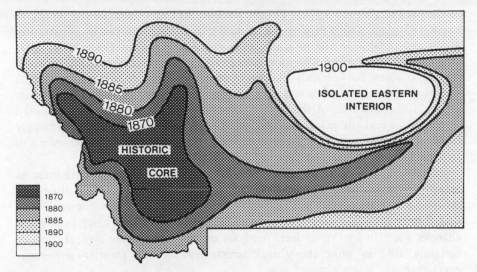

Fig. 7.3   Settlement expansion in Montana, 1865–1900. (After Alwin 1974: 185)

Ontario before 1851. Railways played a key role in the Canadian prairies according to McCormick (1980) despite many construction delays. For parts of Saskatchewan Dick and Greenwood (1979) confirmed the importance of the railway for settlement dates by means of a multiple-regression analysis. Varying land costs, according to the policy of the granting agency, might also have been an influential factor. An analysis of southern Ontario by Gentilcore (1972) argued for a change in the perception of the environment with physical variations initially being of minor relevance but then of increasing relevance as the economy developed. In the prairies and plains, on the other hand, some environmental considerations were significant very early. In a study of one Kansas county, Forsythe (1977) emphasized the importance of water, soil, terrain and of varied environmental hazards such as beaver and grasshopper damage. Hudson (1978) noted the importance of fuel availability for North Dakota settlers. In all cases analyses need to recognize that interpretation of environment varied according to both economic and cultural background. Cultural issues represent a third major area of work.

One example of cultural factors is that by Lehr (1975) concerning early Ukrainian settlement on the Canadian prairies. The Ukrainian settlement was unusual for its concentration on areas of difficult land. 'They settled on marshy, stony and sandy ground in areas often ignored, rejected or abandoned by more discriminating settlers' (Lehr 1975: 51). An explanation of this decision-making required recognition of the desire for a secure social environment. A comparison with Mormon movement to Utah might be appropriate. Elsewhere in the Canadian west Mennonite, Hutterite and Dukhobor groups produced distinctive group settlement areas in response to their cultural and religious requirements. In an area composed largely of dispersed rural settlement, Mennonite villages present a distinctive feature and have largely continued through

121

to the present (Friesen 1977). The settlement of French Canadians in Vermont in the 1850s and 1860s displayed a marked degree of concentration, illustrating a cultural variable in the location decision-making process (Vicero 1971). It is not easy to generalize regarding the relative importance of cultural and economic variables, but certainly analyses of settlement require at least some initial appraisal of both sets of factors. For the San Luis Valley of Colorado, Carlson (1967: 128) observed: 'Although a comparable physical environment existed in the valley and the primary objective of every group was agriculture largely based upon irrigation, each group appraised the valley differently according to its own cultural values.'

A study of one southern Ontario township chose to interpret settlement as an attempt to maintain the social and economic independence of small farmers on the land (Harris *et al*. 1975). Social and economic development was interpreted in terms of the idea of progress meaning essentially the obvious physical changes wrought by the settlers. Analyses of this type are not typical, but are certainly able to offer thoughtful assessments of the frontier settlement experience.

One final emphasis which merits attention relates to explanations of immigration. A major debate is evident for the Canadian prairies concerning the time-lag between settlement policies being established and settlers arriving. Norrie (1975) argued that initial development was limited by lack of railway export facilities and by competition with superior land in the United States. For other areas, of course, such analysis is hardly necessary as settlement often preceded land availability or responded immediately to availability.

BRITISH SETTLEMENT

Although the material presented in this chapter has largely been framed in the context of New World settlement this does not preclude discussion of older settled areas along similar lines. The time-span available for analysis is substantially longer and problems of data availability and reliability arise. Nevertheless, many of the empirical analyses of rural and urban settlement tackle similar problems of spread, growth, retreat and decline and incorporate explanations which rely on immigration, agricultural change, transport improvement and industrialization. Indeed, in Britain the situation may be somewhat simplified in certain instances for there is less chance of a variety of variables operating at the same time. This comment is possibly appropriate prior to the eighteenth century. The following discussion cannot do justice to the enviable research output of historical geographers and others, and all that is attempted is a survey of major themes. For convenience a chronological sequence is employed. One emphasis which is particularly well documented for Britain concerns the question of settlement survival, an emphasis which is noted for each of the chronological stages.

Prehistoric and Roman Britain

'All settlement develops within a matrix composed of two distinct but inter-locking frameworks; on the one hand, there is the physical environment, with the limitations and possibilities inherent in variations in location, altitude, soil quality, local climate and biological response; on the other, there are the man-imposed organizational frameworks of kingdom and honour, estate and manor, parish and township' (Roberts 1976: 300). It is often the case that the former are easier to determine than the latter in studies of early settlement as in the case of prehistoric contributions. Although the pre-Roman component of the contemporary landscape is slight it is important in certain regions. Areas of dense forest were least attractive because of the difficulties of land clearance, while proximity to key raw materials, such as flint, was important (Bowen 1969: 10). However, generalizations are dangerous as the prehistoric period extended from before 10,000 BC to AD 43 and incorporated major technological advances in the transitions from Palaeolithic to Mesolithic to Neolithic to Bronze to Iron ages. This extended period also included climatic changes which affected both soil and vegetation. The establishment of settled villages was intensified by the in-movement of Belgic populations from about 75 BC onwards and their introduction of a heavy wheeled plough opened new areas of the south-east and midlands to agriculture. Despite the limited knowledge of pre-Roman settlement Hodder (1978a) noted that the human geography of the Roman period seemed dependent on that which preceded it.

It is generally agreed that the major Roman towns grew on earlier sites in response to economic and servicing advantages (Hodder 1978a: 37). The smaller Roman towns, while somewhat more difficult to explain, also appear to have been located in response to economic variables with military considerations of greater or lesser relevance. The creation of towns was an integral part of all Roman expansion and Gilbert (1969: 65) summarized towns and related regions and noted their imposition on a previously largely rural landscape. Roman occupation also involved much rural settlement in the area of lowland Britain, but does not appear to have caused the dislocation of earlier settlements. Again, light soils were favoured. Overall, the impact of populations prior to the arrival of the English c. AD 450 was limited: 'the great majority of the English settlers faced a virgin country of damp oak-ash forest, or beech forest on and near the chalk; and what was not thickly forested was likely to be cold, high mist-wrapped moorland, or water-logged wet heath, drowned marshes and estuary saltings, or sterile, thin-soiled dry heath' (Hoskins 1955: 37).

English and Scandinavian occupation

Between about 450 and 1066 English populations moved into Britain and village settlement expanded markedly, especially in the midlands. From about 850 onwards Scandinavians moved into Britain, an immigration which also involved much village settlement. Together these two movements accounted

123

for much of the contemporary British rural landscape as confirmed by place-name evidence. The Scandinavian impact on the Scottish Highlands involved considerable change with new settlements and a new way of life (Small 1968). Throughout most of England the Scandinavians tended to adapt to existing sites, but this also involved much change and Jones (1978: 77) noted: 'The grafting of new on to old, . . ., epitomizes much of the process whereby southern Britain came to be more closely settled during the period between the departure of the Romans and the advent of the Normans.' Most of these conclusions about English and Scandinavian settlement have relied at least partly on placename evidence, and a cautionary comment in this regard has been offered by Arnold (1977) who argued for detailed studies of settlement structure and pattern as the best means of explanation.

The medieval period

As is evident from the preceding comments the pattern of village settlement was essentially complete before the Norman Conquest and the contribution of the medieval period is one of expansion of existing villages plus the addition of hamlets and dispersed farmsteads. Nevertheless, it is this period which has received much attention from historical geographers and three major areas have been researched. First, the expansion of settlement into new and more difficult environments; second, the decline of certain villages and the disappearance of others and third, the growth of towns. Most of this work, however, has been bedevilled by a number of difficulties including that of data. Sawyer (1976: 2–7) emphasized the unreliability of 'Domesday Book' as a guide to eleventh-century settlement; noted that the first recorded mention of a place is not a good indicator of first date of settlement and recognized the antiquity of the rural settlement pattern.

One detailed analysis of northern Ryedale in Yorkshire regarded medieval colonization as: 'A frontier movement, involving the expansion and cultivation into areas that had been little developed in former times. . . .' (Hodgson 1969: 44). Agricultural changes were a principal cause of this colonization as was pressure on resources, and the result was the creation of an organized, settled and exploited landscape. The expansion involved both lay and monastic populations and, while environmental factors were important, differing perceptions also played a role. Expansion and colonization were also emphasized in an analysis of Warwickshire: 'the population increased, the frontier of colonization was pushed forward, new hamlets were born, and at the same time some villages grew into market towns' (Harley 1964: 115). The role of the physical environment was explicitly noted by Jones (1953) in an evolutionary analysis of North Wales. In contrast to England and Wales Whyte (1981) has noted for Scotland a general lack of knowledge between the Iron Age and the late eighteenth century and has suggested directions for future work.

The analysis of village depopulation and related abandonment usually begins with the medieval period although earlier abandonments doubtless occurred. Explanations of abandonment involve causes such as the devastation of the

Norman Conquest and subsequent devastations. Monastic expansion sometimes involved depopulation of earlier villages, especially in northern England. More significantly: 'The great wave of colonization which had spread through the country since the Norman Conquest was at last weakening' and this, in conjunction with the Black Death of 1349–51, proved crucial to subsequent village desertion (Allison 1970: 27).

The medieval town was typically a small market centre with a population of 500 to 1,500 (Butlin 1978: 142). For Warwickshire, the period between 1066 and 1350 saw the growth of a village network and one explanation for settlement growth was the granting of a market charter (Harley 1964: 126). The change from village to market centre to town is related to the appropriate legal status and not to factors of population growth or rural settlement. Further up the urban hierarchy, above the market centres, were ports and industrial towns with populations up to 5,000. At the top of the hierarchy were a few select cities headed by London.

Britain 1500–1700

This period may be characterized as one of relative stability prior to the dramatic consequences of industrialization which were to occur during the eighteenth and nineteenth centuries. Rural settlement changed little and the two themes which need to be emphasized are those of continued village desertion on the one hand and town growth on the other.

From the late fifteenth century onwards deliberate village depopulation occurred as landlords desired to change village lands to sheep pasture for reasons of personal profit. Much of this desertion occurred in the English midlands with Northamptonshire losing perhaps one in every eight villages (Allison 1970: 36). A second cause of desertion evident at the end of this period and beyond involved the expansion of parkland; quite simply a village was removed if it spoiled the view.

Patten (1979: 29) estimated the urban population of England at perhaps 20 per cent of the total in this period. By 1700 London had exceeded 500,000 and the other major regional centres were up to perhaps 20,000. But the vast majority of towns and villages experienced little growth before 1700 and nor were there new centres created. The spatial form changed but little and the basic urban structure was quite stable.

Britain 1700–1900

Major changes occurred in settlement forms at this time in relation to some fundamental economic changes involving agriculture, transport and industry. Rural settlement became increasingly dispersed, towns grew rapidly and new towns emerged.

Dispersion of rural settlement took place where the lack of a single landlord meant control was difficult. More critically, field enclosure encouraged farmers to move away from the nucleated village to their new consolidated farms. In

Scotland the situation was rather different with the dominant trends being the disappearance of some centres and the creation of others, largely as a response to the spread of sheep-farming (Gray 1962: 147). About 150 new planned centres emerged in Scotland between 1745 and 1845. For the year 1800, Perry (1975: 16) noted that: 'A continuance of dispersion characterized the lowland zone' while depopulation was more typical in the upland areas.

With the expansion of agriculture, trade and industry the central place functions of towns became more evident. In the eighteenth century the major growth occurred in the largest towns although some towns, such as Norwich, lost population or failed to grow. Varied growth also characterized the smaller centres depending on the changing communication links. During the nineteenth century urban growth was typical such that by 1900 both England and Wales were predominantly urban; in 1801 the percentage urban was 34, by 1901 it was 78 (Carter 1978: 370). Again, the principal growth accrued to the largest towns. With regard to the processes affecting the urban system, Carter (1978: 382) suggested that a system in dynamic equilibrium became a system in flux and then became a system in dynamic equalibrium once more (Fig 7.4). Relevant processes were those of technological change and of communication development.

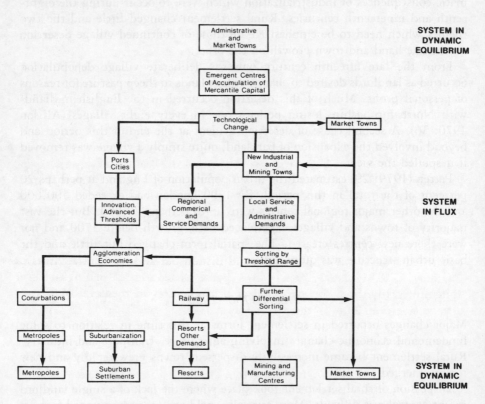

Fig. 7.4 Processes affecting the nineteenth-century urban system of England and Wales.
(After Carter 1978: 382)

OTHER SETTLEMENT ANALYSES

Scandinavian research has dealt extensively with settlement advance and retreat. A conference in 1960 generated contributions on this and related themes and three sets of variables were evident. First, historical factors including technology, second, the resource base and third, economic factors (Enequist 1960: 345). The need to relate settlement and economy is evident in any attempt to explain advance or retreat as is the need to consider cultural factors. A detailed analysis was provided by Jaatinen (1960) for the south-western archipelago of Finland, a marginal area which experienced major colonizations during the nineteenth century only to be succeeded by retreat in the twentieth century. Medieval settlement in Finland involved substantial spread and a marked increase in the number of farms although that spread varied locally (Orrman 1981).

The Mediterranean region has received attention with regard to the impact of conflict on settlement. Thompson (1978), for example, considered Corsican settlement in relation to geopolitical, economic and developmental conflict, and Wagstaff (1978b) demonstrated that warfare encouraged settlement and abandonment in Greece which was occurring primarily because of social and economic processes. The general relationship between settlement and conflict is one which merits attention elsewhere. Many colonial settlements have been located with some strategic consideration in mind and settlement spread or retreat might frequently be a response to changes in security.

Russian movement into eastern Siberia was considered by Vorob'yev (1975) and three stages recognized. First, the seventeenth century when the territory became politically Russian and in-movement commenced such that by 1700 Russians were 40 per cent of the population. Second, from 1700 to 1850 natural increase was substantial and distinctive regions emerged. Third, from 1850 to the revolution there was again little in-movement from outside and further regionalization was evident. A similar focus in a different area was offered by Ramesar (1976) in an analysis of immigration and regional settlement of British West Indians and East Indians in Trinidad between 1851 and 1900. In this example the location of settlement was related principally to economic developments such as the growth of the sugar industry.

Historical geographers have examined urban origins not only for such well-researched areas as the United States and Britain but also for Central America (Mathewson 1977). Maya urban origins appear related to trade and to intensive agriculture. In Africa the evolution of urban centres in medieval Mali conformed to aspects of both the mercantile model and central place theory, but was essentially the product of a variety of cultural factors (Winters 1981). Mobility of populations and rural to urban migrations were considered by Grossman (1971b) for a part of Nigeria. Rural mobility was related to the concept of absorptive capacity, a measure of population and resource balance. One final example of settlement movement referred to Oceania and used the diffusion of a cultivated plant, the sweet potato, as an indicator of movement (Kreisel 1981).

SOME CONCLUDING COMMENTS

The diverse contents of this chapter have concentrated around the themes of rural and urban settlement. The theories, concepts and empirical analyses discussed demonstrate a necessary and healthy diversity of concerns. The historical geographer, while much has been investigated, remains confronted with a series of major tasks. Continued theoretical work is desirable, theoretical work which might prove appropriate for different areas at different times. With only a few exceptions (Carter 1978) the North American theoretical and conceptual contributions have received little application in older settled areas. For Britain and Europe continued contributions from archaeology are likely to explain much about original settlement locations, and continued data analyses can go further towards explanations of change. In this chapter little has been offered concerning the relative values attached to rural and urban existence or concerning the social mechanisms involved in movement and change. The primary emphasis has been towards economic explanations as these are well represented in the available literature and narratives and static descriptions have been largely avoided. Although relatively little of the work is explicitly process and form oriented, a recurring theme is the search for causes of change.

CHAPTER EIGHT

The agricultural landscape

The agricultural component of the economic landscape has received much attention from historical geographers, especially in Britain and Europe where a strong agrarian emphasis has long been evident. Probably the greatest advances in history have stemmed from the *Annales* school with their studies of collective mentalities, of long-term change, of human and land relationships and of spatial, psychological and economic structures. Many of these features were evident in the Languedoc study by Le Roy Ladurie (1974) which showed how population pressure caused land subdivision and how a particular peasant mentality developed. North American work has progressed along rather different lines with a much greater emphasis on theory and statistical manipulation in the new economic history. These differences also prevail in the historical geographic literature, although for both regions a major focus has been agricultural change and landscape evolution. It is this theme which receives the greatest attention in the following discussion. A first concern is with available land-use theory which, although not explicitly evolutionary, has proven valuable as an explanation of both past landscapes and of landscape change. This is followed by two sections which focus on the evolution of the agricultural landscape for areas of European overseas expansion and for Britain and Europe respectively. Such a regional distinction is valid in some respects but redundant in others, for instance the topic of land clearing is a major theme for both areas. These regional discussions are followed by a consideration of the diffusion of agricultural innovations. The chapter concludes with an assessment of agricultural change as one part of wider economic changes.

LAND-USE THEORY

Those who search for causes and consequences soon find themselves involved in the study of processes. What are the processes operating through time that have resulted in the observable association of phenomena now visible on the maps? Of course, the geographer does not proceed to this point in his research study without forming some hypothesis regarding the areal association of factors affecting agriculture (McCarty 1954: 270).

All too often, however, the hypotheses tested were not derived from theory although by geographic standards a substantial body of theoretical concepts was available. Harvey (1966: 368) noted the tendency to ignore theory and observed that: 'There is a broad analogy between the idea of the frontier of settlement sweeping across a country and a dynamic Thünen model where, for example, the seaboard region is regarded as the central market', but at the same time the need for more explicit models of spatial form evolution was acknowledged. It is certainly the case that traditional agricultural land-use theory is essentially static in character, although a variety of empirical analyses have demonstrated that it can be interpreted in evolutionary terms and these are discussed below. It has also been demonstrated that the spatial equilibrium described by Thünen can develop in many different ways and with many different detailed outcomes (Day and Tinney 1969).

Agricultural land-use theory, as conceived by Johann Heinrich von Thünen in the early nineteenth century, has proved of great interest to both economists and economic geographers, particularly since the work was translated (Hall 1966). The theory has in general been well received and the proposed pattern of land use verified given the necessary conditions. It appears, however, that two important areas for investigation have been little studied. First, there have been few analyses of land use in historical context, despite the origins of the theory c. 1800. Second, and more critically, there have been few evolutionary analyses of land use which focus explicitly on change. Both of these omissions stem from the adoption of Thünen concepts by economic geographers, rather than by historians, at a time when geography focused primarily on problems of spatial variation without reference to time. Such analyses are appropriate in that the theory itself is a static equilibrium formulation but their explanatory potential is limited. These omissions are acknowledged and there have been increasing numbers of Thünen analyses in a historical context and, further, an increased awareness of the critical need for evolutionary analyses. This former development resulted from the growing willingness of historical geographers to indulge in both theoretical and quantitative analyses (Norton and Conkling 1974; Ewald 1977). The latter development is one aspect of a significant change in economic geography away from static analyses and towards dynamic analyses which emphasize both spatial patterns and the factors responsible for such patterns.

Further, most studies have been concerned with economies which have had some considerable time to develop and consequently are relatively stable. For pioneer societies change may be dramatic, particularly in areas of European overseas expansion, and land-use surfaces are relatively ephemeral. Land-use theory was conceived for developed areas. In areas undergoing settlement of virgin land and in which frontier conditions prevail, the relevance of theoretical factors of a commercial nature as determinants of land use might be expected to be temporarily reduced. Under such conditions subsistence agriculture may prevail and settlement location with respect to market facilities may not be a determining factor.

One interpretation of Thünen's work which recognized a 'theory of agricultural history' was that of Schlebecker (1960: 188) which saw originally unspecialized agriculture being amended as urban centres grew. The general notion of increasing specialization through time is an important one and has received strong theoretical support from Brinkmann (Benedict 1935) and strong empirical support from a variety of sources. Schlebecker (1960), for example, suggested a world metropolis, the location of which has changed from Athens to western Europe to western Europe and eastern North America combined, and further argued that the history of North American agriculture showed the influence of the world metropolis. These ideas have been substantially advanced and supported by Peet (1969, 1970, 1972) in a series of studies centring on the spreading of commercial grain production during the nineteenth century. The Thünen concepts lend themselves to a dynamic interpretation with the additional realistic inputs of an increasing central market demand and of changing transport costs. These inputs were used by Peet (1969) to facilitate explanation of the global spread of grain, to explain the spread of grain farming in the northern United States (Peet 1970) and to explain the changes in European farming landscapes prior to 1860 (Peet 1972). This work has succeeded in both relating agricultural change to more general economic change and in verifying the value of Thünen theory as both a source of testable hypotheses and as a framework for analysis.

Somewhat similarly, Leonard (1976) calculated the spread of agricultural zones by considering imports to London. Table 8.1 shows the average distances which various agricultural imports to Britain were shipped between 1831 and 1913. These figures show the expansion of zones in response to market size increase and transport cost changes. The sequence of import categories is in close accord with the sequence of zones proposed by Thünen in his original formulation.

For North America a number of studies have confirmed basic Thünen hypotheses. Conzen (1971) in an analysis of one township adjacent to Madison

Table 8.1 Average distances from London, England, to regions of import derivation (miles)

	1831–35	1856–60	1871–75	1891–95	1909–13
Fruit and vegetables	0	324	535	1,150	1,880
Live animals	0	630	870	3,530	4,500
Butter, cheese, eggs	262	530	1,340	1,610	3,120
Feed grains	860	2,030	2,430	3,240	4,830
Flax and seed	1,520	3,250	2,770	4,080	3,900
Meat and tallow	2,000	2,900	3,740	5,030	6,250
Wheat and flour	2,430	2,170	4,200	5,150	5,950
Wool and hides	2,530	8,830	10,000	11,070	10,900

(After Leonard 1976: 28)

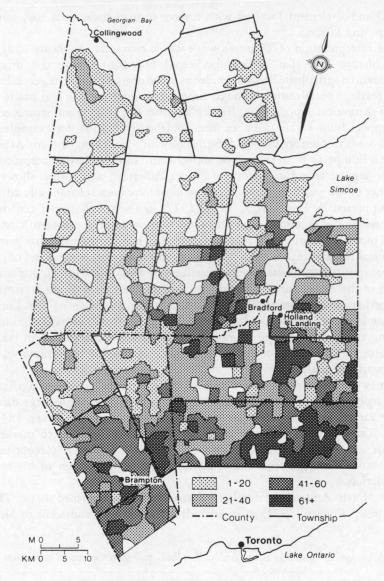

Fig. 8.1 Land values in a part of southern Ontario, 1861 (dollars per acre). (Adapted from Norton and Conkling 1974: 51)

noted that urban fringe farming was essentially wheat until 1870, market gardening during the 1870s and dairy farming by 1880. The hypotheses of declining land values and of changing land use with increasing distance from a major market were confirmed by Norton and Conkling (1974) for a part of southern Ontario in 1861. Figure 8.1 indicates the decline in land values with a simple correlation coefficient between value and distance to Toronto of $r = -0.6502$. Land use was clearly demarcated into a zone of commercial production close

132

Table 8.2   Correlation results for an area of southern Ontario, 1861*

Dependent variable	r value[1]	R value[2]
Total crop acreage	−0.3654	0.3789
Fall wheat	−0.5547	0.5888
Spring wheat	0.4963	0.5110
Peas	−0.3291	0.3558
Oats	−0.1575	0.1703
Potatoes	0.2548	0.3010
Turnips	0.2115	0.3234

(Adapted from Norton and Conkling 1974: 54)
[1] Independent variable is distance to Toronto.
[2] Independent variables are: distances to Toronto; distance to local market; distance to line of principal access and regional subdivision.
* All r and R values are significant at the 1 per cent level.

to the urban market and an outer zone of subsistence production. Typical crops for the inner zone were fall wheat, peas and oats; for the outer zone, spring wheat, potatoes and turnips (Table 8.2).

A study in comparative statics was accomplished by Leaman and Conkling (1975) for western New York State in 1840 and 1860, and the hypothesis that the decline of transport costs through time increased the relevance of environment as a determinant of land use was tested. Use of canonical correlation analysis showed that the 1840 land-use form was one of unspecialized general farming bearing minimal relationship to the physical environment. By 1860 a number of specialized land uses had appeared and a much closer conformity to the environment was apparent.

Muller (1973) analysed net income per unit area, a surrogate for economic rent, in 1,376 counties of the United States and inferred evolution from an essentially static analysis. The surface analysed was for 1964 and the results, and dynamic economic integration theory, were used to discuss the evolution of the surface from the early nineteenth century onwards. Initially, interdependent specialized farming regions developed and focused on the national market. These regions expanded west through time. In addition the eastern seaboard market grew and became the principal national market. 'The spatial expansion of such agricultural development is an expanding system of concentric Thünian regions analogous to spreading ripples, focusing upon the northeastern seaboard and with the frontier as its leading edge' (Muller 1973: 238).

A recent analysis of colonial Mexico recognized agricultural zones which accorded closely to Thünen principles for both Indian and Spanish economies (Ewald 1977). Little indication was offered as to the evolution of the zonal pattern although the process began after the *conquista* and continued during the period of reconstruction. An equilibrium state was suggested for the end of the colonial period.

Even this brief discussion of Thünen theory and the application to selected historical problems does serve to demonstrate the value of having analyses at

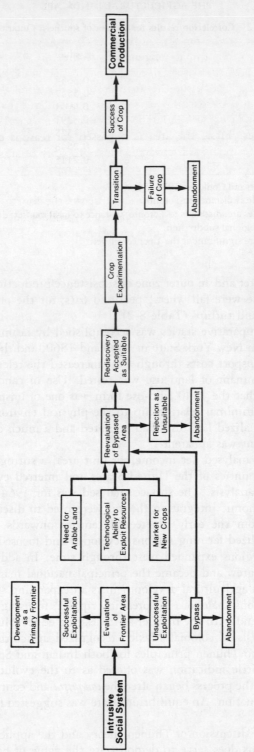

Fig. 8.2 A conceptual framework for agricultural evolution on secondary frontiers. (After Lewis 1979a: 207: from *The Frontier: Comparative Studies*, Volume 2, by William W. Savage Jr. and Stephen I. Thompson. © 1979 by the University of Oklahoma Press).

least partially directed by theoretical constructs. Although Thünen theory does not offer an explicit understanding of landscape evolution, being only an equilibrium account with nominal reference to change, it has been successfully exploited in both a static historical and an evolutionary context.

A conceptual framework for the analysis of agricultural evolution on secondary frontiers, areas of marginal desirability settled later than adjacent areas, has been offered by Lewis (1979a). The framework is indicated in Fig. 8.2 and includes five stages. First, the area is bypassed for reasons of initial unsuitability. Second, the area is rediscovered, most probably because of the need for additional arable land. The third stage includes rapid commercialization and hence a series of crop experiments takes place. Change-over from experimentation to the establishment of a staple crop marks the fourth stage, while the final stage is characterized by fully commercial production. These stages are confirmed with reference to grape, pineapple and citrus fruit industries in Florida.

An innovative approach to agrarian system dynamics was employed for an area of India prior to 1800 and three stages described (Murton 1975). First, from 900 to 1300, settlements were located in relation to water-supply and both permanent and shifting agricultural activities were practised. From 1300 to 1500 population increased, agricultural acreages expanded and shifting cultivation declined. These trends continued to 1800 with intensification of land use and technological advance.

THE EVOLUTION OF THE AGRICULTURAL LANDSCAPE – AREAS OF EUROPEAN OVERSEAS EXPANSION

Rapid change has been characteristic in areas settled by Europeans as the economy has progressed from aboriginal to frontier to commercial. Typically, the later the first settlement by Europeans the more rapid the changes, with many areas of nineteenth-century settlement undergoing especially dramatic developments in relation to mass population movements and major technological advances. Although the details of agricultural landscape evolution vary from place to place it is possible to recognize typical sequences of activity from early subsistence to later commercial enterprises. This section considers early agriculture and the process of land clearing, the subsistence to commercial transition and the spread of commercial agriculture. The section concludes with an assessment of the relevance of cultural variables in the process of evolution and some summary observations.

Early agriculture and land clearing

The significance of agricultural activities for North American Indians, for first settlers and for supporting the fur trade has received little attention despite the fact that 'agriculture pervaded the history of Indian–white contact' (Wessel

1976: 9). Indian agriculture was responsible for supporting early American colonists in both Plymouth and Jamestown and a farming way of life was pursued over large areas at the time of European settlement. Both the Huron and Iroquois were largely supported by agriculture during the fur trade and the westward expansion can be related to the location of agricultural groups (Wessel 1976: 13). According to Moodie (1980: 275) the fur trade relied on company agriculture, colonial agriculture and Indian agriculture. Company agriculture was practised at many trading posts, colonial agriculture was important at specific locations such as the Red River settlements, while Indian agriculture 'provided a pre-existing agricultural base for the development of the European trade in eastern Canada' (Moodie 1980: 275). Thus it can be argued that Indian agriculture was a key to both the expansion and the success of fur trading. More substantial conclusions await further substantive research.

For incoming settlers a primary concern was that of land clearing. Indeed, the perceived time, effort and cost of needed clearing was often a relevant variable in the location decision-making process (Kelly 1970). The details of land clearing, including the rate of clearing, the methods employed and the types of land prepared for agriculture, varied. Two examples are now noted as being largely representative of more general developments. In a discussion of the South Australian landscape Williams (1974) detailed clearing of woodland and draining of swamps. For most areas of overseas expansion the former was instrumental for the evolution of landscape and it was typically a process of individual actions. Woodland clearing was an integral first step because areas with a forest vegetation were the favoured agricultural locations. Land was cleared to allow for crop cultivation, to provide fencing, building material and domestic and industrial fuel. Areas of scrub in South Australia were largely cleared in the 1880s as a result of the introduction of new techniques although much initial clearing was only preliminary – for example, stumps might be left in an effort to cut down on costs. In southern Ontario most settlement occurred in forested areas with the general attitude for most of the nineteenth century being one of hostility to forest. Initially, forests were viewed as an impediment to farming and to development in general; they were perceived as depressing and as of only short-term benefit. Land clearance provided materials for both fencing and shelter and also furnished an immediate source of cash income from the export of potash and pearl-ash. Nearly all farms had potash factories and small nucleated centres had pearl-ash areas where the potash could be further refined for the European market. Rates of clearing were of course highly variable, but 5 acres per annum is an appropriate figure. Primarck (1962: 487) calculated the median labour costs involved in land clearing for areas of forest and of prairie. Expressed as man-days per acre, forest required 33 and prairie 1.5 c. 1850; by 1900 these statistics had reduced to 25 and 0.75 respectively.

The subsistence to commercial transition

Definitions of such terms as 'subsistence' and 'commercial' are somewhat arbitrary. For purposes of discussion, subsistence implies farming to supply the

136

minimum food to survive and also implies that the farm unit is self-contained. Commercial implies farming aimed at converting products to cash in an exchange economy. Clearly there is a continuum between these two extremes, with early agriculture being relatively subsistence oriented and subsequent developments approaching a fully commercial orientation. Despite this general trend towards increasing commercialization there are still areas of the world which remain essentially subsistence. Three general explanations can be offered. First, in a Thünian sense, these areas lie beyond the Isolated State. Second, traditional pursuits may be difficult to reject if the society does not value cash in the manner of western society. Third, subsistence practices are related to areas of difficult environment. In a historical context it is evident that the character of agriculture can be related to these three factors of economy, culture and physical environment. Discussions of any transition from subsistence to commercial need to consider these variables, especially if explanations of the pace of change are being sought.

Certainly much of the disagreement in the literature concerning this issue can be readily resolved by acknowledging regional variations in economy, culture and environment. The relatively rapid transition in southern Ontario, for example, was related to a rapidly growing population and economy and a favourable environment, while the relatively slow transition in South Africa was related to limited in-movement and to a more difficult environment (Norton 1977b, 1982b). Nevertheless there remains much disagreement, with some recent work emphasizing the commercial character of the earliest agriculture and arguing that any subsistence phase was merely an undesirable economic necessity while population was increasing, agriculture expanding, markets growing and communications improving. Mitchell (1972: 485–6), for the early Shenandoah Valley, noted that 'there was no clear cut division in newly settled areas between subsistence and commercially oriented economies, but gradual change toward greater agricultural specialization and commercialization accompanied by some elaboration of secondary and tertiary functions'. In a detailed study of one county in Indiana, Kiefer (1969) observed that initial subsistence was soon replaced by commercial activities and Conzen (1971) arrived at a similar conclusion for an area adjacent to Madison, Wisconsin. It has already been noted that southern Ontario pioneers frequently received cash in return for potash and pearl-ash. Each of these examples has argued that a subsistence phase is either brief or non-existent such that even the earliest activities were of an incipient commercial variety.

Such a conclusion is not, however, universally accepted. According to Stiverson (1976) the aim of early agriculture may have been commercial, but this ideal was hindered by poor transport, an inadequate technology and limited marketing facilities such that the reality was a definite subsistence period. An analysis of South Africa and of the Appalachians encouraged Guelke (1979: 3) to argue that frontier settlement was characterized by much subsistence economic activity. To a significant extent this apparent disagreement can be explained, as suggested, by reference to other variables. Areas of rapid commercial growth were areas in the main stream of economic change, areas of prolonged subsistence were often relative backwaters. Again, the areas of limited change were characteristically areas of more difficult environment and were also, perhaps, those areas occupied by societies less concerned with commercial concerns. Interior South Africa, for example, was settled by Dutch-speaking groups where primary motivation for movement was political not economic. The character of frontier agriculture and the extent of any subsistence phase is, then, a function of specific aspects of the character of a given region with the more typical sequence being one of rapid commercialization and specialization as one aspect of economic growth.

The spread of commercial agriculture

As one component of the expansion of European settlement the spread of commercial agriculture, especially wheat cultivation, has received much attention. Both geographers and historians have recognized the significance of the phenomena and a valuable comparison of their typically varying approaches was provided by Heathcote (1963), noting that historians focus on local studies while geographers focus on regional studies. Wheat or pastoral activity was typical in grassland areas, and wooded areas frequently passed through a stage of wheat cultivation. In southern Ontario the first commercial crop was wheat, typically alternating with fallow. Initial commercial agriculture was both for local urban markets and for export overseas. Colonial North Carolina agriculture also involved wheat as a major commercial crop (Merrens 1964). It was the grassland environments, however, which were the areas of spectacular wheat expansion. For most nineteenth-century pioneers in the mid-latitude zones wheat was the key cash crop as it was usually in demand and commanded an adequate price. The expansion of wheat was related to railway links, for wheat is a bulky product relative to value and, accordingly, benefits appreciably from any decline in transport costs. For Queensland, Camm (1976: 177) noted that a distance of 16–20 km was about the maximum a wheat farmer could afford to locate from a railway line. Changes in transportation, especially, could increase the potential wheat area and Fig. 8.3 indicates the expansion of suitable wheat areas in Queensland between 1892 and 1898. Similar developments occurred in New South Wales where the actual wheat area increased only marginally between 1860 and 1870. 'It was when the railways provided cheaper access to Sydney in the 1870s that the inland wheat industry took on a colonial rather than a local significance' (Jeans 1972: 201–2). Other variables which help explain the movement of the commercial wheat frontier included immigration, new cultivation technologies and the development of environmentally suitable wheat varieties. Each of these variables was noted by Cant (1968: 166) for the Canterbury Plains area of New Zealand where in the 1870s the price of wool was falling, railway expansion was typical, immigration was high and the demand for wheat was 'apparently insatiable'.

Over-expansion did occur such that in Queensland, for example, the wheat area of the Darling Downs declined from 47 per cent in 1905 to 31 per cent in 1914 (Camm 1976: 179). In southern Ontario the wheat monoculture of

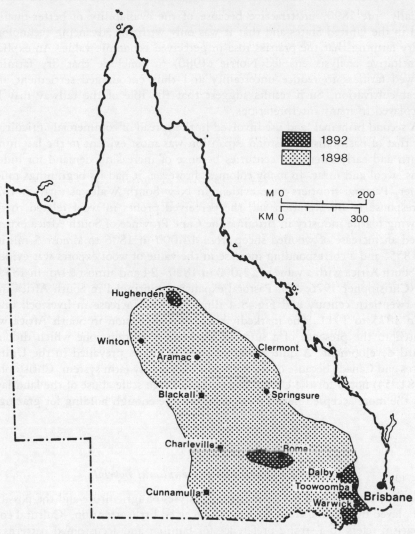

Fig. 8.3 Areas perceived as suitable for wheat, Queensland, Australia. (After Camm
1976: 179)

the mid-nineteenth century was soon replaced by a more diversified economy.
During the difficult years between 1931 and 1945 wheat-growing was abandoned in a pioneer zone of Western Australia (Dahlke 1975). Such retreats
typically occurred because of world market conditions, because over-expansion
into marginal areas had taken place or because the area was better suited to
more valuable land uses.

Much of the above discussion has failed to focus explicitly on the question
of timing, other than to note the emergence of appropriate variables. For the
Canadian prairies the traditional explanation of a suitable coincidence of factors
is somewhat unsatisfactory. Norrie (1975, 1977) argued that the prairies were

initially, pre-1890, unattractive because of the availability of better-quality land in the United States and that it was only with the advancing technology of dry farming that the prairies rose in perceived economic value. An explicit quantitative analysis enabled Norrie (1980) to conclude that dry farming allowed farmers to reduce uncertainty and thus encouraged settlement and wheat cultivation. Such results suggest that the role of the railway may be overplayed in many interpretations.

A second principal land use involved in the spread of commercial agriculture was that of pastoralism. Pastoral expansion was most evident in the late nine-teenth and early twentieth centuries because of increasing demand for hides, skins, wool and meat. In many colonies, however, it had its beginnings much earlier. Pastoral frontiers were evident in New South Wales as early as 1820 in response to immigration and the perceived profits in wool related to the growing textile industry in Britain. The Cape Province of South Africa experi-enced an increase of woolled sheep from 14,000 in 1806 to almost 5 million in 1855, and a corresponding increase in the value of wool exports was evident for South Africa with a value of £2,000 in 1820–24 and almost £1m. in 1855– 59 (Christopher 1976: 59). Pastoral expansion continued in South Africa into the twentieth century and Fig. 8.4 illustrates the increase in livestock units from 1875 to 1911. The markedly successful expansion in South Africa was related to the presence of a suitable land-tenure system, one which did not retard development. A quite different state of affairs prevailed in the United States and Canada because of the emphasis on a family farm system. Christopher (1981: 54) noted for the United States that: 'Large scale abuse of the land laws was the more accepted means of securing a large enough holding for grazing.'

New World agriculture: the cultural imprint

Economic explanations have dominated analyses of agriculture and the possible role played by cultural conservatism has received little attention. 'Cultural con-servatism refers to a strong preference for familiar and accustomed patterns of behavioural and material manipulation which becomes most pronounced when these patterns are challenged by a pressing need to adapt to new conditions' (Lewis 1979b: 622). Such conservatism is liable to be most effective if a frontier environment is similar to the homeland, if the distance between the two does not restrict all contact, if established techniques continue to work and if there is a reasonable accord between image and reality. Lewis (1979b) considered two areas of commercial viticulture in nineteenth-century Florida and showed that one area was successful because the behaviour associated with conservatism was economically appropriate, while the second area was subject to change because initial conservative behaviour proved unsatisfactory.

Certainly some form of cultural conservatism is relevant in many cases and has been explicitly acknowledged by Jordan (1966) and Wacker (1968) among

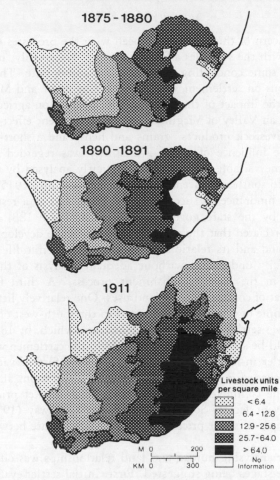

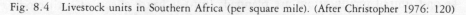

Fig. 8.4   Livestock units in Southern Africa (per square mile). (After Christopher 1976: 120)

others. An analysis of parts of Kansas between 1875 and 1925 by McQuillan (1978b) showed that three ethnic groups were faring somewhat differently in terms of economic success. In two areas of Nebraska Baltensperger (1980) showed that cultural conservatism was one of four overlapping processes influencing agriculture and that a process of rapid assimilation of new practices was more significant. It appears that cultural conservatism was restricted in areas of commercial agriculture. In southern Ontario, for example, mixed farming was an exception to the prevalent monoculture of wheat and 'not only was a reflection on the land of the transfer of ideas about agriculture from Britain, but also was a manifestation of the attempt to implant in Ontario the total life-style of British gentry' (Kelly 1973: 205). Such mixed farming was not especially profitable and was not associated with an ethnic group but rather with a group of hopeful gentry.

Summary observations

A principal concern of this section has been with the processes of agricultural evolution and with the variables affecting change. Necessarily, much has been left unsaid and some concluding comments are appropriate. The influence of conflict situations on settlement was noted in Chapter 7 and Mitchell (1973) has considered the impact of the American Revolution on agricultural change in the Shenandoah Valley of Virginia. The most apparent effect was increased production of livestock products, grains and hemp and a short-term decrease in tobacco. The influence of credit availability was regarded by Heathcote (1963) as a prime variable and has been explicitly analysed by Camm (1974) with reference to southern Queensland between 1890 and 1915. The absence of credit was a hindrance to successful settlement and as a result credit was made available by the state government. Camm (1974: 188) concluded: 'It needs to be appreciated that the economic aspects of the development of farming in Queensland and its relations to the larger economic life of the colony are not to be fully understood without adequate analysis of the costs which selectors faced in the farm establishment process.' A third factor, largely ignored, was that of competition for land uses. One relatively little-known but interesting example of competition occurred in the south-west of the Canadian prairies which was settled *c.* 1880 by cattlemen and which, by 1882, was being coveted by would-be settlers. At least until 1896 the cattlemen were successful in resisting settler in-movement (Breen 1973). One further variable relevant to agricultural change is the effects of economic depressions and booms. For the spread of the commercial wheat frontier, high market prices have been noted as a relevant factor. Somewhat similarly, Galloway (1975) noted the effects of a collapse in sugar prices on Brazilian agriculture between 1700 and 1750.

A scheme for analysing human and land relationships was offered by Kelly (1978) with five stages being suggested. First, initial settler evaluation occurs; second, initial modifications are planned; third, adverse effects of such modifications are acknowledged; fourth, new and more efficient landscapes are conceived and, finally, these new landscapes are developed. Kelly (1978) also proposed a three-stage sequence for the evolution of the landscape. First, a brief early settler landscape emerges; second, early commercial wheat farming dominates and third, a post-railway wheat landscape is evident. Although both of the above were developed on the basis of local evidence within southern Ontario they appear to merit some application in a wider context.

THE EVOLUTION OF THE AGRICULTURAL LANDSCAPE – BRITAIN AND EUROPE

This section is similar to the corresponding section of Chapter 7 in that a substantial chronological account is not possible. Rather, the intention is to highlight major research themes and to attempt to reflect the considerable quantity of work accomplished by historical geographers and others. Wherever feasible the mechanics of change are emphasized although it is evident that, in many cases, both the details and more general trends remain unclear. The subsequent discussion is organized within six basic themes. The first three themes involve processes of land clearing, field systems prior to enclosure and selected aspects of agricultural colonization and agricultural land use prior to *c*. 1700. The process and effects of enclosure are then considered and followed by discussions of the agricultural revolution and nineteenth-century depression periods.

Land clearing, field systems and medieval agriculture

'The clearing of the woodland is recognized as one of the most important themes in the historical geography of all the countries of medieval Europe' (Brandon 1969: 135). It resulted in a significant extension of cultivated land and the cultivation of much marginal land which was later to revert to pasture. Broad accounts of colonization and associated clearing have been provided for western Europe by C. T. Smith (1967) and for Germany by Mayhew (1973). The role of the Church was significant in this process and much of the clearing was not of haphazard and individual origin. A detailed analysis of the Weald by Brandon (1969) emphasized the extent of clearance, the sequence of developments and the extent of remaining woodland *c*. 1500. A major limiting factor was relief, with land above 150 m remaining largely as uncleared. A second detailed analysis of one area of the English midlands, the Forest of Arden, focused on the clearing of waste and woodland between the eleventh and fourteenth centuries (Roberts 1968). The motives for clearing included a need for more land and the stimulation offered by large landowners in an attempt to increase incomes and perhaps political power.

Britain and Europe displayed a wide variety of field systems into the medieval period as a result of a complex variety of agrarian systems (Baker and Butlin 1973). A basic distinction in Britain is evident between the predominantly arable south and east and the predominantly pastoral north and west. The south and east were highly manorialized while the north and west had field systems related to kinship bonds. However, such a simple regionalization necessarily masks important features. Harvey (1980), for example, argued that a particular field morphology for the Holderness region of Yorkshire was a result of eleventh-century planning possibly caused by economic depression and changes in land-ownership. The characteristic field system for arable areas was one of large fields divided into unenclosed strips although many varieties were possible (Baker and Butlin 1973). Nevertheless, French (1969, 1970) emphasized that a three-field system was widespread throughout lowland Europe. For one area, Lithuania, the system appeared as late as 1557 as a result of a royal decree, but evolution elsewhere was more gradual and hence is more difficult to discern. Thirsk (1964, 1966) explained the origins of common fields in terms of population pressure and McCloskey (1975) explained their stability in terms of a risk minimization very similar to that proposed by Norrie (1980) for Canadian prairie settlement. In some areas the process of enclosure began prior to 1500 for a variety of regional reasons such as rationalization, land-use change and depression (Butlin 1978: 138–9).

Agricultural land use in the early modern period prior to *c*. 1700 has received much attention with interest in technical advances and increased commercialization, productivity and intensification. Crop combinations and rotations in east Worcestershire have been mapped and described by Yelling (1969) and for the same area livestock farming trends have been established by use of probate inventories (Yelling 1970). Probate inventories have also been innovatively employed to calculate estimates of grain yields when other reliable data are unavailable and the results found to be satisfactory (Overton 1979). Overall, this early modern period is now seen as strongly influenced by markets and market conditions (Yelling 1978). Market area size increased although major change was limited because of the limited transport development. Subsistence problems varied between countries. Before 1740 France experienced a number of subsistence crises, whereas no such phenomena occurred in England. Appleby (1979) explained this in terms of the English cultivation of both spring and winter grains which ensured that not all cereals failed in any one year.

Enclosures, changes, depressions

The processes of enclosure are complex in terms of causes, mechanics of change and consequences. Two forms of enclosure are usually acknowledged and have been confirmed by Yelling (1977). The two are general, often parliamentary, enclosure and piecemeal enclosure. It is the former which was most evident and which has received most attention. Piecemeal enclosure was characteristic where the common fields were not involved in any regulated organization and was especially evident before 1760. The distinction between these two is important because 'usually general enclosures involved the complete removal of common field' (Yelling 1978: 153).

Enclosure affected common fields, common pastures, wasteland and moorland. In a series of articles Williams (for example, 1971) discussed waste reclamation throughout England and Wales and for the one county of Somerset. Much of this reclamation and enclosure occurred between 1780 and 1880 and nearly 13.8 per cent of Somerset was affected. Moorland enclosures often involved many separate parliamentary Acts and incorporated both permissive and compulsory change, the former resulting in gradual enclosure and the latter in more rapid enclosure. Both types were evident in the North Yorkshire Moors (Chapman 1976).

Eighteenth- and nineteenth-century agricultural change took place against a background of rapid industrialization, urbanization and transport improvements. Included were a series of changes often regarded as revolutionary and periods of nineteenth-century depression. Essentially the series of changes which became known as the agricultural revolution involved technological advances and increases in output. Enclosure continued, new livestock breeds diffused rapidly, new fodder crops were introduced and farm-management techniques advanced. The single most famous development was the introduction of a Norfolk four-course rotation which basically involved wheat, turnips, barley and clover. As early as 1700 British agriculture was both regionally specialized and market oriented, a trend which intensified as agriculture responded to the rapid increases in demand. Specialization was especially evident adjacent to urban centres and land use evolved in accord with basic Thünian principles (Walton 1978: 255). Discussions of the agricultural revolution have acknowledged the diffusion of innovations as being fundamental to any explanation of developments. Pawson (1979: 63) suggested that: 'In England, at least, it appears that the larger tenantry and independent farmers were the most important agents of change. It was they who had the resources to experiment and often the time to travel and read.' Examples of diffusion were provided by Walton (1978: 260), and on the basis of evidence relating to pedigree Shorthorn cattle it was argued that logical spatial diffusion forms applied in the cases of most innovations.

Continuing advance and change prevailed during the nineteenth century although periods of prosperity, namely the Napoleonic Wars and mid-century, alternated with periods of depression, post-war and late nineteenth century. It is the 'great agricultural depression', 1870–1914 approximately, which has received particular attention. Using data on agricultural bankruptcies Perry (1972) mapped the extent of the depression and related the impact to environmental factors. The depression included declines in wool and cereal prices and a substantial reduction in grain yields. An analysis of parts of Yorkshire and Nottinghamshire argued that depression was caused by the low prices and was not closely related to climatic difficulties (Bunce 1972). Depression periods notwithstanding, the eighteenth and nineteenth centuries were times of expanding acreage, increasing yields, much rationalization and major change. These or related developments were apparent in many different cases such as the evolution of market gardening in Bedfordshire (Beavington 1975), the history of flax cultivation in Scotland (Turner 1972) and the early-nineteenth-century cattle trade (Blackman 1975).

DIFFUSION OF AGRICULTURAL INNOVATIONS

Origins of agriculture

Plant and animal domestication qualify as a revolution in human technology, possibly the first purely cultural revolution. Details of origin, however, remain a source of much debate because of the paucity of evidence. It is generally agreed that domestication was a process, not an event, and was the culmination of many years of human and vegetation relationships. Early attempts at explanation included those by Childe (1951) and Sauer (1952), both of which were largely speculative and not based on sound data. Sauer (1952) argued that domestication was not a response to hunger, for starving people do not have the leisure time for the needed experimentation. Accordingly, initial domestication could not have occurred in grassland areas or on floodplains because of problems of thick sod and flooding respectively. Rather, a hilly area with a variety of plants was favoured and south-east Asia was specifically advocated. Others have traditionally leaned towards the south-west Asia region at a time when conditions were somewhat moister. A principal contemporary emphasis is towards ecological theory which requires 'a set of environmental circumstances that will upset the negative feedback of the food-foraging adaptation and lead a group step-by-step into a radically new subsistence pattern' (Richerson 1979: 639). Typical independent variables in the theory are climatic change, population pressure, specific patterns of resources that favour minimal movement and the availability of suitable plants and animals. The role of climatic change in particular is especially contentious. As far as locations are concerned the relevance of tropical areas is poorly understood primarily as a result of the difficulty of data preservation.

Grigg (1974: 9) recognized six centres of early agriculture, each of which was a possible centre of independent domestication. The six are south west Asia, south-east Asia and north China with early cereal cultivation, and south-east Asia, West Africa and South America as areas of early vegeculture. The origins of agriculture may be regarded as a precursor to urban development in many areas. Through time agriculture diffused remarkably until hunting economies became marginally located in isolated areas.

Diffusion of techniques and land uses

Diffusion analyses have been both descriptive and general on the one hand, and explanatory and specific on the other. Most recent studies are of the latter variety and have been stimulated by the spatial analytic developments in human geography.

One example of a large-scale diffusion study considered the expansion of an Arab agricultural revolution between 700 and 1100 (Watson 1974). This revolution originated in India and involved many new crops and new farming practices such as irrigation. Diffusion of the revolution was a result of Arab expansion and strong demand factors prior to the discovery of supply areas beyond the Islamic world of the Middle East and the Mediterranean.

The diffusion of ideas, techniques, crops and livestock both beyond and during the British agricultural revolution is a major area of research. In Wales, for example, new legumes were being adopted from 1650 onwards even by smaller farmers, and Emery (1976) observed that no major difficulties in either accessibility or information were apparent. Diffusion of wheel-houses in Northumberland has been related to potential adopters, to diffusion centres, to large landowners and to agricultural societies (Hellen 1972). A series of typically S-shaped growth curves have been calculated by Walton (1978) for such innovations as improved sheep breeds (Fig. 8.5) and a wide range of technical

146

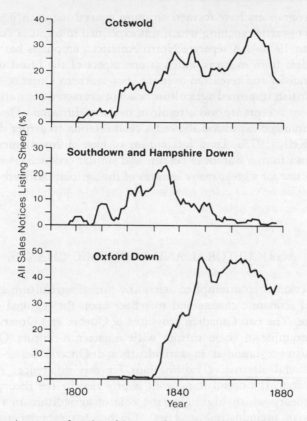

Fig. 8.5 Adoption curves for selected improved sheep breeds in Oxfordshire, England (five-year moving means). (After Walton 1978: 247)

advances. Overall, this body of literature confirms conceptual expectations regarding both growth and spread although formal analyses of the communication process are less rigorous. Emery (1976: 48) proposed an original three-step flow of communication. First, information about new procedures is received and accepted by the innovative opinion leaders. These leaders quickly influence their tenants, followed by a dispersal of information to other opinion leaders. This suggestion is in accord with Hellen's (1972) recognition of the important role played by large landowners. For the period of the 'great agricultural depression' Robinson (1981) analysed horticultural diffusion in an area of the English midlands. Relevant variables included railway expansion and individual innovators. It is expected that further research on aspects of agricultural diffusion will lead to improved knowledge of distributions and improved knowledge of relevant processes. The examples cited strongly suggest that the role of individuals is especially important in the early stages.

Comparable North American analyses have been conducted primarily by economic historians and for the diffusion of mechanical reapers both individual and technological variables have been identified (Colman 1968; Pomfret 1976).

Historical geographers have focused on more general issues such as the expansion of types of cattle ranching which was explained in terms of cultural movements (Jordan 1977a). A separate North American emphasis has involved the transfer of ideas from overseas which is one aspect of the broad research issue of cultural transfer and retention overseas. For southern Ontario, Kelly (1976) noted that British improved agriculture was not characteristic until after 1850, and subsequent acceptance was a result of overseas diffusion. The specific case of artificial drainage expansion showed a clear relation to earlier developments in Britain (Kelly 1975). Long lots appear to have diffused through parts of North America from a European hearth, and similar conclusions would appear to be appropriate for a great many features of the agricultural landscape (Jordan 1974).

AGRICULTURAL AND ECONOMIC CHANGE

This final section is an attempt to assess the role of agriculture as one part of more general economic change and to reflect upon the regional development of agriculture. The two Canadian provinces of Quebec and Ontario serve as an interesting example of these themes with nineteenth-century Quebec being largely subsistence oriented in agriculture and Ontario being commercial. There are several alternative explanations for this difference. According to Isbister (1977: 674) a useful framework is provided by the theory of balanced growth: 'a theory which highlights the role of agriculture in the economic development of preindustrial societies'. Quebec has experienced unbalanced economic development while Ontario's experience has been balanced. This framework allows the role of agriculture to be considered in the form of labour transfer, commodity exchange or exports, with commodity exchange being crucial for balanced growth. From at least 1850 onwards Ontario farmers were both producing and selling a surplus to support non-farm populations, while the surplus rate in Quebec was virtually nil before 1900. Part of the explanation for this difference between the two provinces can be attributed to cultural factors; for example, average family size in Quebec was 7.1 and in Ontario was 6.2 c. 1850 (Isbister 1977: 681). Also, Ontario farmers displayed a higher productivity per farm, perhaps two and a half times higher, a fact which can be attributed to a different attitude to farming life (Isbister 1977: 681). Environmental variations were ascribed little significance. The differences between the two provinces, one subsistence and one commercial, were not adequate to impede industrial growth in Quebec which in the twentieth century involved exporting manufactured goods. It can be argued, however, that the traditional subsistence orientation of Quebec agriculture had effects on Quebec society. An alternative approach to Quebec–Ontario differential growth focused largely on economic factors with Ontario having advantages for the production of a staple (wheat) and multiplier effects subsequently generating industrial and urban growth (McCallum 1980).

148

The spread and growth of agriculture was closely related to world markets, and distance minimization between supply and demand locations was important. The American Pacific coastal region in the 1850s has been likened to Australia in terms of the distance to world markets, although the similarity terminates by the 1860s (Rothstein 1975). The Pacific region rapidly transformed into an area of staple production with the emergence of wheat farming for the British market and then gradually transformed to an area of more diversified activity. 'The mercantile firms that had dominated trade in that commodity also performed important functions in the transformation toward greater diversity' (Rothstein 1975: 279).

Relationships between agricultural change and economic growth in general have been extensively analysed in the European context with major questions relating to the complex links with aspects of transport, industry, urban growth and populations (Parker and Jones 1975). There is every suggestion of further research in these areas by historical geographers judging by the accounts of Perry (1975) and Pawson (1979). It is hardly necessary to observe that a major difficulty in all such work relates to the task of identifying cause and effect in complex multivariate problems.

CHAPTER NINE

Transportation, industrial and urban landscapes

TRANSPORT

In common with other aspects of the economic and cultural landscape, transportation networks change with periods of evolution and periods of revolution. Spasmodic growth is characteristic as evidenced by terms such as 'canal boom' and 'railway mania'. No frameworks are available to explain the process of network change beyond a series of partial models and one result of this failure is a general paucity of work which focuses explicitly on the economic and social consequences of transport patterns.

Network evolution

Although much recent work has progressed beyond the descriptive and reconstruction stages there are often data deficiencies which effectively limit analysis for these early stages. Such is particularly the case prior to the eighteenth century. The road network of medieval England, for example, has been reconstructed by Hindle (1976) using a mix of cartographic and indirect evidence provided by the travel itineraries of three English monarchs. The result is an admittedly tentative map of roads c. 1348 which might be improved by use of further indirect approaches. Difficulties of reconstruction are compounded by the fact that: 'Much of the transport system of pre-industrial England was informal and small scale, in the case of land as opposed to river carriage it was not likely even always to be along fixed lines, for roads in the modern sense hardly existed' (Patten 1979: 33). During the eighteenth and nineteenth centuries the increased demand generated by the process of industrialization spurred the creation of more permanent systems, although technological advance resulted in changes in the dominant transport mode. These changes have been chronologically assessed by Fullerton (1975) from 1750 to 1970, although the early turnpike road system was largely excluded, and by Moyes (1978) from 1730 to 1900.

The evolution of transport networks has been approached as a series of discrete stages by means of basic model construction. Taafe et al. (1963) proposed a sequence of six stages based on empirical evidence from Ghana and Nigeria. A series of scattered ports is followed by the disappearance of some ports related to inland expansion. Feeder routes then evolve leading to initial interconnections prior to a completely interconnecting system. The final stage involves the appearance of high-priority routes. This model was considered inadequate for the Niagara peninsula (Burghardt 1969) and might be criticized for requiring specific local conditions. Other stage-of-growth models are those of Lachene (1965) and Ekström and Williamson (1971), both of which employed a deductive approach. The former suggested an initial network of trails, urban growth at trail intersections and related road links and, finally, the emergence of dominant centres and corresponding routes. The latter recognized a new transport innovation, spread of that innovation and subsequent integration into the various transport networks. These model formulations were detailed by Lowe and Moryadas (1975: 114–20).

Analyses of network evolution frequently focus on a traditional concern, that of the relationship between the development of transport and economic development. In addition, the relative importance of different systems has been debated. Freeman (1980) argued that the early English industrial revolution involved both canal and road improvement and advocated that analyses focus on demand considerations. A detailed regional study of stage-coach routes in south Hampshire suggested that reduced journey times contributed to regional economic development (Freeman 1975). This theme has been particularly articulated for North America in a wide variety of research. For the Niagara peninsula region of southern Ontario Burghardt (1969) considered the evolution of the entire basic road system. Roads were closely related to earlier Indian trails and to the stream network, but urban growth was largely dependent not on nodality but on the location of port and milling sites. North of Toronto McIlwraith (1970) noted that a successful agricultural life relied on an adequate road system during the 1790–1850 period. A close link between railway expansion and economic change was noted for northern Michigan (Krog 1977). The railway network responded to demand factors with the pre-1890 routes serving sawmill towns and subsequent changes in the availability of lumber necessitating network change. Hubbard (1974) analysed the Jamaican road network until 1846 and noted a close relationship between roads and plantation agriculture expansion. Equating railways with national development has been an especially popular topic in Canada. A traditional view argued that railways played a key role in the emergence of Canada as an industrialized and unified country (Innis 1923). Baskerville (1979: 69) anticipated a continuing concern with such grand themes, albeit an increasingly critical and analytic concern.

The importance of ocean transport availability for countries exporting staple products was discussed by Broeze (1975) for the regional development of wool in Australia. Wool expanded about 1830 once ocean freight rates declined adequately, suggesting that a key factor in the profitability of wool production was the cost of export to Britain. Although staple export theory is a popular framework there is rarely detailed consideration of the export cost component.

An original analysis of turnpike roads in England by Pawson (1977) consid-

151

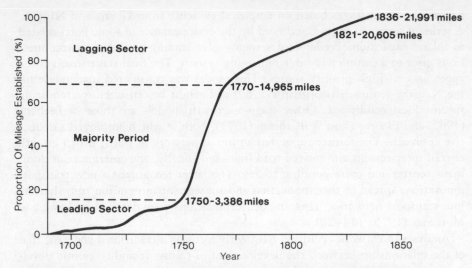

Fig. 9.1 Diffusion curve of turnpike road mileage, England and Wales. (After Pawson 1977: 115)

ered the question of a transport and economy relationship with the explicit use of temporal and spatial diffusion concepts. The S-shaped curve, an empirical regularity for innovation growth, was confirmed (Fig. 9.1). Explanation of the growth process involved demand, supply and resistance considerations. Spatial diffusion, the spread of the innovation, involved both expansion and hierarchical diffusion. Figures 9.2 and 9.3 respectively show the network for 1740, in the early years of the spread, and for 1770, following the main period. By 1770 'a well integrated turnpike road network had been developed' (Pawson 1977: 154). The success of this analysis was largely related to the availability of a consistent and comprehensive data source, namely the Acts passed in Parliament which established each turnpike trust. The precise reconstructions which were permitted facilitated process discussion. Economic consequences of the growth and spread of turnpiking included declining travel times and declining travel costs. Wider effects were a general improvement in road quality and an extension of markets which encouraged industrial and agricultural expansion. Pawson (1977: 339) concluded that the turnpike road system was responsible for initiating many of the major economic changes usually related to railway expansion.

Contributions from new economic history

Relating transport and economy has been a long-standing concern of economic history, and the traditional view held that improvements in transport were a prerequisite to economic growth and contributed directly to growth. New economic historians have disputed these ideas, which they saw as unproven and largely invalid assertions. This reappraisal of the role of transport has not, how-

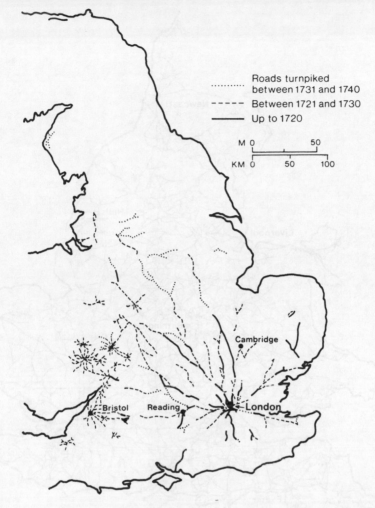

Fig. 9.2   Turnpike road network in 1740, England and Wales. (After Pawson 1977: 139)

ever, been conducted without considerable debate over methods, both between the traditional and the new economic historians and between the new economic historians themselves. This section reviews the new interpretations and attempts an assessment of their validity. Although the style and character of such work is rather different to that typically employed by historical geographers, with much emphasis on theory, quantification and counterfactuals, it is apparent that the questions posed and resultant answers are of direct relevance.

Economic historians have long recognized the varied improvements in transport associated with industrialization, related freight cost declines, related cost reductions of fuels and raw materials and related market area expansion. New economic historians argued that 'the influence of railways upon the long term

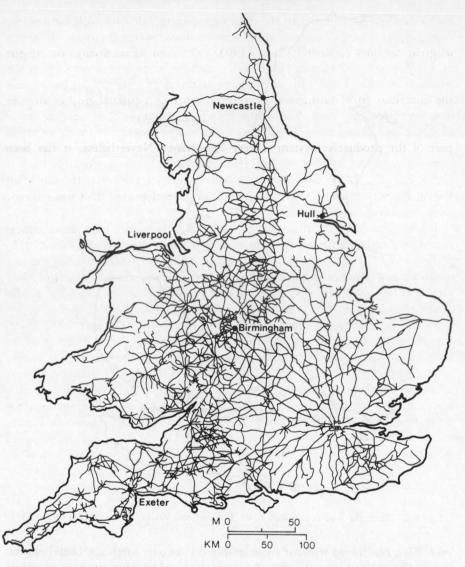

Fig. 9.3 Turnpike road network in 1770, England and Wales. (After Pawson 1977: 150)

growth of any economy can only be properly assessed by measuring reductions in the cost of sending freight by rail compared to alternative forms of transport' (O'Brien 1977: 22). Further, it was necessary to evaluate railways in terms of impact on capital, labour and production technique availability. Resultant analyses relied heavily on the concept of social savings, which essentially refers to the difference between actual national income and the national income without railways. Using this concept Fishlow (1965) estimated social savings for the United States in 1859 at $134m. while Hawke (1970) estimated £28m. for England and Wales in 1865. Much of the criticism directed at new economic history has referred to the data necessary to calculate such figures, for example the assumed costs of alternative road and water transport. In terms of gross national product Fishlow (1965) calculated social savings on freight at 3.3 per cent and Hawke (1970) calculated the savings at 4 per cent of the national income. These and other comparable results certainly suggested that the contribution of railways to nineteenth-century industrializing economies was not overly significant. Such a simple conclusion might be misleading, however, for, as O'Brien (1977: 261) noted: 'Providing substitutes exist, no single part of the productive system is very important.' Nevertheless, it has been demonstrated that specific modes of transport were not indispensable to economic growth. In the Canadian context it has been argued that the Canadian Pacific Railway played a smaller role in prairie development than was conventionally assumed (George 1975).

Understanding the contribution of new economic history requires awareness of the two rather different types of counterfactual employed. Fishlow (1965) and Hawke (1970), on the one hand, adopted the *ceteris paribus* condition and excluded any adjustments to the hypothesized railway closure. Fogel (1964), on the other hand, allowed both agriculture and transport to adjust to the absence of railways, with agricultural land locating close to navigable waterways and both water and road routes being improved. O'Brien (1977: 35–9) considered the implications of removing railways for the period 1859–90. The actual growth rate was 4 per cent, the growth rate adopting a *ceteris paribus* counterfactual was calculated at 3.76 per cent and the growth rate with a counterfactual allowing adjustments was 3.84 per cent. Overall, work in new economic history has not succeeded in using the concept of social savings to arrive unequivocally at conclusions concerning railways and economic growth. Rather more success has been achieved in discussions of the effects of railways on industrial growth where it has been shown that railways were not crucial to emerging industrialization. Indeed, no one input can be regarded as necessary for nineteenth-century growth.

Gateways, ports and regional development

Gateways, and ports as a subset of gateways, can be viewed as basic to the economic development of emerging regions. The mercantile model proposed by Vance (1970) assumed such exogenous factors, thus highlighting the role of transportation from the gateway to the established areas and from the gateway into the new area. Conzen (1975) analysed transport, in the form of passenger service, and showed that a mercantile system evolved prior to a central place system in the case of the American midwest. A city such as Chicago quickly developed a transport network for staple export purposes and for more general service considerations.

Ports are perhaps the most studied gateways to regions (Bird 1980). A model of port evolution suggested five stages: an initial dispersed pattern; inland penetration and some port piracy; interconnection of ports and concentration of activities; increased centralization; and finally, decentralization (Rimmer

1967). These stages were confirmed in the Australian context from 1861 to 1961. The somewhat contradictory fifth stage was necessary to accommodate recent changes resulting from the inability of some large ports to cope with traffic volumes. For an analysis of Ghanaian ports, Hilling (1977) adopted the Taafe *et al.* (1963) model of transport expansion and equated transport and port development. These and related port or inland gateway analyses are valuable both as specific empirical studies and as contributions to the issue of regional landscape change.

Network analyses and simulations

Network analysis was employed by Dicks (1972) in a study of the Roman road system of Britain with a starting assumption of the primacy of London. Simplified networks were generated and were argued to be a suitable basis for intensive analysis. Such procedures were criticized by Hutchinson (1972) on the grounds that no new knowledge is made available. Further applications of network techniques are necessary to clarify the value of an established technique in transport geography to historical matters.

Simulation procedures are a well-established tool for handling problems of historical decision-making and represent an addition to the well-established tools of intimate knowledge and detailed archival research. The problem is well indentified by Fig. 9.4 which indicates both proprosed and actual railway routes in the Isle of Wight off southern England. For a similar problem in Maine, Black (1971) assumed certain key variables and then proceeded to simulate a railway network for 1851 which corresponded closely to the actual net-

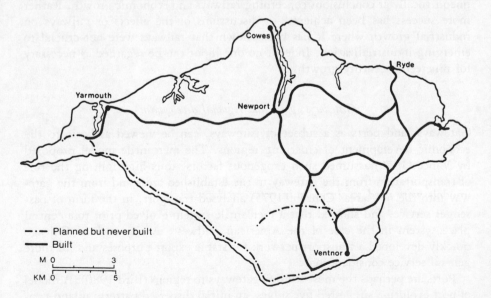

Fig. 9.4 Proposed and actual railway networks, Isle of Wight.(After Ashworth and Bradbeer 1977: 13)

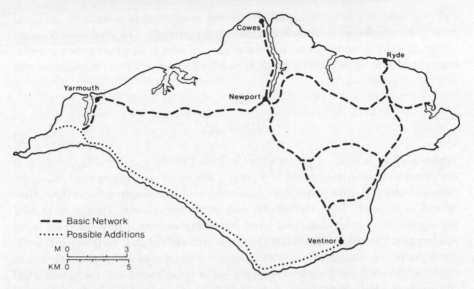

Fig. 9.5   Simulated railway network, Isle of Wight. (After Ashworth and Bradbeer 1977: 16)

work. This network was simulated link by link. Other analyses have preferred to simulate an entire network in an effort to replicate a specific form following an initial specification of the assumed process. This procedure was used by Kansky (1963) for the Sicilian railway network of 1908, by Kolars and Malin (1970) for the Turkish network as it evolved from 1860 to 1964 and by Ashworth and Bradbeer (1977) for the Isle of Wight. Figure 9.5 indicates the Isle of Wight simulated network and is based upon a set of assumptions including relief factors. Each of these simulations is open to criticisms of over-simplification. Ashworth and Bradbeer (1977) assumed the Isle of Wight to be a closed system while Kolars and Malin (1970) used the 1960 population distribution as an independent variable, thus indulging in issues of circularity. Nevertheless, each of these examples has provided insights into networks in addition to those offered by detailed reconstructions. A somewhat different use of simulation was employed in a study of investment choices between railways and canals c. 1840 in the United States (Schaefer and Weiss 1971). Models of decision-making were constructed based, again, on assumptions, and these models were used to simulate investment data output.

Although network analyses and simulations have been applied to historical transport problems the applications are rather limited and often areally specific. It appears that much more can be accomplished by means of these procedures as historical geographers increase their conceptual and technical sophistication. Indeed, Quastler (1978) has argued that the historical geographer has contributed relatively little, by whatever means, to questions about American railways. Further studies of network evolution were advocated focusing on processes, regional variations, the locational strategies of corporations and the influence of individuals. A second research area advocated involved railway rate-making, including discriminatory pricing. The relatively nominal attention paid to transport by historical geographers is surprising, but increasing concerns about regional growth are likely to lead to a more substantial and diversified literature.

INDUSTRY

Technological progress is perhaps best reflected in the industrial landscape and the process of industrialization is a central theme of the eighteenth- and nineteenth-century British experience and of the later nineteenth-century New World experience. Industrialization and urbanization were closely correlated during this time with cause and effect operating in both directions. Historical geographers have focused on both the economic and cultural variables involved, particularly the economic. Cultural analyses have recognized the emergence of class distinctions, the increased segregation of populations and the loss of local control over production (Goheen 1973: 57–8). Gregory (1978b) has provided a substantive account of cultural change related to the emergence of the working classes and the rise of the middle classes. The processes of cultural change continue to be largely the concern of social historians despite the significance of regional variations.

Industrial location theory and economic growth

Industrialization may be explained in terms of production changes or in terms of location theory. The former focuses on the institutions which encourage capital accumulation while the latter emphasizes issues of comparative advantage. In common with other location concepts, industrial theory is essentially static although it has been applied in a variety of ways to analyse change. Brook (1976) noted that issues such as entrepreneurial activity, diffusion, concentration, capital, technology and pricing systems can all be successfully applied, but that there is also a need to emphasize and relate organization, behaviour and location. The clearest discussion of the value of industrial theory as a framework for historical analyses has been provided by Langton (1979). Least-cost approaches and market-area approaches were distinguished and limitations noted. The least-cost approach of Weber (1929) is especially limited because of the concern with but one firm, but neither approach can cope with both cost and demand as spatial variables. Despite stated reservations Langton (1979) successfully exploited the market-area concepts of Lösch (1954) as a means of highlighting and ranking relevant variables.

Two sets of concepts widely used by economic historians are those of take-off and of staple export influences. Take-off approaches are especially unsatisfactory in the New World where industrialization was often a gradual process, often relying on initial agricultural growth. The staple export model has been found to be more useful to explain industrialization.

The industrial revolution in Britain

Manufacturing prior to the industrial revolution has primarily been studied by economic historians, and analyses have emphasized cloth, iron and coal in addition to recognizing that manufacturing was directed at providing basic necessities (Coones 1979; Patten 1979). Generalizations about the pre-industrial period are difficult and Coones (1979: 130–1) noted the ambiguities involved in discussions of growth and change, the two often being unrelated.

The industrial revolution was, of course, much more than industrial change with dramatic consequences for population growth, towns, agriculture, transport, trade and cultural life. The causes of industrial change are subject to much debate, but may be summarized as rising demand for products and increasing supply of raw materials, capital, labour and entrepreneurship (Pawson 1978, 1979). Industrial growth accelerated c. 1730 and continued essentially unabated until the late nineteenth century. The effects were selective with some industries being especially subject to change and some regions receiving especially large inputs. Cotton and iron were major growth industries while the coalfield regions of the north and midlands of England, of central Scotland and of South Wales became centres of industry. By 1900 the growth centres of Britain were iron, steel and shipbuilding towns close to supplies of ore and not too distant from coalfields.

The changing geography of the south-west Lancashire coalfield before 1800 involved production largely for local industries, and increasing supply was stimulated by industry and not by domestic demands. Other factors influencing output were transport cost and availability, physical considerations, drainage problems, capital and labour. Competition was also crucial to the emergence of functioning economic systems and was related to the rise of distinct regions within the coalfield (Langton, 1979: 239–40). The Tyneside coal industry provides a good example of the effect on space economies of matters of economic power and organization. In 1750 the industry was dominated by a monopolistic group, a domination which ended about 1770 only to be replaced by an alternative cartel which was effective until the end of the century. These changes in control were explained by Cromar (1977, 1979) in terms of technological advances, which allowed concealed areas to be exploited, in terms of the emergence of a banking system which encouraged capital inflow and in terms of desires by the post-1770 cartel to minimize risk. It is clear that analyses which consider issues of power and organization generally can help to explain regional and other changes.

More conventional economic geographic analyses of British heavy industry have been provided by Warren (1970, 1976) for the period 1800 to the present. These analyses combined economic and behavioural principles to explain location decision-making and particularly emphasized the locational inertia which constrains contemporary planning. An increased commitment by historical geographers to national, regional and local analyses seems evident and promises not only to clarify many issues but also to generate frameworks for research integrating economic and cultural analyses.

Industrialization in the New World

Historical geographic analyses of New World industry have been less concerned with causes of change, which have largely related to overseas diffusion and less concerned with cultural aspects of industrial growth. Manufacturing activity has received most attention and analyses have been framed within staple export concepts. For southern Ontario, Gilmour (1972) noted the growth of manufacturing·industry between 1851 and 1891 and the increasing importance of producer goods industries relative to consumer goods industries. Spatial variations were related to temporal variations in the initiation of industrial activity and to established location-theory concepts with multiplier effects also operating. Nevertheless, some components of southern Ontario manufacturing were subject to major structural and locational changes in the late nineteenth and early twentieth centuries. Urban locations became increasingly attractive – an attraction which was encouraged by discriminatory freight rates. Bland (1975) emphasized changes in metal fabricating and clothing industries as measured by shift analysis and showed the increasingly important role played by the western cities, especially those at the western end of Lake Ontario.

Relations between industrial growth, transport expansion and economic growth were noted by Walsh (1978) with reference to the pork industry of the American midwest. Initial locations were the Ohio river towns, but by the 1850s railway centres dominated and by the 1870s larger towns controlled the industry. Pork processing was one of several important processing industries in the midwest which were complemented by some heavy industrial and consumer goods activity. Walsh (1978: 22) concluded that new agricultural regions industrialized quite rapidly, a conclusion which can be readily confirmed by reference to other areas. Industrial foundations were laid in South Africa from 1860 onwards in the form of diamond-, gold- and coal-mining. The related development of precious metals and of coal was noted by Williams (1972). Linge (1975) began a discussion of Australian manufacturing as early as 1788, recognizing that local activity was essential from the outset, given the travel time from Europe. Initially, industry catered to everyday needs, but by the second half of the nineteenth century industry was growing at twice the rate of the gross domestic product (Linge 1975: 158). Again, there was appreciable regional variation. Industrial spread to areas of recent frontier character was even evident in the case of steel with the American industry moving west as early as 1850 (Warren 1973).

Summary comments

Industrial historical geography has generally fared rather poorly in comparison to rural settlement and agricultural interests. This relative neglect can be explained in part by the traditional interests of British and European historical geographers which have always leaned towards the countryside and not the industrial town, and in part by the pre-twentieth-century interests of New World historical geographers which have restricted the concern with industry.

There are, however, signs of an increasing concern with industrial issues both economic and cultural. In addition there have been analyses of the images held of industrial landscapes. According to Peters and Anderson (1976) the perception of such a landscape is highly variable, with artists and poets responding with an initial optimism succeeded by questioning and concern.

TOWNS

This section is concerned primarily with the internal structure of cities, questions of settlement spacing having been covered in Chapter 7. Urban historical geography is flourishing and has, according to Gregory (1974: 27), reached the stage where techniques are being employed on sophisticated problems. This recent maturing of urban historical geography beyond the descriptive and beyond the occasionally inappropriate use of techniques owes much to developments in urban history. An edited volume by Dyos (1968) provides a clear indication of the then current trends in urban history with contributions focusing on data problems, reconstructions and the potential use of quantitative methods and computers. Today, the final concern has emerged into the reasonably distinctive field of 'new urban history', a field which explicitly advocates theory and quantitative methods and which involves a variety of disciplines, including historical geography. An edited volume by Schnore (1975) on the new urban history has contributions from geographers, historians, economists and a sociologist. However, the current vitality of urban historical geography is not entirely reliant on this new urban history. A valuable stimulus has also come from social history, and another from urban geography. The remainder of this section considers some historical concepts of urban form, pre-industrial cities, aspects of the nineteenth-century city and residential differentiation.

Historical theories of urban form

There are several examples of attempts to explain form evolution, largely by formulating a process model. Hanley (1974) developed a model designed to ascertain the relative importance of public and official demands to urban development. The model was largely derived with reference to one town, Invercargill, New Zealand, and was evaluated for that same centre. Four stages were suggested. First, the need for some change is recognized and the situation is assessed by both public and officials. Second, the channels which express most concern and take most action are identified. Third, both groups first make decisions, then consult and reach a compromise position. Fourth, decisions are made and incorporated into legislation. Hanley (1974: 73) concluded that the model facilitated understanding of Invercargill during the 1870s and acknowledged the need for applications elsewhere in order to determine whether growth and development patterns have a degree of conformity.

A second example of a model-based approach to the evolution of urban form

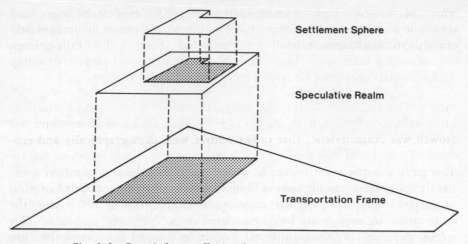

Fig. 9.6 Growth factors affecting form. (After Sargent 1972: 358)

focused on residential land use and on the spatial and temporal factors affecting location (Sargent 1972). Three distinct spatial entities were proposed as influencing form, namely a transportation frame, a speculative realm and a settlement sphere. As Fig. 9.6 suggests, these three are nested, with transportation determining the outer limits of growth, speculation determining the sequence and location of building activity and settlement taking place within these constraints. An empirical analysis of the evolution of Buenos Aires largely supported the conceptual framework, a framework which appears to be appropriate for many New World towns.

The role of individual landowners and of institutions as factors determining urban form was stressed by Vance (1978). This view emphasized the decision-making processes of government and financial institutions and the significance of housing policy. Perhaps the most developed discursive explanations are those which have argued that urban development is related to capital availability and demand factors (Whitehand 1975) and to the timing of innovations (Whitehand 1977). Arguments involving capital and demand were criticized by Daunton (1978) for being overly conceptual and simplified, although they have been partially supported by Rodger (1979),while the arguments relating to innovations have received empirical support from Gordon (1981). Whitehand (1975) argued that a general process of urban expansion was applicable which was related to a pricing mechanism in the land market. Whitehand (1977) identified the role played by innovations relating to constructional activity, functional innovations, transport innovations and planning innovations. Extension and testing of these arguments has linked the elements of morphology to the causal variables of, first, landowners, builders and others, and second, site characteristics, innovations and so forth (Gordon 1981).

The evolution of urban form has thus been approached from a variety of directions and conceptual advances are notable. Future work seems likely to integrate decision-making and formative variables and to continue striving for empirical verification of conceptual statements. The explicit process–form approach adopted appears to owe much to the related methodological developments in human geography.

Pre-industrial cities

In both Old and New Worlds the pre-industrial town has received relatively little attention. For England, Patten (1978) emphasized that change and not growth was characteristic, that urban centres were demographically and economically weak and that the impact of rural areas was significant. Analyses are necessarily constrained by data limitations, but these have not proven sufficiently severe to curtail all analysis. Indeed, recent work has succeeded in evaluating some of the established assumptions about pre-industrial towns proposed by both Sjoberg (1960) and by Vance (1971).

Sjoberg (1960) argued for a basic division within towns between the élite areas and other areas. The élite typically occupied the central core which was the economic, cultural and political focal point while a distance decay factor operated with decreasing living standards related to increasing distance from the core. Vance (1971) contended that the guild system was more crucial to urban differentiation than was the feudal system. Accordingly, towns were differentiated according to occupation rather than social class. These widely divergent assumptions about town structure were tested by Langton (1975) using seventeenth-century hearth-tax data and found not only to be oversimplified, which was to be expected, but also to be inappropriate. For Newcastle, a mercantile zone was evident as were other occupational districts emphasized by class factors. Comparable conclusions, largely rejecting both sets of concepts, were derived from an analysis of Gloucester in the mid-fifteenth century (Langton 1977b). Although these empirical conclusions are necessarily limited in application they do demonstrate the inadequacy of existing conceptual frameworks.

The economy of pre-industrial English towns was dominated by individuals rather than by firms (Patten 1978: 150) and was largely unspecialized. Patten (1977) asserted that it was necessary to consider the economic behaviour of individuals to arrive at legitimate conclusions, but that the true nature of urban occupations was liable to remain elusive.

For the United States Warner (1968) argued that privatism, an attitude focusing on individuals and their search for wealth, was the dominant factor determining the character of the pre-industrial colonial town. The privatism of speculators, for example, influenced town growth. According to Bridenbaugh (1938), colonial United States centres exerted an influence far beyond that suggested by their size, unlike their British equivalents. These and other generalizations remain largely unproven, but there is little doubt that there were major differences between the Old and New Worlds in this respect. New World towns were much less constrained by either class or occupational constraints and were growing in response to overseas movement and not merely rural to urban migration. For North Carolina, Merrens (1964: 142) acknowledged that there were few towns and that they were small, but that they were of considerable significance for the local economy.

Nineteenth-century towns

Rapid population growth and relocation characterized the nineteenth-century or Victorian town, both in Britain and Europe and overseas. This growth and relocation had important consequences for both the cultural and economic landscapes and for residential differentiation. In North America a recurring emphasis in urban cultural analyses has been that of ethnic identity resulting from the large-scale immigration of a variety of groups. Urban destinations were discussed by Ward (1971) while Conzen (1976) emphasized the German origins of Milwaukee and illustrated their role in the evolution of the town. Both prior to and succeeding the Civil War, ethnic differentiation in Charleston was determined by the White élite and not by conventional market forces (Radford 1976). Somewhat similarly, the evolution of nineteenth-century Jerusalem was intimately bound up with the distribution of Muslims, Christians and Jews (Ben-Arieh 1975, 1976).

The economic landscape of the nineteenth-century town was characterized by expansion and emergence. Industrial districts evolved in Baltimore between 1833 and 1860 in relation to centrifugal and localizing tendencies among large firms (Muller and Groves, 1979). Retailing districts evolved in some English towns in response to population and transport variables (Wild and Shaw 1971, 1976). Commercial areas increased in size and in complexity with Tucson, for example, being dominated by one function, saloons, in 1883, but being highly diversified by 1914 (Gibson 1975). Edwards (1981) proposed an outward movement of the Sydney business frontier which involved both changes of building use and constructional change. Although these and other analyses have not as yet identified a body of concepts adequate to serve as a framework for such diversified studies it seems probable that continuing research will move in that direction.

Residential differentiation in both pre-industrial and industrial towns has proved a major theme with analyses of slum development, ethnic segregation and migrant location preferences. For the pre-industrial town the characteristic form was one of an élite located in the core area and lower-class populations beyond. One interesting contradiction was Pittsburgh which had upper-class dwellers on the outskirts of the town in addition to others occupying the core (Swauger 1978). This reversal of preferences involved those élite members who did not travel to work on a regular basis and hence were relatively unaffected by the poor transport system of 1815. In this sense the basic groundwork for the characteristic residential differentiation of the industrial town was well established prior to industrialization. Curson (1974) has shown that a small colonial pre-industrial town, Auckland in the 1840s, exhibited a high degree of residential differentiation comparable to that of modern towns with the working classes largely in the central area.

The emergence of slums and of distinct ethnic areas was a feature of the nineteenth-century city which experienced growth and in movement. The presence of substantial alley populations in Washington was noted by Groves (1974: 275) involving at least 15 per cent of the Black population at the end of the century. The emergence of slums as a feature of residential differentiation occurred simultaneously in several areas and prompted Ward (1976) to relate this apparent emergence to social attitudes concerning property rather than to clearly defined spatial change. Black residential areas in late-nineteenth-century eastern American towns emerged as small enclaves coalesced in a discriminatory environment (Groves and Muller 1975).Temporal details of such emergence appear to be related to town location and size, with the larger towns and southern towns exhibiting earliest concentrations. A high degree of residential differentiation was evident in Liverpool where, in 1871, both Irish and Welsh immigrants were segregated in response to both socio-economic factors and aspects of cultural similarity (Pooley 1977). The situation appeared quite different in Sydney where ethnic ghettos did not develop despite a variety of minority groups being evident (Wolforth 1974). Rather there was an ethnic preference for certain employment which led to some spatial differentiation.

The picture of the nineteenth-century town is not clear. During this period of rapid technological advance and substantial town growth residential differentiation was itself subject to change within a given town and also varied between towns. Ward (1975b: 151) questioned the simple characterization of an emerging slum core and affluent suburbs and emphasized the need to consider social stratification and the causes of intra-urban mobility. A specific suggestion by Gordon and Robb (1981) concerned the scale of analysis with a recommendation that small-scale issues received greater attention. Certainly, the increasing sophistication of historical geography, both statistical and conceptual, promises continuing advances in this area.

CHAPTER TEN

Population and social analyses

Population history is concerned with births, deaths, marriages and the structure of populations. The family is the basic unit of such demographic activity and is also a basic unit of social activity. Socialization takes place largely in a family context and demographic and social issues are closely related. Further, there are close links between populations and economic change. These relationships, between population, society and economy, are the central concern of this chapter. Recent trends have promoted the population variable from dependent to independent status with fertility, mortality and other demographic characteristics now regarded as causes of social and economic development and not mere consequences. The four subdivisions of this chapter are demographic analyses, social change, social analyses and population and society on the frontier.

DEMOGRAPHIC ANALYSES

The contribution of historical geographers to questions of population has been somewhat limited, except for analyses of movement (Lawton 1978). Indeed, the study of population history has only recently achieved a status comparable to, say, economic history, but current trends are suggestive of increasing recognition. A principal drawback to historical population research has always been a lack of data comparable to that available for modern societies and development of the discipline has been dependent on the emergence of new procedures. Contemporary historical demography utilizes two principal techniques, aggregative analysis and family reconstitution, in order to overcome data limitations. Aggregative analysis can provide summaries of fertility and mortality change at a variety of scales. Family reconstitution permits statements regarding the likelihood of individual demographic events, but is restricted to a local scale. Both procedures are discussed and assessed by Wrigley (1981). In addition to this impetus from within population history there have also been new techniques devised by economists and mathematicians (Eversley 1977). These concerns have emphasized behavioural and statistical model-building.

A major stimulus was provided by Wrigley (1966) with the development of a hypothesis of voluntary fertility control in the early eighteenth century. Such controls can be seen as a response to changing economic conditions and involved marriage decisions, age of marrying and intervals between births. The more traditional alternative view argued that family limitation was mainly related to lack of food. The hypothesis of controlled fertility has important implications for the demographic revolution as it suggests that increases in fertility may have played a major role. A substantial testing of the hypothesis by Crafts and Ireland (1976) simulated family reproduction behaviour using the data provided by Wrigley (1966) for the village of Colyton. Results suggested that the fertility control hypothesis accounted for some 60 per cent of the fertility changes. This leaves the intriguing question as to what variables influence desired fertility. A similar suggestion regarding reduced fertility was made by McInnis (1976) with reference to late-nineteenth-century rural Ontario. Reduced birth-rates were presumed to be caused by an excess population which was also causing emigration.

According to Wrigley (1981: 216) the relationship between demographic and economic trends worked in both directions. The influence of social and economic variables on family size was minimal for one southern Ontario county in 1871 (Denton and George 1973), but the more general influences of the economy are well established. Marriage is accorded a key role and can be related to both price and wage trends in pre-industrial England. This same issue was considered by Easterlin (1976) in the context of American frontier farm settlement and several relationships noted. First, a low land cost encourages in-movement and high fertility which, in turn, cause an increase in costs. Second, the increased costs prompt reduced in-movement and reduced fertility. These trends were noted in a variety of states until all relevant variables stabilized. The basic conclusion to be noted is that large families prevail in good economic circumstances and vice versa. Large families in nineteenth-century Britain meant an increasingly large labour force at a time of rising demand for labour.

Undoubtedly, the most substantive and most important contribution to population history is the volume by Wrigley and Schofield (1981) which succeeds in reconstructing English population history at a national scale from 1541 to 1871. Such a reconstruction was justified on the grounds that 'long-term changes in the balance between a people and the means of sustenance and economic activity available to them had profound effects both upon individual welfare and upon the course of institutional and attitudinal change' (Wrigley and Schofield 1981: 1). Using the considerable data on baptisms, marriages and deaths provided by 404 parish registers, aggregative results were presented followed by a modelling of the population history. In accomplishing the latter task Wrigley and Schofield (1981: 457) acknowledged the conflict between 'clarity and comprehensiveness'. To achieve some clarity four models were evolved and discussed for the late sixteenth, the seventeenth, the early nineteenth and the late nineteenth centuries. Each of the four summarized relationships between population and economic variables.

Historical geographers, in addition to movement and redistribution analyses have contributed to population history with studies of mortality decline in nineteenth-century Birmingham (Woods 1978), of disease and related mortality in early Virginia (Earle 1979) and of urban rural demographic contrasts (Bromley 1979). Such varied studies have little in common in terms of procedures and techniques. However, further analyses focusing on population, social and economic relationships seem probable in the light of trends elsewhere.

SOCIAL CHANGE–METHODOLOGICAL DEVELOPMENTS

Until the 1970s the links between social history and historical geography were quite limited. Social historians concentrated attention on the analysis of social institutions, such as family and church, and described social structure. Historical geographers preferred a regional approach integrating social and economic landscapes. Kulikoff (1973) advocated closer ties, with social historians benefiting from geographic emphases on scale of analysis and economic exchange while historical geographers could benefit from the use of a biographical approach and employment of more rigorous chronological frameworks. Similar pleas from Cook (1980) referred to the geographic advances in a variety of areas including behavioural developments. Current trends in historical geography confirm that the links with social history have improved. The biographical approach, for example, is incorporated within time geography and was innovatively applied to the development of a factory mode of production as it related to family and individual behaviour (Pred 1981). Perhaps the greatest stimulus to historical geographic work, however, has emanated from an increasing awareness and application of conceptual advances in social history, including those of marxism and structuralism.

Historical geographers have relied heavily on the works of marxist writers such as Thompson (1968), Foster (1974) and Jones (1976) in attempts at achieving greater sophistication. This trend in social history can be summarized by reference to a study of the skilled working classes in the southern Ontario town of Hamilton between 1860 and 1914 (Palmer 1979). The study had three aims: first, to outline industrial capitalist development and the role of the skilled worker; second, to investigate the culture of the skilled worker; and third, to analyse the evolution of class conflict. Impressionistic data, such as newspapers, were interpreted within a tradition of empirical marxism. The significance of such work has been clearly stated by Baker (1979a: 565–7) and was seen to include the dynamics of historical change, of social group conflict and of social justice. The interest in marxian analysis is perhaps the principal contribution of social history to historical geography. Within the historical geography literature an analysis of housing tenure and social classes in late-nineteenth-century Kingston, Ontario, is indicative of these trends (Harris *et al*. 1981). Between 1881 and 1901, home-ownership dropped from 37 per cent to 32 per cent and the related increase in tenancy affected landlord–tenant interaction with an increase in the number of absentee landlords. New tenants felt a loss of security, but a polarization between capital and labour did not arise because private tenancy and class were not closely related.

A final development in historical geography which can be related to social history concerns the question of community. This is noted by Gregory (1978b: 304) with reference to labour processes. An innovative discussion by Sutter (1973) focused on historical communities in North America and probed the issue of people in relation to their surroundings, especially that of quality of life. A detailed discusssion of the data and analytic problems involved in the historical reconstruction of communities included many suggestions for future work such as size and structure of household, kinship ties and marriage patterns (MacFarlane 1977). An increasingly sophisticated and varied historical geography is likely to continue borrowing and utilizing such concepts from social history. The following section on analyses of social change does not pursue these methodological developments, focusing instead on a variety of empirical examples.

SOCIAL ANALYSES

Many social analyses relate population, economy and social characteristics, and most are explicitly concerned with issues of data collection and validity. Popular themes include those of occupation, household structure, kinship and marriage although such a list is by no means exhaustive.

For an area of varied occupations in northern England Hall (1974) sampled the census enumerators' books of 1861 and demonstrated that age was an insignificant variable and that males predominated in most occupations. Ninety per cent of farmers were household heads and other traditional occupations had a similar high figure. Textiles, however, was relatively new to the area and was mainly pursued by other than household heads. Lead-mining proved to be a traditional family occupation with many families having two or more miners. Occupation and township size were related as evidenced by Table 10.1. Farmers' households were larger than those of non-farmers in all areas sampled. The concern with household size and composition, especially as they change through time, was outlined by Williams (1977). Again, a central theme related to the effects of economic change. Major economic changes affecting the family included the town growth and increased mobility of the industrial revolution, while changes in birth- and death-rates have affected the household in terms of numbers of young and old people. For the late eighteenth century Williams (1977: 4–8) noted an average family size of 4.78 for pre-industrial British communities with the typical household being restricted to the nuclear family. The lack of co-resident kin can be explained by reference to the low life expectancy, the availability of housing and the social norm that married couples establish their own household. An analysis of Auckland, New Zealand, in 1842 showed 337 households with a mean size of 5.48 (Curson 1974: 114). The higher socio-

Table 10.1   Household size by township group, 1861, in a part of Derbyshire

Township group	Mean household size	Standard deviation	Mean household size with at least one farmer	Mean household size with at least one agricultural labourer	Mean size of non-agricultural households
Eyam	4.20	2.48	5.16	4.18	4.02
Tideswell	5.04	3.11	5.12	3.48	4.74
Longstone	4.75	2.50	4.87	6.48	4.63
Edensor	5.05	2.50	6.73	4.95	4.63
Baslow	4.81	2.22	4.93	4.59	4.83
Hathersage	5.15	2.47	6.57	4.84	4.76
Hope	4.76	2.34	6.00	4.18	3.52
Bradwell	4.85	2.36	6.00	4.34	4.57
Youlgreave	4.74	2.34	6.36	4.00	4.55
Brassington	4.29	2.36	6.05	4.10	3.91
Bakewell	4.81	2.50	5.67	5.65	4.60
Tissington	5.21	2.63	6.89	4.24	4.54
Edale	4.48	2.32	5.11	4.34	4.13
Wormhill	5.00	2.23	5.94	4.33	5.17
Hartington	4.83	2.19	5.37	4.15	4.74

(After Hall 1974: 76)

economic status households had larger households because of the presence of domestic servants. Using several data sources and family reconstitution methods, Mills (1978) analysed one English village in 1841 and showed that, on marriage, people made a residential location decision which was influenced by proximity to kin.

Generalizations about industrial periods are difficult as there was increased spatial variation. Industrial towns were characterized by a young family structure and a separation of residence and workplace (Williams 1977: 8–9). Mean household size remained essentially unchanged as did nuclear family size, although the number of households with co-resident kin increased as did the number with lodgers.

Analyses of social interaction have emphasized both migration and marriage. Investigations of marriage-distance relationships have confirmed a distance decay bias with friction decreasing through time (Perry 1969). The isolation of communities as determined by marriage distances and the relative immobility of peasant groups was confirmed for an area of rural France through until 1945 (Ogden 1980). For the urban centre of Huddersfield Dennis (1977) showed that marriage declined with both physical and social distance.

Data problems have been especially evident in much of this work. Concerning the methods by which nineteenth-century populations can be stratified into social classes Royle (1977) outlined a method of data classification which succeeded in avoiding twentieth-century assumptions. Parish registers were used by Rice (1978b) to measure late-nineteenth-century social change in Sweden and proved a valuable data source. In addition to an increasing variety of data sources, historical geographers might benefit from an increasing diversity of themes to include such topics as the effects of inheritance and individual life histories.

POPULATION AND SOCIETY ON THE FRONTIER

Demographic and social analyses of frontier environments are limited. Regional historical geographies have paid little attention to these themes, relative to economic considerations, and much of the available work has been accomplished by local and social historians. Necessarily, then, this section is largely exploratory in character.

One crucial difficulty for any demographic analysis concerns data availability. By definition a frontier is typically outside of any areas of organized data collection, particularly for such detailed data as births, deaths, marriages and migration. Lefferts (1977: 38) distinguished between two aspects of the demography of the frontier: interaction with an external population in the form of in- and out-movement, and internal developments. On the basis of empirical research on twentieth-century Asian frontiers Lefferts (1977) proposed a number of empirical regularities (Fig. 10.1). Curve A describes three developments with parallel trends: first, the overall growth rate is initially high but decreases and stabilizes at a low rate; second, the sex ratio is initially biased towards males but changes to one of equality; and third, migration is initially a major growth factor but decreases to a nominal level. Curve B describes population growth and eventually assumes an S-shape form. The two curves labelled C describe the broadening of the age structure with the lower line referring to the changing sex ratio and fertility rise and the upper line referring to a longer life-span and indigenous expansion of older people. Curve D is descriptive of marital fertility and suggests a heightened fertility for the post-pioneer phase of settlers, some of whom were born on the frontier.

These regularities have varying degrees of confirmation. An analysis of eighty-eight agricultural frontier counties in the United States between 1840 and 1860 concluded that the frontier characteristics were evident for perhaps only twenty years and an average sex ratio of 125 was calculated (Eblen 1965). Imbalanced sex ratios were reported by Thompson (1974) for a variety of seventeenth-century regions. The initial high growth rate succeeded by zero growth was noted for the northern United States, as was a decline of in-movement and reduction in fertility (Easterlin 1976). As noted earlier in this chapter the fertility changes can be related to economic opportunity. Closely related to these ideas are the assertions of Boserup (1965) concerning the effects of population growth on economy being those of development rather than declining living standards.

For the very different frontier area of eighteenth-century South Africa Ross (1975) described the character and mechanics of European population growth.

171

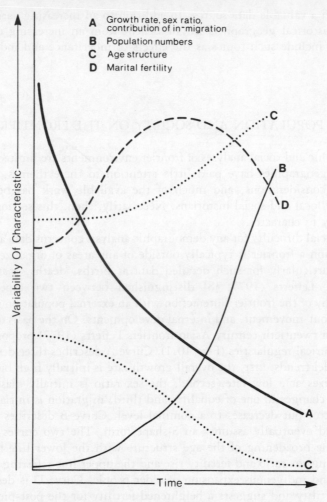

A Growth rate, sex ratio, contribution of in-migration
B Population numbers
C Age structure
D Marital fertility

Fig. 10.1 Some regularities of frontier demography. (After Lefferts 1977: 46): from *The Frontier: Comparative Studies*, by David Harry Miller and Jerome O. Steffen. © 1977 by the University of Oklahoma Press.

Growth was rapid with the annual rate averaging 2.6 per cent as a result of both in-movement and natural increase (Fig. 10.2). Immigration was primarily male, sex ratios varied between 144 and 180 and hence natural increase was the principal contributor to growth (Ross 1975: 223). Women married young and the mean number of children was 5.8. The South African case appears atypical in terms of the long time-span, but otherwise exhibits several characteristic frontier features.

The social geography of the frontier has recently begun to receive attention by historical geographers but remains a largely neglected topic. The role of institutions, social and otherwise, in the frontier settlement process was noted in Chapter 6 and institutions have also played a role in the social life of settlers.

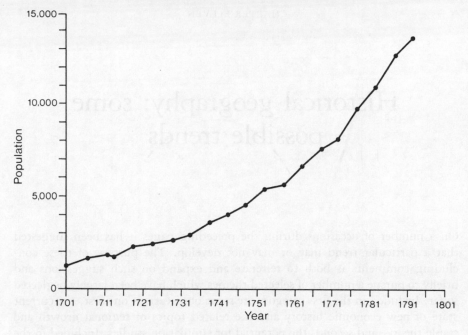

Fig. 10.2   White population in South Africa. (After Ross 1975: 222)

The significance of the Orange Order for Ontario settlement and life involved a political role and a social and community role but did not involve the organization of colonization schemes (Houston and Smyth 1978). A more general discussion of Ontario related the distinctiveness of the society largely to a desire for self-improvement (Wynn 1979). By the mid-nineteenth century Ontario was also proving to be less attractive than the United States and the relatively conservative settlers remained while the more adventurous moved. Similar comments can be directed at many of the regions of North America which experienced a passing frontier.

For the frontiers of Lower Canada and of South Africa, both of which received below-average immigration and both of which experienced relatively slow economic growth, Harris and Guelke (1977) have proposed an explanation of social change which relies on the availability of cheap land and the limited commercial links. The emerging frontier society was both egalitarian and homogeneous and largely comprised moderately well-off peasants without the extremes of either riches or poverty (Harris and Guelke 1977: 151). The argument was extended by Harris (1977) to include the example of New England. This suggestion of the emergence of homogeneous rural societies as a response to economic conditions merits consideration and rigorous analysis elsewhere.

CHAPTER ELEVEN

Historical geography: some possible trends

On a number of occasions during the preceding pages it has been suggested that a particular trend may or may not develop. The purpose of these concluding comments is both to reiterate and expand on such suggestions and briefly to pursue a number of selected themes which have been largely neglected so far. Included in the first category are some observations on, first, the current state of new economic history and the related topics of regional growth and staple theory, and second, the potential for simulation studies. Included in the second category are a discussion of intellectual history and of attitudes and behaviour.

CONTRIBUTIONS FROM NEW ECONOMIC HISTORY

The future of the new economic history appears rather uncertain with two recent commentators arriving at somewhat different conclusions (Supple 1981; Temin 1981). Temin (1981: 179) advocated a change in analytical focus to the topic of the second industrial revolution and to a methodology which emphasized diverse modes of behaviour. Supple (1981: 199) preferred to envisage closer ties with social and cultural history which were seen as achieving a new popularity as a result of including the most recent radical approaches. The future success of new economic history as a discipline directed at theory construction and explicit statistical modelling and testing is open to discussion, despite the explanations of American economic change achieved by Williamson (1974).

Perhaps the most widely used set of concepts intended to explain economic change in areas settled by Europeans are those usually labelled the staple export theory. The growth of a new area is explained in terms of available natural resources which are in demand by a developed region. Both capital and labour are moved to the new area and production of the staple export begins. Demand changes can lead to expansion of the new area or, possibly, to a settlement collapse if demand drops before a more diverse economy emerges. Staple export concepts are not a complete explanation. Political and religious motives for colonization are omitted (Galenson and Menard 1980: 5), the thesis is not of universal applicability and there is a need to broaden research to include both growth and character of the export (Pomfret 1981). Nevertheless, these concepts are appropriate for initial economic development in areas settled by Europeans. It might be argued that the slow growth, in terms of both people and economy, of South Africa after 1652 was related to the lack of a staple where areas of relatively rapid growth relied heavily on a staple. Pomfret (1981: 135) noted that the time-lag between discovery and subsequent European settlement for both Australia and Canada was explicable in terms of the timing of the perception of a land-based staple. The nature of the staple is important in terms of the related creation of an economic infrastructure. Fur in Canada did not encourage permanent settlement, whereas wheat prompted urban growth because of the need for processing and transportation facilities. The export of wool from Australia was the first staple and the rapid growth of that area compared to the Canadian fur country can be directly attributed to the differing requirements of the two staples. Any change in staple, or addition to existing staples, is also important for growth. Canada, for example, incorporated two staples in the early nineteenth century, with the addition of timber which required population increase and settlement. In Australia gold emerged as a staple in the 1850s and large population increases resulted. Pomfret (1981: 142) argued that the applicability of the concept declines after c. 1850 with the development of more mature and diversified economies in both countries. Consideration of initial staples might also be employed to explain differences in labour practices, with some regions producing labour-intensive staples and other regions having staples with minimal short-lived labour requirements (Earle 1978). Somewhat surprisingly, there are only limited links between the approaches of new economic history and the staple thesis. Staple thesis analyses have not employed counterfactuals or quantification, possibly as a consequence of the relatively loose framework provided by the thesis.

Historical geographers might be encouraged and stimulated by a recent focus on regional, as opposed to national, economic structures in Victorian Britain (Lee 1981). This analysis centred on population and employment in an attempt to measure regional change and utilized both factor analysis and shift and share techniques. Results indicated three major types of growth region, textile regions, mining and metal-working regions and a metropolitan region based on London. A fourth type was the slow-growing rural and peripheral region. Both the textile and mining activities can be interpreted as staple pursuits, but it is the metropolitan region which Lee (1981: 449) recognized as the major growth region with a diversity of activities.

A final area of concern in economic history which has close ties with historical geographic interests concerns the role of government and political decisions. Dick (1976: 38) raised the question of the indispensability of government participation to the settlement and economic growth of the Canadian west. The Canadian Pacific Railway was heavily subsidized, but there is minimal evidence that railway availability was a prerequisite of expansion. Somewhat differently,

Owram (1980) considered the growth of the west in terms of the emergence of an Expansionist movement which developed in the east and which regarded the western frontier as a key to national prosperity. It seems appropriate to anticipate a continuing concern with questions of institutional impact and a growing appreciation of contributions from related disciplines.

SIMULATION

The technique of simulation and the related topic of the counterfactual have been discussed in some detail both methodologically and empirically. The intention here is briefly to reiterate the value of the technique and to note the advances being made in archaeology. Simulation is widely used in natural, social and behavioural sciences and typically, but not necessarily, involves a stochastic approach to the evolution of forms. In historical geography the procedure has been used in a variety of ways to analyse a variety of topics. A process – form analysis of southern Ontario settlement (Norton 1976), a model of social and economic organization for Sweden during the early Iron Age (Widgren 1979) and a township-scale analysis of population distribution (J. D. Wood 1974) have each turned to simulation as an appropriate and rewarding technique. Despite these advances the technique has not achieved the degree of success evident elsewhere. In archaeology, simulation was first discussed in 1970 (Doran 1970) and has experienced considerable growth since that time with two recent edited volumes (Hodder 1978b; Sabloff 1981). Aldenderfer (1981: 47) recognized the real benefits to be derived from attempts at simulation-model construction in a discipline such as archaeology which is characterized by inadequate concepts and laws. It is tempting to categorize historical geography in much the same way.

Four basic stages for a typical simulation exercise can be recognized (Hammond, 1978: 4). First, hypotheses are conceptualized on the basis of available knowledge. Second, a process model is formulated by means of synthesizing the hypotheses and incorporating additional necessary constraints. Third, the process model is used to generate as many varied outcomes as are required. Finally, the validity of the formulated process is assessed and the results are interpreted. Such a sequence of activities can contribute in two major directions. Empirical knowledge of the particular topic may be increased and theoretical appreciation is likely to be advanced. In disciplines, such as archaeology and historical geography, which lack explicit theories, this second contribution can be crucial. Because simulation is able rigorously to test hypotheses theoretical knowledge is gained.

Examples of simulation studies in archaeology are increasing and increasingly varied. Examples include those of prehistoric location behaviour (Zimmerman 1978) and dynamic systems change (Day 1981), both of which bear close resemblance to concerns in historical geography. A consideration of recent archaeological research might prompt historical geographers to reconsider the merits of a simulation approach for appropriate research topics.

INTELLECTUAL HISTORY

It is generally recognized that the interdisciplinary area of intellectual history has been in decline since approximately 1960 in relation to a decline in traditional philosophy (Bouwsma 1981). In particular decline is the attempt by historians to convey the intellectual spirit of an age, a decline which Colton (1981) linked to the current unpopularity of élitist studies. Despite these conditions there appears to be potential for an intellectual history approach to historical geographic problems. The most probable stimulus concerns the idea of progress.

'No single idea has been more important than, perhaps as important as, the idea of progress in Western civilisation for nearly three thousand years' (Nisbet 1980: 4). This idea of progress argues that humans have advanced, are advancing and will continue to advance. Although this notion is also somewhat out of favour today it may serve as a useful framework for past studies. Indeed, the importance of progress to frontier communities was referred to by Williams (1974: 124) and by Kelly (1974: 64) in studies of South Australia and southern Ontario respectively. The most explicit discussion to date was that of Harris *et al.* (1975). For one southern Ontario township it was argued that mid-nineteenth-century settlers regarded their age as one of progress, saw their success as dependent on hard work and perceived a future in the new environment. Support for the notion of progress was provided by the rapidly evolving and developing landscape and thus: 'Progress became external to society and was associated with the physical environment' (Harris *et al.* 1975: 14). Elsewhere in the New World less conservative pioneers might have conceived progress in both societal and physical environmental terms.

The notion of progress is not easy. The argument that it was central to the settlement experiences of immigrants requires detailed analysis in a variety of settings before the more general merits of this approach can be confirmed.

ATTITUDES AND BEHAVIOUR

Contemporary trends towards an idealistic historical geography have relied heavily on such historians as Collingwood, but might also turn to Dilthey for inspiration. Rose (1981) outlined the work of Dilthey and noted close links between historical geographic syntheses and idealistic approaches on the one hand, and Dilthey's emphasis on the significance of ideas, values and beliefs for past events on the other. Development of a humanistic historical geography

177

might also rely on this philosophy of historical understanding. The acknowledgement of Dilthey's contribution in these areas is another indication of the increasing conceptual sophistication of historical geography.

An emerging humanistic emphasis was confirmed by Baker (1981) in a discussion of the viability of time geography. Emphasis was placed on studies of the groups which mediate between individuals and societies, on both time constraints and time choices and on a new kind of historical regional geography. For Baker (1981: 441) the way ahead appeared to involve studies of periods and places rather than notions of time and space.

Interestingly, many of the conceptual suggestions included in idealist, humanist, marxian and progress studies share a common problem – that of determining past attitudes. A strictly positivist approach avoids this difficulty by electing not to analyse attitudes, focusing instead on their outcomes, namely behaviour. A. Wilson (1981) proposed a method of inferring attitudes from behaviour which involved the use of popular behaviour as an indicator of popular attitudes. The method requires that any inference made should be empirically testable, which in turn implies that the attitudinal statement predict behaviour and that it is the behaviour which is tested.

During the discussion of simulation approaches the contribution of archaeology was emphasized. Archaeologists have also been explicitly concerned with humans and environment and with the developing and testing of frameworks for evolutionary analyses. In a study of Nigeria from earliest human times to the present Connah (1981) used an ecological and ethnographic framework which emphasized environmental stresses and environmental opportunities. Connah (1981: 254) suggested that the long-standing practices of the people could be employed to explain the behaviour that created the available, in this case archaeological, evidence. Rather similarly, Dulov (1980) described human and environment interaction in Russia from the fourteenth to the seventeenth century.

Analyses of individual behaviour in the past lend themselves to discussions of attitudes. Birch (1981) studied a collection of 280 letters written by two brothers describing their nineteenth-century frontier movements in the United States. Reasons for a series of moves were clarified and prior experience shown to be as important as perceptions of new areas. Again, McIntosh (1981) showed that particular emotions and preconceptions influenced the behaviour of one American settler. Using a somewhat fictionalized biography and relevant land records it was argued that movement was a result of social factors and of the need to locate in a place which was satisfying to the individual.

THE WAY AHEAD?

Throughout, this volume has focused on issues of cultural and economic landscape evolution and both the spatial and temporal aspects of such issues have been identified. Traditional historical geographic notions of horizontal or vertical themes have largely been ignored in favour of an explicit process – form approach. Warkentin (1978: 211) argued that: 'There is a danger that geographers will ignore essential spatial relationships if they persist in looking at change through time alone. A constant placing of geographical phenomena into a dynamic spatial context is necessary because the interactions give a worldwide territorial perspective to geography.' The discussions in this volume have attempted to satisfy the requirement of both a spatial and a temporal component. Further, in an attempt to package the material discussed in a coherent and meaningful manner one methodology has been especially advocated. The favoured methodology focuses on spatial form evolution and might incorporate process formulations, simulation and counterfactuals. Such an approach has been noted wherever possible. It is clear that this emphasis is not being advocated as a panacea for historical geography, if such were required. Rather, it is one viable approach which has been largely undeveloped and has been particularly ignored in the current debates on methodologies. A further component of such an emphasis is theory construction. Most historical geography is short on theory and, accordingly, this volume is also short on theory. Again, however, this volume has attempted to accord with an observation by Warkentin (1978: 211): 'Theory in geography should not be dragged in, nor should it be eschewed; rather, it should be sought for and used where it can advance understanding.' It is argued here that there are many opportunities for increased understanding as a consequence of additional theoretical content, but it is not argued that all historical geography needs to be theoretical. Hopefully, a balanced view has been presented which recognizes a need for further generalization, conceptualization, model-building and theory construction, but which does not insist on such developments for all problems. The value of theory is especially evident in works on agriculture by Conzen (1971), on settlement by Muller (1977) and on industry by Langton (1979). Such works not only adopt a theoretical standpoint but also demonstrate by example the value of theory in advancing knowledge. Historical geographers might also be stimulated by the theoretical content of such work in new economic history and by the contributions of Martin *et al.* (1978) and A. G. Wilson (1981) on space–time modelling and catastrophe theory respectively. While it is unlikely that such abstract and mathematical work will ever be at the forefront of historical geography it is material which needs to be recognized as a contribution to historical geography.

This concluding chapter has discussed a few selected themes which appear likely to be relevant approaches for future historical geographic research. As has been the case in the past, the trends identified are of divergent character, being both social scientific and humanistic. Historical geography seems liable to progress on a number of different fronts as suggested and, no doubt, also along lines which this volume has not identified.

Bibliography

Aalen, F. H. A. (1973) 'Vernacular architecture of the British Isles', *Yearbook*, Association of Pacific Coast Geographers, Vol. 35, 27–48.

Abler, R., Adams, J. S. and Gould, P. R. (1971) *Spatial Organization*. Prentice-Hall: Englewood Cliffs, NJ.

Adams, I. H. (1976) 'The changing face of Scotland and the role of emigration, 1760–90', in B. S. Osborne (ed.), *The Settlement of Canada: Origins and Transfer*. Queen's University: Kingston, 2–11.

Adelman, H. (1974) 'Rational explanation reconsidered: case studies and the Hempel–Dray Model', *History and Theory*, 13, 208–24.

Adrian, C. (1977) 'The nineteenth century gazette corn returns from East Anglian markets', *Journal of Historical Geography*, 3, 217–36.

Aldenderfer, M. S. (1981) 'Computer simulation for archaeology: an introductory essay', in J. A. Sabloff (ed.), *Simulation in Archaeology*. Albuquerque: University of New Mexico Press, 11–49.

Allardt, E. (1974) 'A Comment on Hollingsworth', *Historical Methods Newsletter*, 7, 245–8.

Allen, J. L. (1972) 'An analysis of the exploratory process: the Lewis and Clark expedition of 1804–06', *Geographical Review*, 62, 13–39.

Allen, J. L. (1975) 'Thomas Jefferson and the passage to India: A pre-exploratory image', in R. E. Ehrenberg (ed.), *Pattern and Process: Research in Historical Geography*. Howard University Press: Washington, 103–13.

Allison, K. J. (1970) *Deserted Villages*. Macmillan: London.

Alwin, J. A. (1974) 'Post Office locations and the historical geographer: a Montana example', *Professional Geographer*, 26, 183–6.

Amedeo, D. and Golledge, R. G. (1975) *An Introduction to Scientific Reasoning in Geography*. Wiley: New York.

Amson, J. C. (1974) 'Equilibrium and catastrophic models of urban growth', in E.L. Cripps (ed.), *Space Time Concepts in Urban and Regional Models*. Pion: London, 108–28.

Anderle, O. F. (1964) 'A plea for theoretical history', *History and Theory*, 4, 27–56.

Andrews, J. (1966) 'The emergence of the wheat belt in southeastern Australia to 1930', in J. Andrews (ed.), *Frontiers and Man*. F. W. Cheshire: Melbourne, 5–65.

Annenkov, V. V. (1979) 'Spatial organization: Its historical changes and trends of historico-geographical research', abstract circulated at the Symposium on Research Methods in Historical Geography, International Geographical Union's Working Group on Historical Changes in Spatial Organization, Cambridge, 1979.

Appleby, A. B. (1979) 'Grain prices and subsistence crises in England and France, 1590–1740', *Journal of Economic History*, 39, 865–87.

Arnold, C. J. (1977) 'Early Anglo-Saxon settlement patterns in southern England', *Journal of Historical Geography*, 3, 309–15.

Arthur, C. J. (1968), 'On the historical understanding', *History and Theory*, 7, 203–16.

Ashworth, G. J. and Bradbeer, J. B. (1977) 'Predicting the past: a study of the railway network of the Isle of Wight', *South Hampshire Geographer*, 9, 12–18.

Association of American Geographers (1977) 'Applied historical geography directory', *Newsletter*, 12 (9), 4.

Aydelotte, W. O. (1971) *Quantification in History*. Addison Wesley: Reading, Mass.

Aydelotte, W. O., Bogue, A. G. and Fogel, R. W. (eds) (1972) *The Dimensions of Quantitative Research in History*. Princeton University Press: Princeton.

Bailey, D. T. and Haulman, B. E. (1977), 'Ethnic differences on the southwestern United States frontier', in D. H. Miller and J. O. Steffen (eds), *The Frontier*. University of Oklahoma Press: Norman. 243–58.

Baker, A. R. H. (1966) 'Field systems in the vale of Holmesdale', *Agricultural History Review*, 14, 386–92.

Baker, A. R. H. (1972a) *Progress in Historical Geography*. David and Charles: Newton Abbott.

Baker, A. R. H. (1972b) 'Rethinking historical geography', in A. R. H. Baker (ed.), *Progress in Historical Geography*. David and Charles: Newton Abbott, 11–28.

Baker, A. R. H. (1972c) 'Historical geography in Britain', in A. R. H. Baker (ed.), *Progress in Historical Geography*. David and Charles: Newton Abbott, 90–110.

Baker, A. R. H. (1974), 'In pursuit of Wilbur Zelinksy and other hysterical geographers', *Historical Geography Newsletter*, 4, 17–19.

Baker, A. R. H. (1976) 'The limits of inference in historical geography', in B. S. Osborne (ed.), *The Settlement of Canada: Origins and Transfer*. Queen's University: Kingston, 169–183.

Baker, A. R. H. (1977) 'Historical geography', *Progress in Human Geography*, 1, 465–74.

Baker, A. R. H. (1978), 'Historical geography: understanding and experiencing the past', *Progress in Human Geography*, 2, 495–504.

Baker, A. R. H. (1979a) 'Historical geography: a new beginning', *Progress in Human Geography*, 3, 560–570.

Baker, A. R. H. (1979b), 'Settlement pattern evolution and catastrophe theory: a comment', *Transactions of the Institute of British Geographers*, 4, 435–7.

Baker, A. R. H. (1980) 'On the historical geography of France', *Journal of Historical Geography*, 6, 69–76.

Baker, A. R. H. (1981) 'An historico-geographical perspective on time and space and on period and place', *Progress in Human Geography*, 5, 439–43.

Baker, A. R. H. and Butlin, R. A. (eds) (1973) *Studies of Field Systems in the British Isles*. Cambridge University Press: London.

Baker, A. R. H. *et al.* (1970), 'Introduction', in A. R. H. Baker *et al.* (eds), *Geographical Interpretation of Historical Sources*, David and Charles: Newton Abbott, 13–25.

Baltensperger, B. H. (1980), 'Agricultural change among Nebraska immigrants, 1880–1920', in F. C. Luebke (ed.), *Ethnicity on the Great Plains*. University of Nebraska Press: Lincoln, 170–89.

Barraclough, G. (1979) *Main Trends in History*. Holmes and Meier Publications: New York.

Bartholomew, D. J. (1967) *Stochastic Models for Social Processes*. Wiley: New York.

Bartlett, M. S. (1962) *An Introduction to Stochastic Processes With Special Reference to Methods and Applications*. Cambridge University Press: Cambridge.

Bartlett, R. A. (1974) *The New Country: A Social History of the American Frontier*. Oxford University Press: New York.

Baskerville, P. (1979) 'On the rails: trends in Canadian railway historiography', *American Review of Canadian Studies*, 9, 63–72.

Bauer, F. H. (1963) 'Significant factors in the White settlement of northern Australia', *Australian Geographical Studies*, 1, 39–48.

Beavington, F. (1975), 'The development of market gardening in Bedfordshire, 1799–1939', *Agricultural History Review*, 23, 23–47.

Beer, S. H. (1963) 'Causal explanation and imaginative reenactment', *History and Theory*, 3, 6–29.

Ben-Arieh, Y. (1975) 'The growth of Jerusalem in the nineteenth century', *Annals of the Association of American Geographers*, 65, 252–69.

Ben-Arieh, Y. (1976) 'Patterns of Christian activity and dispersion in nineteenth-century Jerusalem', *Journal of Historical Geography*, 2, 46–69.

Benedict, E. T. (ed.) (1935) *Theodor Brinkmann's Economics of the Farm Business*. University of California Press: Berkeley.

Bennett, R. J. (1975) 'The representation and identification of spatio-temporal systems: an example of population diffusion in North West England', *Transactions of the Institute of British Geographers*, 66, 73–94.

Bennett, R. J. (1979), 'Space–Time models and urban geographical research', in D. T. Herbert and R. J. Johnston (eds), *Geography and the Urban Environment: Research and Applications*, Vol. II. Wiley: New York, 27–58.

Bennett, R. J. and Haining, R. P. (1976) *Space Time Models: An Introduction to Concepts*. University College, Department of Geography: London, Occasional Papers, No. 28.

Berkhofer, R. F., jun. (1969) *A Behavioral Approach to Historical Analysis*. Free

Press: New York, 1969.

Berry, B. J. L. (1973), 'A paradigm for modern geography', in R. J. Chorley (ed.), *Directions in Geography*. Methuen: London, 3–21.

Billinge, M. (1976) 'The other neighbours', *Historical Geography Newsletter*, 6 (2), 16–18.

Billinge, M. (1977) 'In search of negativism: phenomenology and historical geography', *Journal of Historical Geography*, 3, 55–68.

Billington, R. A. (1966), *America's Frontier Heritage*. Holt, Rinehart and Winston: New York.

Birch, B. P. (1967), 'The measurement of dispersed patterns of settlement', *Tijdschrifte voor Economische en Sociale Geografie*, 58, 68–75.

Birch, B. P. (1981) 'An English approach to the American frontier', *Journal of Historical Geography*, 7, 397–406.

Bird, J. (1980) 'Seaports as a subset of gateways for regions: a research survey', *Progress in Human Geography*, 4, 360–70.

Black, W. R. (1971) 'An iterative model for generating transportation networks', *Geographical Analysis*, 3, 283–8.

Blackman, J. (1975) 'The cattle trade and agrarian change on the eve of the railway age', *Agricultural History Review*, 23, 48–62.

Blainey, G. (1966) *The Tyranny of Distance*. Macmillan: London.

Bland, W. R. (1975) 'The changing location of metal fabrication and clothing industries in southern Ontario: 1881–1932', *Ontario Geography*, 9, 34–57.

Blaut, J. M. (1961) 'Space and process', *Professional Geographer*, 13, 1–7.

Blaut, J. M. (1970), 'Geographic models of imperialism', *Antipode*, 2, 65–83.

Bogue, A. G., Clubb, J. C. and Flanigan, W. H. (1977) 'The new political history', *American Behavioral Scientist*, 21, 201–20.

Bohland, J. R. (1972), 'Behavioral aspects of rural settlement', in W. P. Adams and F. M. Helleiner (eds), *International Geography*, Vol. 2. IGU: Montreal, 704–6.

Boots, B. N. and Getis, A. (1977) 'Probability model approach to map pattern analysis', *Progress in Human Geography*, 1, 264–86.

Borchert, J. R. (1967) 'American metropolitan evolution', *Geographical Review*, 57, 301–32.

Boserup, E. A. (1965) *The Conditions of Agricultural Growth*. George Allen and Unwin: London.

Bouwsma, W. J. (1981) 'Intellectual history in the 1980s: from history of ideas to history of meaning', *Journal of Interdisciplinary History*, 12, 279–91.

Bowden, L. W. (1965), *Diffusion of the Decision to Irrigate*. Department of Geography, University of Chicago: Chicago, Research Paper No. 97.

Bowden, M. J. (1969) 'The perception of the western interior of the United States, 1800–70: a problem in historical geosophy', *Proceedings of the Association of American Geographers*, 1, 16–21.

Bowen, E. G. (1969) 'Introductory background: prehistoric South Britain', in H. C. Darby (ed.), *An Historical Geography of England Before A.D. 1800*. Cambridge University Press: Cambridge, 1–29.

Bowen, M. (1976) 'Mormon land selection in the Greybull Valley, Wyoming:

rationale and implications', *Ecumene*, 8, 40–9.

Bowen, W. A. (1978) *The Willamette Valley: Migration and Settlement on the Oregon Frontier*. University of Washington Press: Seattle.

Bowman, I. (1931) *The Pioneer Fringe*. American Geographical Society: New York.

Brandon, P. F. (1969) 'Medieval clearances in the East Sussex Weald', *Transactions of the Institute of British Geographers*, 48, 135–153.

Braudel, F. (1972) *The Mediterranean and the Mediterranean World of Philip II*. Harper and Row: New York.

Breen, D. H. (1973) 'The Canadian prairie west and the "harmonious" settlement interpretation', *Agricultural History*, 47, 63–75.

Bridenbaugh, C. (1938) *Cities in the Wilderness*. Knopf: New York.

Broek, J. O. M. (1932) *The Santa Clara Valley, California: A Study in Landscape Change*. Oosthoek: Utrecht.

Broek, J. O. M. (1965) *Compass of Geography*. Merrill: Columbus.

Broeze, F. J. A. (1975) 'The cost of distance: shipping and the early Australian economy, 1788–1850', *Economic History Review*, 28, 582–97.

Bromley, R. D. F. (1979) 'Urban–rural demographic contrasts in highland Ecuador: town recession in a period of catastrophe, 1778–1841', *Journal of Historical Geography*, 5, 281–95.

Brook, A. (1976) 'Industry, history and location theory', *Journal of Historical Geography*, 2, 165–8.

Brookfield, H. C. (1972) *Colonial Development and Interdependence*. Cambridge University Press: Cambridge.

Brown, L. A. (1966) *Diffusion Processes and Location*. Regional Science Research Institute: Philadelphia, Bibliography Series, No. 4.

Brown, L. A. and Moore, E. G. (1969) 'Diffusion research: a perspective', in C. Board *et al.* (eds), *Progress in Geography*, Vol. 1. Edward Arnold: London, 120–57.

Brown, R. H. (1943), *Mirror for Americans*. American Geographical Society: New York.

Bunce, M. F. (1972) 'The agricultural depression in South Yorkshire and North Nottinghamshire, 1875–1900: climatic hazard and price competition', *Canadian Geographer*, 16, 323–37.

Burghardt, A. (1969) 'The origin and development of the road network of the Niagara Peninsula, Ontario, 1770–1851', *Annals of the Association of American Geographers*, 59, 417–440.

Butlin, R. A. (1978) 'The late Middle Ages, *c.* 1350–1500', in R. A. Dodgshon and R. A. Butlin (eds), *An Historical Geography of England and Wales*. Academic Press: London, 119–150.

Bylund, E. (1960) 'Theoretical considerations regarding the distribution of settlement in inner North Sweden', *Geografiska Annaler*, 42B, 225–31.

Bylund, E. (1972) 'Generation waves and spread of settlement', in W. P. Adams and F. M. Helleiner (eds), *International Geography*, Vol. 2. IGU: Montreal, 1306–9.

Cameron, J. M. R. (1972) 'Scottish emigration to Upper Canada, 1815–55:

a study of process', in W. P. Adams and F. M. Helleiner (eds), *International Geography*, Vol. 1. International Geographical Union: Montreal, 404–6.

Cameron, J. M. R. (1974) 'Information distortion in colonial promotion: the case of Swan River Colony', *Australian Geographical Studies*, 12, 57–76.

Camm, J. C. R. (1967) 'The Queensland Agricultural Purchase Act, 1894, and rural settlement: a case study of Jimbour', *Australian Geographer*, 10, 263–74.

Camm, J. C. R. (1974) 'Farm making costs in southern Queensland, 1890–1915', *Australian Geographical Studies*, 12, 173–89.

Camm, J. C. R. (1976) 'Commercial wheat growing in Queensland, 1870–1915', *Australian Geographer*, 13, 173–81.

Cant, R. G. (1968) 'The agricultural frontier in miniature: a microstudy on the Canterbury Plains, 1850–75', *New Zealand Geographer*, 24, 155–67.

Cant, R. G. (1969) 'The dilemma of historical geography', in W. B. Johnston (ed.), *Human Geography: Concepts and Case Studies*. University of Canterbury Press: Christchurch, 40–60.

Careless, J. M. S. (1954) 'Frontierism, metropolitanism, and Canadian history', *Canadian Historical Review*, 35, 1–21.

Carlson, A. W. (1967) 'Rural settlement patterns in the San Luis Valley: a comparative study', *The Colorado Magazine*, 44, 111–28.

Carlstein, T. (1978) 'Innovation, time allocation and time–space packing', in T. Carlstein, D. Parkes and N. Thrift (eds), *Timing Space and Spacing Time*, Vol. 1. Edward Arnold: London, 146–61.

Carlstein, T. *et al* (eds) (1978), *Timing Space and Spacing Time*. 3 vols. Edward Arnold: London.

Carney, G. O. (1974) 'Country music and the radio: a historical geographic assessment', *Rocky Mountain Social Science Journal*, 11, 19–32.

Carr, E. H. (1961) *What is History?* Penguin: Harmondsworth.

Carter, F. W. (1969) 'An analysis of the medieval Serbian oecumene: a theoretical approach', *Geografiska Annaler*, 51B, 39–56.

Carter, F. W. (ed.) (1977) *An Historical Geography of the Balkans*. Academic Press: London.

Carter, H. (1978) 'Towns and urban systems, 1730–1900', in R. A. Dodgshon and R. A. Butlin (eds), *An Historical Geography of England and Wales*. Academic Press: London, 367–400.

Chapman, J. (1976) 'Parliamentary enclosure in the uplands: the case of the North York Moors', *Agricultural History Review*, 24, 1–17.

Chappell, J. E. (1976) 'Comment in reply', *Annals of the Association of American Geographers*, 66, 169–73.

Childe, V. G. (1951) *Man Makes Himself*. Mentor: New York.

Christopher, A. J. (1970) 'The closer-settlement movement in Natal, 1875–1910', *Journal for Geography*, 3, 569–578.

Christopher, A. J. (1971) 'Land policy in Southern Africa during the nineteenth century', *Zambezia*, 2, 1–9.

Christopher, A. J. (1973) 'Environmental perception in Southern Africa', *South African Geographical Journal*, 55, 14–22.

Christopher, A. J. (1976) *Southern Africa*. Dawson: Folkestone.

Christopher, A. J. (1981) 'Southern Africa and the United States: a comparison of pastoral frontiers', *Journal of the West*, 20, 52–9.

Christopher, A. J. (1982) 'Partition and population in Southern Africa', *Geographical Review*, 72, 127–38.

Clark, A. H. (1954) 'Historical geography', in P. James and C. F. Jones (eds), *American Geography: Inventory and Prospect*. Syracuse University Press: Syracuse, 70–105.

Clark, A. H. (1959), *Three Centuries and the Island*. Toronto University Press: Toronto.

Clark, A. H. (1972) 'Historical geography in North America', in A. R. H. Baker (ed.), *Progress in Historical Geography*. David and Charles, Newton Abbott, 129–43.

Clark, A. H. (1975a) 'The conceptions of "empires" of the St. Lawrence and the Mississippi: an historico-geographical view with some quizzical comments on environmental determinism', *American Review of Canadian Studies*, 5, 4–27.

Clark, A. H. (1975b) 'First things first', in R. E. Ehrenberg (ed.), *Pattern and Process: Research in Historical Geography*. Howard University Press: Washington.

Clark, A. H. (1975c) 'Foreword: the Great Plains, perception by any name', in B. W. Blouet and M. P. Lawson (eds), *Images of the Plains*, University of Nebraska Press: Lincoln, ix–xiv.

Clark, E. A. G. (1977) 'Port sites and perception: the development of the southern and eastern Cape coast in the nineteenth century', *South African Geographical Journal*, 59, 150–62.

Clarke, J. (1972) 'Spatial variations in population density: southwestern Ontario in 1851', in W. P. Adams and F. M. Helleiner (eds), *International Geography*, Vol. 1. IGU: Montreal, 408–11.

Clarke, J. (1975) 'The role of political position and family and economic linkage in land speculation in the Western District of Upper Canada, 1788–1815', *Canadian Geographer*, 19, 18–34.

Cliff, A. D. (1977) 'Quantitative methods: time series methods for modelling and forecasting', *Progress in Human Geography*, 1, 503–11.

Cliff, A. D. *et al.* (1975) *Elements of Spatial Structure*. Cambridge University Press: Cambridge.

Climo, A. T. and Howells, P. G. A. (1976) 'Possible worlds in historical explanation', *History and Theory*, 15, 1–20.

Cloher, D. U. (1979) 'Urban settlement process in lands of "recent settlement": an Australian example', *Journal of Historical Geography*, 5, 297–314.

Clout, H. D. (ed.) (1977) *Themes in the Historical Geography of France*. Academic Press: London.

Clubb, J. M. and Bogue, A. G. (1977) 'History, quantification and the social sciences', *American Behavioral Scientist*, 21, 167–85.

Colenutt, R. J. (1971) 'Building models of urban growth and spatial structure', in C. Board *et al.* (eds), *Progress in Geography,* Vol. 2. Edward Arnold:

London, 109–152.

Colman, G. P. (1968) 'Innovation and diffusion in agriculture', *Agricultural History*, 42, 173–88.

Colton, J. (1981) 'Intellectual history in the 1980s: the case for the defense', *Journal of Interdisciplinary History*, 12, 293–8.

Connah, G. (1981) *Three Thousand Years in Africa*. Cambridge University Press: London.

Conrad, A. H. and Meyer, J. R. (1957) 'Economic theory, statistical inference and economic history', *Journal of Economic History*, 17, 524–44.

Conrad, A. H. and Meyer, J. R. (1958) 'The economics of slavery in the antebellum South', *Journal of Political Economy*, 66, 95–130.

Conzen, K. N. (1976) *Immigrant Milwaukee*. Harvard University Press: Cambridge, Mass.

Conzen, M. P. (1971) *Frontier Farming in an Urban Shadow*. State Historical Society of Wisconsin: Madison.

Conzen, M. P. (1974) 'Local migration systems in nineteenth century Iowa', *Geographical Review*, 64, 339–61.

Conzen, M. P. (1975) 'A transport interpretation of the growth of urban regions: an American example', *Journal of Historical Geography*, 1, 361–382.

Conzen, M. P. (1977) 'The maturing urban system in the United States, 1840–1910', *Annals of the Association of American Geographers*, 67, 88–108.

Conzen, M. P. (1980) 'Historical geography: North American progress during the 1980's', *Progress in Human Geography*, 4, 549–559.

Cook, E. M., jun. (1980) 'Geography and history: spatial approaches to early American history', *Historical Methods*, 13, 19–28.

Coones, P. (1979) 'Manufacture in pre-industrial England: a bibliography', *Journal of Historical Geography*, 5, 127–55.

Cosgrove, D. (1978) 'Place, landscape and the dialectics of cultural geography', *Canadian Geographer*, 22, 66–72.

Cox, K. R. (1972) *Man, Location and Behavior: An Introduction to Human Geography*. Wiley: New York.

Crafts, N. R. F. and Ireland, N. J. (1976) 'Family limitation and the English demographic revolution: a simulation approach', *Journal of Economic History*, 36, 598–623.

Cromar, P. (1977) 'The coal industry on Tyneside, 1771–1800: oligopoly and spatial change', *Economic Geography*, 53, 79–94.

Cromar, P. (1979) 'Spatial change and economic organization: the Tyneside coal industry, 1751–1770', *Geoforum*, 10, 45–57.

Crone, G. R. (ed.) (1962) *The Explorers: An Anthology of Discovery*. Cassell: London.

Crosby, A. W. (1978) 'Ecological imperialism: the overseas migration of Europeans as a biological phenomenon', *Texas Quarterly*, 21, 10–22.

Crowley, W. K. (1978) 'Old order Amish settlement: diffusion and growth', *Annals of the Association of American Geographers*, 68, 249–64.

Crush, J. S. (1980) 'On theorizing frontier underdevelopment', *Tijdschrifte voor Economische en Sociale Geografie*, 71, 343–50.

Cumberland, K. B. (1949) 'Aotearoa Maori: New Zealand about 1780', *Geographical Review*, 39, 401–24.

Curry, L. (1964) 'The random spatial economy: an exploration in settlement theory', *Annals of the Association of American Geographers*, 54, 138–46.

Curry, L. (1966) 'Chance and landscape', in J. W. House (ed.), *Northern Geographical Essays in Honour of G. H. J. Daysh*. Oriel Press: Newcastle, 40–55.

Curry, L. (1967) 'Central places in the random spatial economy', *Journal of Regional Science*, 7, 217–38.

Curry, L. (1977) 'Stochastic spatial distributions in equilibrium settlement theory', in R. C. Eidt *et al.* (eds), *Man, Culture and Settlement*. Kalyani: New Delhi, 228–37.

Curson, P. H. (1974) 'Auckland in 1842', *New Zealand Geographer*, 30, 107–28.

Dahlke, J. (1975) 'Evolution of the wheat belt in Western Australia: thoughts on the nature of pioneering along the dry margin', *Australian Geographer*, 13, 3–14.

Daly, M. T. (1972) *Techniques and Concepts in Geography*. Nelson: Melbourne.

Danks, P. (1977) 'Some observations on medieval and postmedieval artefact distributions: a spatial model at the regional scale (macro)', in D. L. Clarke (ed.), *Spatial Archaeology*. Academic Press: New York, 353–81.

Darby, H. C. (1948), 'The regional geography of Thomas Hardy's Wessex', *Geographical Review*, 38, 426–43.

Darby, H. C. (1951), 'The changing English landscape', *Geographical Journal*, 117, 377–98.

Darby, H. C. (1952), *The Domesday Geography of Eastern England*. Cambridge University Press: Cambridge.

Darby, H. C. (1953) 'On the relationships of geography and history', *Transactions of the Institute of British Geographers*, 19, 1–11.

Darby, H. C. (1962) 'Historical geography', in H. P. R. Finberg (ed.), *Approaches to History: A Symposium*. Routledge and Kegan Paul: London, 127–56.

Darby, H. C. (1973) *The New Historical Geography of England*. Cambridge University Press: Cambridge.

Darby, H. C. (1977) *Domesday England*. Cambridge University Press: Cambridge.

Daunton, M. J. (1978) 'The building cycle and the urban fringe in Victorian cities: a comment', *Journal of Historical Geography*, 4, 175–81.

Davidson, W. V. (1974) *Historical Geography of the Bay Islands, Honduras: Anglo-Hispanic Conflict in the Western Caribbean*. Southern University Press: Birmingham, Ala.

Davis, F. J. (1974) 'The role of the railroad in the settling of Nebraska 1860–1900', in R. G. Ironside *et al.* (eds), *Frontier Settlement*. University of Alberta: Edmonton, Studies in Geography, Vol. 1, 164–77.

Davis, L. E. (1970) '"And it will never be literature" – the new economic history: a critique', in R. P. Swierenga (ed.), *Quantification in American History*. Atheneum: New York, 274–82.

Dawson, A. H. (1975) 'Are geographers indulging in a landscape lottery', *Area*, 7, 42–5.

Day, M. and Tivers, J. (1979) 'Catastrophe theory and geography: a Marxist critique', *Area*, 11, 54–8.

Day, R. H. (1981) 'Dynamic systems and epochal change', in J. A. Sabloff (ed.), *Simulations in Archaeology*. University of New Mexico Press: Albuquerque, 189–227.

Day, R. H. and Tinney, E. H. (1969) 'A dynamic von Thünen model', *Geographical Analysis*, 1, 137–51.

Dennis, R. J. (1977) 'Distance and social interaction in a Victorian city', *Journal of Historical Geography*, 3, 237–50.

Denton, F. T. and George, P. J. (1973) 'The influence of socio-economic variables on family size in Wentworth County, Ontario, 1871: a statistical analysis of historical micro data', *Canadian Revue of Sociology and Anthropology*, 10, 334–44.

Deveneaux, G. C. (1978) 'The frontier in recent African history', *The International Journal of African Historical Studies*, 11, 63–85.

Dick, L. and Greenwood, D. (1979) 'A quantitative analysis of settlement in the Abernethy and Neudorf districts, 1880–1920', paper presented at the Northern Great Plains History Conference, Winnipeg.

Dick, T. J. O. (1976) 'Frontiers in Canadian economic history', *Journal of Economic History*, 36, 34–9.

Dicken, S. and Dicken, E. (1979) *The Making of Oregon: A Study in Historical Geography*. Oregon Historical Society: Portland.

Dicks, T. R. B. (1972) 'Network Analysis and historical geography', *Area*, 4, 4–9.

Dickson, K. B. (1969) *A Historical Geography of Ghana*. Cambridge University Press: London.

Dickson, K. B. (1972) 'Historical geography reconsidered', in W. P. Adams and F. M. Helleiner (eds), *International Geography*, Vol. 1, IGU: Montreal, 412–15.

Dodge, R. E. (1938) 'The interpretation of sequent occupance', *Annals of the Association of American Geographers*, 28, 233–7.

Dodgshon, R. A. and Butlin, R. A. (eds) (1978) *An Historical Geography of England and Wales*. Academic Press: London.

Dollar, C. M. and Jensen, R. J. (1971) *Historians' Guide to Statistics: Quantitative Analysis and Historical Research*. Holt, Rinehart and Winston: New York.

Donagan, A. (1964) 'Historical explanation: the Popper–Hempel theory reconsidered', *History and Theory*, 4, 3–26.

Doran, J. (1970) 'Systems theory, computer simulations and archaeology', *World Archaeology*, 1, 289–98.

Dray, W. H. (1964) *Philosophy of History*. Prentice-Hall: Englewood Cliffs, NJ.

Dray, W. H. (1971) 'On the nature and role of narrative in historiography', *History and Theory*, 10, 153–71.

Dulov, A. V. (1980) 'Man and nature in Russia from the 14th to the 17th centuries', *Soviet Geography: Review and Translation*, 21, 604–19.

Duncan, J. S. (1980) 'The superorganic in American cultural geography', *Annals of the Association of American Geographers*, 70, 181–98.

● Dunlevy, J. A. (1980) 'Nineteenth century European immigration to the United States: intended versus lifetime settlement patterns', *Economic Development and Cultural Change*, 29, 77–90.

Dunlevy, J. A. and Gemery, H. A. (1976) 'Some additional evidence on settlement patterns of Scandinavian migrants to the United States: dynamics and the role of family and friends', *Scandinavian Economic History Review*, 24, 143–52.

Dutton, J. M. and Starbuck, W. H. (eds) (1971) *Computer Simulation of Human Behavior*. Wiley: New York.

Dyos, H. J. (ed.) (1968) *The Study of Urban History*. Edward Arnold: London.

Earle, C. V. (1977) 'The first English towns of North America', *Geographical Review*, 67, 34–50.

Earle, C. V. (1978) 'A staple interpretation of slavery and free labor', *Geographical Review*, 68, 51–65.

Earle, C. V. (1979) 'Environment, disease and mortality in early Virginia', *Journal of Historical Geography*, 5, 365–90.

Easterlin, R. A. (1976) 'Population change and farm settlement in the northern United States', *Journal of Economic History*, 36, 45–75.

Eblen, J. E. (1965) 'An analysis of nineteenth-century frontier populations', *Demography*, 2, 399–413.

Eccles, W. J. (1969) *The Canadian Frontier*. Holt, Rinehart and Winston: New York.

Eckstein, A. *et al*. (1974) 'The economic development of Manchuria: the rise of a frontier economy', *Journal of Economic History*, 34, 239–64.

● Edwards, K. J. and Jones, P. (1976) 'The methodology of historical geography', *Journal of Interdisciplinary History*, 8, 187–9.

Edwards, N. (1981) 'The Sydney business frontier, 1865–1892: a building stock approach', *Australian Geographical Studies*, 19, 78–98.

Eichenbaum, J. and Gale, S. (1971) 'Form, function and process: a methodological inquiry', *Economic Geography*, 47, 525–44.

Eidt, R. C. (1975) 'Towards a unified methodology in abandoned settlement analysis: contributions from geography and archaeology', *National Geographical Journal of India*, 21, 135–50.

Eidt, R. C. and Woods, W. I. (1974) *Abandoned Settlement Analysis: Theory and Practice*. Field Text Associates: Sherwood, Wis.

Eigenheer, R. A. (1973–74) 'The frontier hypothesis and related spatial concepts', *California Geographer*, 14, 55–89.

Ekström, A. and Williamson, M. (1971) 'Transportation and Urbanization', in A. G. Wilson (ed.), *Urban and Regional Planning*. Pion: London, 37–46.

Elazar, D. (1970) *Cities of the Prairie: The Metropolitan Frontier and American Politics*. Basic Books: New York.

Emery, F. (1976) 'The mechanics of innovation: clover cultivation in Wales before 1750', *Journal of Historical Geography*, 2, 35–48.

Enequist, G. (1960) 'Summary of discussions: advance and retreat of rural settlement', *Geografiska Annaler*, 42, 345–6.

Ennals, P. M. (1972) 'Nineteenth-century barns in southern Ontario', *Canadian Geographer*, 16, 256–70.

Ernst, J. A. and Merrens, H. R. (1978) 'Praxis and theory in the writing of American historical geography', *Journal of Historical Geography*, 4, 277–90.

Everitt, A. (1977) 'River and wold: reflections on the historical geography of regions and pays', *Journal of Historical Geography*, 3, 1–20.

Eversley, D. E. C. (1977) 'Review of: *Population Patterns in the Past*, R. D. Lee (ed.)', *Demography*, 14, 539–48.

Ewald, V. (1977) 'The von Thünen principle and agricultural zonation in colonial Mexico', *Journal of Historical Geography*, 3, 123–34.

Fain, H. (1970) 'History as science', *Histroy and Theory*, 9, 154–73.

Fair, T. J. D. and Browett, J. G. (1979) 'The urbanization process in South Africa', in D. T. Herbert and R. J. Johnston (eds), *Geography and the Urban Environment*, Vol. II. Wiley: Toronto, 259–94.

Fielding, G. J. (1974) *Geography as Social Science*. Harper and Row: New York.

Fishlow, A. (1965) *American Railroads and the Transformation of the Ante-Bellum Economy*. Harvard University Press: Cambridge, Mass.

Fishlow, A. and Fogel, R. W. (1971) 'Quantitative economic history: an interim evaluation. Past trends and present tendencies', *Journal of Economic History*, 31, 15–42.

Florin, J. (1977) 'The advance of frontier settlement in Pennsylvania, 1638–1850: a geographic interpretation', paper in Geography No. 14, Department of Geography, Pennsylvania State University, University Park, Pennsylvania.

Floud, R. (ed.) (1973) *An Introduction to Quantitative Methods for Historians*. Princeton University Press: Princeton.

Floud, R. (1974) *Essays in Quantitative Economic History*. Clarendon Press: Oxford.

Fogarty, J. P. (1981) 'The comparative method and the nineteenth-century regions of recent settlement', *Historical Studies*, 19, 412–29.

Fogel, R. W. (1964), *Railroads and American Economic Growth. Essays in Econometric History*. Johns Hopkins Press: Baltimore.

Fogel, R. W. (1966) 'The new economic history: its findings and methods', *Economic History Review*, 19, 642–56.

Fogel, R. W. and Engerman, S. L. (1974) *Time on the Cross: Evidence and Methods. A Supplement*. Little, Brown: Boston.

Forrester, M. (1976) 'Practical reasoning and historical enquiry', *History and Theory*, 15, 133–40.

Forsythe, J. L. (1977), 'Environmental considerations in the settlement of Ellis County, Kansas', *Agricultural History*, 51, 38–50.

Foster, R. J. (1974) *Class Struggle and the Industrial Revolution: Early Nineteenth Century Capitalism in Three Towns*. Methuen: London.

Francaviglia, R. V. (1978) 'Western hay derricks: cultural geography and folklore as revealed by vanishing agricultural technology', *Journal of Popular*

Culture, 11, 916–27.

Freeman, M. J. (1975) 'The stage-coach system of South Hampshire, 1775–1851', *Journal of Historical Geography*, 1, 259–81.

Freeman, M. J. (1980) 'Road transport in the English industrial revolution: an interim assessment', *Journal of Historical Geography*, 6, 17–28.

French, R. A. (1969) 'Field patterns and the three field system: the case of sixteenth century Lithuania', *Transactions of the Institute of British Geographers*, 48, 121–34.

French, R. A. (1970) 'The three field system of sixteenth century Lithuania', *Agricultural History Review*, 18, 106–25.

French, R. A. (1972) 'Historical geography in the U.S.S.R.', in A. R. H. Baker (ed.), *Progress in Historical Geography*. David and Charles: Newton Abbott, 111–28.

Fried, M. H. (1962) 'Land tenure, geography and ecology in the contact of cultures', in P. L. Wagner and M. W. Mikesell (eds), *Readings in Cultural Geography*. University of Chicago Press: Chicago, 302–17.

Friesen, R. J. (1977) 'Saskatchewan Mennonite settlements: the modification of an Old World settlement pattern', *Canadian Ethnic Studies*, 9, 72–90.

Friis, H. (1975) 'Original and published sources in research in historical geography: a comparison', in R. E. Ehrenberg (ed.), *Pattern and Process: Research in Historical Geography*. Howard University Press: Washington, 133–59.

Fullerton, B. (1975) *The Development of British Transport Networks*. Oxford University Press: London.

Gaede, H. L. (1973) 'Periodic markets: some comments', *Professional Geographer*, 25, 82–3.

Galenson, D. W. and Menard, R. R. (1980) 'Approaches to the analysis of economic growth in colonial British America', *Historical Methods*, 13, 3–18.

Gallie, W. B. (1963), 'The historical understanding', *History and Theory*, 3, 149–202.

Galloway, J. H. (1975) 'Northeast Brazil, 1700–50: the agricultural crisis re-examined', *Journal of Historical Geography*, 1, 21–38.

Garrison, W. L. (1962) 'Towards simulation models of urban growth and development', *Land Studies in Geography*, 24B, 92–108.

Gentilcore, R. L. (1972) 'Change in settlement in Ontario (Canada), 1800–50: a correlation analysis of historical source materials', in W. P. Adams and F. M. Helleiner (eds), *International Geography*, Vol. 1. IGU: Montreal, 418–19.

George, P. (1975) 'Rates of return and government subsidization of the Canadian Pacific Railway: some further remarks', *Canadian Journal of Economics*, 8, 591–600.

Gerhard, P. (1972) *A Guide to the Historical Geography of New Spain*. Cambridge University Press: Cambridge.

Gerlach, R. L. (1976) *Immigrants in the Ozarks: A Study of Ethnic Geography*. University of Missouri Press: Columbia.

Getis, A. (1974) 'Representation of spatial point pattern processes by Polya models', in M. Yeates (ed.), *Proceedings of the I.G.U. Commission on Quantitative Geography*. McGill–Queen's University Press: Montreal, 76–100.

Getis, A. (1977) 'On the use of the term "random" in spatial analysis', *Professional Geographer*, **29**, 59–61.

Gibson, L. J. (1975), 'Tucson's evolving commercial base, 1883–1914: a map analysis', *Historical Geography Newsletter*, **5** (2), 10–17.

Gilbert, E. W. (1966) *The Exploration of Western America, 1800–50. An Historical Geography*. Cooper Square Publishers: New York.

Gilbert, E. W. (1969), 'The human geography of Roman Britain', in H. C. Darby (ed.), *An Historical Geography of England Before A.D. 1800*. Cambridge University Press: Cambridge, 30–87.

Gilliam, H. (1976) 'The dialectics of realism and idealism in modern historiographic theory', *History and Theory*, **15**, 231–56.

Gilmour, J. M. (1972), *Spatial Evolution of Manufacturing: Southern Ontario, 1851–1891*. University of Toronto Press: Toronto.

Glasscock, R. E. (1975) *The Lay Subsidy of 1334*. British Academy: London.

Goheen, P. G. (1973) 'Industrialization and the growth of cities in nineteenth-century America', *American Studies*, **14**, 49–66.

Goldenberg, L. A. (1972) 'About the place of historical geography in the system of sciences', in W. P. Adams and F. M. Helleiner (eds), *International Geography*, Vol. 1. IGU: Montreal, 420–22.

Goodrich, C. (1960) 'Economic history: one field or two?', *Journal of Economic History*, **20**, 531–38.

Gordon, G. (1981) 'The historico-geographic explanation of urban morphology: a discussion of some Scottish evidence', *Scottish Geographical Magazine*, **97**, 16–26.

Gordon, G and Robb, J. (1981) 'Small-scale residential differentiation in nineteenth-century Scottish cities', *Scottish Geographical Magazine*, **97**, 77–84.

Gould, P. R. (1964) 'A note on research into the diffusion of development', *Journal of Modern African Studies*, **2**, 124.

Gould, P. R. (1969) *Spatial Diffusion*. Association of American Geographers: Washington, Commission on College Geography, Resource Paper No. 4.

Gray, M. (1962) 'Settlement in the Highlands, 1750–1950', *Scottish Studies*, **6**, 145–54.

Green, G. W. (1979) 'The agricultural colonization of temperate forest habitats', in W. W. Savage, jun. and S. I. Thompson (eds), *The Frontier*, Vol. 2. University of Oklahoma: Norman, 69–104.

Gregory, D. (1974) 'New towns for old: historical geography at the I.B.G.', *Historical Geography Newsletter*, **4** (2), 27–30.

Gregory, D. (1976) 'Rethinking historical geography', *Area*, **8**, 295–8.

Gregory, D. (1978a) 'The discourse of the past: phenomenology, structuralism and historical Geography', *Journal of Historical Geography*, **4**, 161–73.

Gregory, D. (1978b) 'The process of industrial change, 1730–1900', in R. A. Dodgshon and R. A. Butlin (eds), *An Historical Geography of England and Wales*. Academic Press: London, 291–311.

Gregory, D. (1978c) *Ideology, Science and Human Geography*. Hutchinson: London.

Grigg, D. B. (1974) *The Agricultural Systems of the World: An Evolutionary Approach*. Cambridge University Press: London.

Grigg, D. B. (1977) 'E. G. Ravenstein and the laws of migration', *Journal of Historical Geography*, 3, 41–54.

Grossman, D. (1971a) 'Do we have a theory for settlement geography?', *Professional Geographer*, 23, 197–203.

Grossman, D. (1971b) 'The process of frontier settlement: the case of Nikeland (Nigeria)', *Geografiska Annaler*, 53B, 107–28.

● Groves, P. A. (1974) 'The "hidden" population: Washington alley dwellers in the late nineteenth century', *Professional Geographer*, 3, 270–6.

● Groves, P. A. and Muller, E. K. (1975) 'The evolution of Black residential areas in late-nineteenth-century cities', *Journal of Historical Geography*, 1, 169–91.

Guelke, L. (1971) 'Problems of scientific explanation in geography', *Canadian Geographer*, 15, 38–53.

Guelke, L. (1974) 'An idealist alternative in human geography', *Annals of the Association of American Geographers*, 64, 193–202.

Guelke, L. (1975) 'On rethinking historical geography', *Area*, 7, 135–8.

Guelke, L. (1976a) 'Commentary: the philosophy of idealism', *Annals of the Association of American Geographers*, 66, 168–9.

Guelke, L. (1976b) 'Frontier settlement in early Dutch South Africa', *Annals of the Association of American Geographers*, 66, 25–42.

Guelke, L. (1977) 'Regional geography', *Professional Geographer*, 29, 1–7.

Guelke, L. (1978) 'Geography and logical positivism', in D. T. Herbert and R. J. Johnston (eds), *Geography and the Urban Environment*, Vol. 1. Wiley: New York, 35–61.

Guelke, L. (1979) 'European expansion and the meaning of frontier settlement', paper presented to CUKANZUS, An International Conference for Historical Geographers, Los Angeles.

Hagerstrand, T. (1967) *Innovation Diffusion as a Spatial Process*, trans. A. Pred. University of Chicago Press: Chicago.

Haggett, P. (1965) *Locational Analysis in Human Geography*. Edward Arnold: London.

Halevy, E. (1971) *The Birth of Methodism in England*, trans. and ed. B. Semmell. University of Chicago Press: Chicago.

Hall, P. G. (ed.) (1966) *Von Thünen's Isolated State*. Pergamon: Oxford.

Hall, R. (1974) 'Occupations and population structure in part of the Derbyshire Peak District in the mid-nineteenth century', *East Midland Geographer*, 6, 66–78.

Hammond, F. W. (1978) 'The contribution of simulation to the study of archaeological processes', in I. Hodder (ed.), *Simulation Studies in Archaeology*. Cambridge University Press: London, 1–9.

Hamshere, J. D. and Blakemore, M. J. (1976) 'Computerizing Domesday Book', *Area*, 8, 289–94.

Handcock, W. G. (1976) 'Spatial patterns in a trans-Atlantic migration field: the British Isles and Newfoundland during the eighteenth and nineteenth centuries', in B. S. Osborne (ed.), *The Settlement of Canada: Origins and Transfer*. Queen's University: Kingston, 13–40.

Handcock, W. G. (1977) 'English migration to Newfoundland', in J. J. Mannion (ed.), *The Peopling of Newfoundland: Essays in Historical Geography*. Memorial University of Newfoundland: St John's, Institute of Social and Economic Research, 15–48.

Hanley, W. S. (1974) 'Invercargill in the 1870s: the application of an historical model', *New Zealand Geographer*, 30, 66–74.

Hanna, J. F. (1971) 'Information theoretic techniques for evaluating simulation models', in J. M. Dutton and W. H. Starbuck (eds), *Computer Simulation of Human Behavior*. Wiley: New York, 682–92.

Harbaugh, J. W. and Bonham-Carter, G. (1970) *Computer Simulation in Geology*. Wiley: New York.

Harley, J. B. (1964) 'The settlement geography of early medieval Warwickshire', *Transactions of the Institute of British Geographers*, 34, 115–130.

Harley, J. B. (1973) 'Change in historical geography: a qualitative impression of quantitative methods', *Area*, 5, 69–74.

Harley, J. B. (1982) 'Historical geography and its evidence: reflections on modelling sources', in A. R. H. Baker and M. Billinge (eds), *Period and Place: Research Methods in Historical Geography*. Cambridge University Press: Cambridge, 261–73.

Harris, R. *et al.* (1981) 'Housing tenure and social classes in Kingston, Ontario, 1881–1901', *Journal of Historical Geography*, 7, 271–89.

Harris, R. C. (1967) 'Historical geography in Canada', *Canadian Geographer*, 11, 235–50.

Harris, R. C. (1971) 'Theory and synthesis in historical geography', *Canadian Geographer*, 19, 157–72.

Harris, R. C. (1977) 'The simplification of Europe overseas', *Annals of the Association of American Geographers*, 67, 469–483.

Harris, R. C. (1978) 'The historical mind and the practice of Geography', in D. Ley and M. S. Samuels (eds), *Humanistic Geography*. Maaroufa Press: Chicago, 123–37.

Harris, R. C. and L. Guelke (1977) 'Land and society in early Canada and South Africa', *Journal of Historical Geography*, 3, 135–53.

Harris, R. C. and J. Warkentin (1974) *Canada Before Confederation: A Study in Historical Geography*. Oxford Universtiy Press: New York.

Harris, R. C. *et al.* (1975) 'The settlement of Mono township', *Canadian Gerapheer*, 19, 1–17.

Hart, J. F. (1974) 'The westward movement of the frontier. 1820–60', *Geoscience and Man*, 5, 73–81.

Hartshorne, R. (1939) 'The nature of geography: a critical survey of current thought in the light of the past', *Annals of the Association of American Geographers*, 29.

Hartshorne, R. (1959) *Perspective on the Nature of Geography*. Rand McNally:

Chicago.

Harvey, D. W. (1966) 'Theoretical concepts and the analysis of agricultural land-use patterns in geography', *Annals of the Association of American Geographers*, 56, 361–74.

Harvey, D. W. (1967) 'Models of the evolution of spatial patterns in human geography', in R. J. Chorley and P. Haggett (eds), *Models in Geography*. Methuen: London, 549–608.

Harvey, D. W. (1968) 'Pattern, process and the scale problem in geographical research', *Transactions of the Institute of British Geographers*, 45, 71–78.

Harvey, D. W. (1969) *Explanation in Geography*. Edward Arnold: London.

Harvey, D. W. (1970) 'Supplementary note to locational change in the Kentish hop industry and the analysis of land use patterns', in A. R. H. Baker, J. D. Hamshere and J. Langton (eds), *Geographical Interpretations of Historical Sources*. David and Charles: Newton Abbott, 264–5.

Harvey, D. W. (1973) *Social Justice and the City*. Edward Arnold: London.

Harvey, M. (1980) 'Regular field and tenurial arrangements in Holderness, Yorkshire', *Journal of Historical Geography*, 6, 3–16.

Hawke, G. R. (1970) *Railways and Economic Growth in England and Wales, 1840–1970*. Clarendon: Oxford.

Hay, A. M. (1979) 'Positivism in geography: response to critics', in D. T. Herbert and R. J. Johnston (eds), *Geography and the Urban Environment*, Vol. 2. Wiley: New York, 1–26.

Hayward, R. and Osborne, B. S. (1973) 'The "British colonist" and the immigration to Toronto of 1847: a content analysis approach to newspaper research in historical geography', *Canadian Geographer*, 17, 391–402.

Head, C. G. (1976) *Eighteenth Century Newfoundland*. McClelland and Stewart: Toronto.

Heathcote, R. L. (1963) 'Bread or cake? A geographer and a historian on the nineteenth century wheat frontier: a review', *Economic Geography*, 39, 176–82.

Heathcote, R. L. (1965) *Back of Bourke: A Study of Land Appraisal and Settlement in Semi-Arid Australia*. Melbourne University Press: Melbourne.

Heathcote, R. L. (1972) 'The evolution of Australian pastoral land tenures: an example of challenge and response in resource development', in W. P. Adams and F. M. Helleiner (eds), *International Geography*, Vol. 1. IGU: Montreal, 1311–13.

Hellen, J. A. (1972) 'Agricultural innovation and detectable landscape margins: the case of wheelhouses in Northumberland', *Agricultural History Review*, 20, 140–54.

Helmfrid, S. (1972) 'Historical geography in Scandinavia', in A. R. H. Baker (ed.), *Progress in Historical Geography*. David and Charles: Newton Abbott, 63–89.

Hempel, C. G. (1942) 'The function of general laws in history', *Journal of Philosophy*, 39, 35–48.

Henderson, J. R. (1978) 'Spatial reorganization: a geographical dimension in acculturation', *Canadian Geographer*, 12, 1–21.

Hennessy, A. (1978) *The Frontier in Latin American History*. Edward Arnold: London.

Hepple, L. W. (1967) 'Epistemology, model building and historical geography', *Geographical Articles*, 10, 42–8.

Hepple, L. W. (1974) 'The impact of stochastic process theory upon spatial analysis in human geography', in C. Board *et al.* (eds), *Progress in Geography*, Vol. 6. Edward Arnold: London, 89–142.

Higgs, R. L. (1969) 'The growth of cities in a midwestern region', *Journal of Regional Science*, 9, 369–75.

Hilling, D. (1977) 'The evolution of a port system: the case of Ghana', *Geography*, 62, 97–105.

Hindle, B. P. (1976) 'The road network of medieval England and Wales', *Journal of Historical Geography*, 2, 207–21.

Historical methods (1980) 'Editorial: historical methods for the 1980s', *Historical Methods*, 13, 1.

Hodder, I. R. (1978a) 'The human geography of Roman Britain', in R. A. Dodgshon and R. A. Butlin (eds), *An Historical Geography of England and Wales*. Academic Press: London, 29–56.

Hodder, I. R. (1978b) *Simulation Studies in Archaeology*. Cambridge University Press: London.

Hodder, I. R. and Orton, C. R. (1976) *Spatial Analysis in Archaeology*. Cambridge University Press: Cambridge.

Hodgson, R. I. (1969) 'Medieval colonization in northern Ryedale, Yorkshire', *Geographical Journal*, 135, 44–54.

Hollingsworth, J. R. (1974) 'Some problems in theory construction for historical analysis', *Historical Methods Newsletter*, 7, 225–44.

Holtgrieve, D. G. (1976) 'Land speculation and other processes in American historical geography', *Journal of Geography*, 75, 53–64.

Hornbeck, D. (1979), 'The patenting of California's private land claims, 1851–1855', *Geographical Review*, 69, 434–48.

Hoskins, W. G. (1955) *The Making of the English Landscape*. Hodder and Stoughton: London.

Houston, C. and Smyth, W. J. (1978) 'The Orange Order and the expansion of the frontier in Ontario, 1830–1900', *Journal of Historical Geography*, 4, 251–64.

Hubbard, R. (1974) 'The development of the Jamaican road network by 1846', *Journal of Tropical Geography*, 38, 31–6.

Hudson, J. C. (1969) 'A location theory for rural settlement', *Annals of the Association of American Geographers*, 59, 461–95.

Hudson, J. C. (1973) 'Two Dakota homestead frontiers', *Annals of the Association of American Geographers*, 63, 442–62.

Hudson, J. C. (1976) 'Migration to an American frontier', *Annals of the Association of American Geographers*, 66, 242–265.

Hudson, J. C. (1977) 'Theory and methodology in comparative frontier studies', in D. H. Miller and J. O. Steffen (eds), *The Frontier*. University of Oklahoma Press: Norman; 11–32.

Hudson, J. C. (1978) 'North Dakota's frontier fuels', *Bulletin of the Association of North Dakota Geographers*, **28**, 1–15.

Hufferd, J. (1980) 'Idealism and the participants' world', *Professional Geographer*, **32**, 1–5.

Hutchinson, P. (1972) 'Networks and Roman roads', *Area*, 4, 279–80.

Huttenback, R. A. (1976) *Racism and Empire: White Settlers and Coloured Immigrants in the British Self-Governing Colonies, 1830–1910*. Cornell University Press: Ithaca.

Innis, H. A. (1923) *A History of the Canadian Pacific Railroad*. University of Toronto Press: Toronto.

Ironside, R. G. *et al.* (1974) 'Frontier development and perspectives', in R. G. Ironside *et al.* (eds), *Frontier Settlement*. University of Alberta: Edmonton: Studies in Geography, Vol. 1, 1–45.

Isaac, J. (1947) *Economics of Migration*. Oxford University Press: Oxford.

Isbister, J. (1977) 'Agriculture, balanced growth, and social change in central Canada since 1850: an interpretation', *Economic Development and Cultural Change*, **25**, 673–97.

Jaatinen, S. (1960) 'Expansion and retreat of settlement in the southwestern archipelago of Finland', *Fennia*, 84, 39–65.

Jackson, D. (1966) *Custer's Gold*. Yale University Press: New Haven.

Jackson, R. H. (1978), 'Mormon perception and settlement', *Annals of the Association of American Geographers*, **68**, 317–34.

Jager, H. (1972) 'Historical geography in Germany, Austria and Switzerland', in A. R. H. Baker (ed.), *Progress in Historical Geography*. David and Charles: Newton Abbott, 45–62.

Jakle, J. A. (1971) 'Time, space and the geographic past; a prospectus for historical geography', *American Historical Review*, 76, 1084–1103.

Jakle, J. A. (1974) 'In pursuit of a wild goose: historical geography and the geographic past', *Historical Geography Newsletter*, 4, 13–16.

Jakle, J. A. (1977) *Images of the Ohio Valley: A Historical Geography of Travel*. Oxford University Press: New York.

Janelle, D. G. (1968) 'Central place development in a time–space framework', *Professional Geographer*, 20, 5–10.

Jankunis, F. J. (1977) 'Perception, innovation and adaptation: the Palliser triangle of western Canada', *Yearbook*, Association of Pacific Coast Geographers, Vol. 39, 63–76.

Jeans, D. N. (1972) *An Historical Geography of New South Wales to 1901*. Reed Education: Sydney.

Jelecek, L. (1980) 'Current trends in the development of historical geography in Czechoslovakia', in *Historical Geography*, Vol. 19. Institute of Czechoslovak and World History of the Czechoslovak Academy of Sciences: Prague, 59–102.

Joachim, M. and Hambloch, H. (1977) 'The applicability of the phosphate method in problems of historical geography: the deserted town of Blankenrode as an example', *Geographische Zeitschrift*, 65, 23–38 (English abstract).

Johnson, H. B. (1974) 'A historical perspective on form and function in upper Midwest rural settlement', *Agricultural History*, 48, 11–25.

Johnston, J. A. (1979) 'Image and reality: initial assessments of soil fertility in New Zealand, 1839–55', *Australian Geographer*, 14, 160–5.

Johnston, R. J. (1979) *Geography and Geographers*. Edward Arnold: London.

Jones, E. L. (1974) 'Review of Darby *et al.*: A new historical geography of England', *Annals of the Association of American Geographers*, 64, 460–1.

Jones, G. R. J. (1953) 'Some medieval rural settlements in North Wales', *Transactions of the Institute of British Geographers*, 19, 51–72.

Jones, G. R. J. (1978) 'Celts, Saxons and Scandinavians', in R. A. Dodgshon and R. A. Butlin (eds), *An Historical Geography of England and Wales*. Academic Press: London, 57–80.

Jones, G. S. (1976) *Outcast London: A Study in the Relationship Between Classes in Victorian Society*. Penguin: Harmondsworth.

Jones, M. (1977) *Finland: Daughter of the Sea*. Dawson: Folkestone.

Jordan, T. G. (1966) *German Seed in Texas Soil*. University of Texas Press: Austin.

Jordan, T. G. (1974) 'Antecedents of the long lot in Texas', *Annals of the Association of American Geographers*, 64, 70–86.

Jordan, T. G. (1975) 'Vegetational perception and choice of settlement site in frontier Texas', in R. E. Ehrenberg (ed.), *Pattern and Process: Research in Historical Geography*. Howard University Press: Washington, 244–57.

Jordan, T. G. (1977a) 'Early northeast Texas and the evolution of western ranching', *Annals of the Association of American Geographers*, 67, 66–87.

Jordan, T. G. (1977b) 'Land survey patterns in Texas', in R. C. Eidt *et al.* (eds), *Man, Culture and Settlement*. Kalyani: New Delhi, 141–6.

Jordan, T. G. (1980) 'A religious geography of the hill country Germans of Texas', in F. C. Luebke (ed.), *Ethnicity on the Great Plains*. University of Nebraska Press: Lincoln, 109–28.

Jordan, T. G. and Rowntree, L. C. (1979) *The Human Mosaic: A Thematic Introduction to Cultural Geography*, 2nd edn. Harper and Row: New York.

Joynt, C. B. and Rescher, N. (1961) 'The problem of uniqueness in history', *History and Theory*, 1, 150–62.

Judt, T. (1979), 'A clown in regal purple: social history and the historians', *History Workshop Journal*, 7, 66–94.

Kahk, J. and Kovalchenko, I. E. (1974) 'Methodological problems of the application of mathematical methods in historical research', *Historical Methods Newsletter*, 7, 217–24.

Kain, R. J. P. (1979) 'Compiling an atlas of agriculture in England and Wales from the tithe surveys', *Geographical Journal*, 145, 225–35.

Kansky, K. (1963) *The Structure of Transportation Networks*. Department of Geography, University of Chicago: Chicago, Research Paper No. 84.

Kay, G. (1971) 'Stage of technology and economic development: an approach to the study of human geography', *Proceedings of the Geographical Society of Rhodesia*, 4, 3–14.

199

Kay, J. (1979) 'Indian responses to a mining frontier', in W. W. Savage, jun. and S. I. Thompson (eds), *The Frontier*, Vol. 2. University of Oklahoma Press: Norman, 193–204.

Kelley, A. C., Williamson, J. G. and Cheetham, R. J. (1972) *Dualistic Economic Development: Theory and History*. University of Chicago Press: Chicago.

Kelly, K. (1970) 'The evaluation of land for wheat cultivation in early nineteenth century Ontario', *Ontario History*, 62, 57–64.

Kelly, K. (1973) 'Notes on a type of mixed farming practised in Ontario during the early nineteenth century', *Canadian Geographer*, 17, 205–219.

Kelly, K. (1974) 'The changing attitude of farmers to forest in nineteenth century Ontario', *Ontario Geographer*, 8, 64–77.

Kelly, K. (1975) 'The artificial drainage of land in nineteenth century southern Ontario', *Canadian Geographer*, 19, 279–298.

Kelly, K. (1976) 'The transfer of British ideas to nineteenth century Ontario', in B. S. Osborne (ed.), *The Settlement of Canada: Origins and Transfer*. Queen's University: Kingston, 70–93.

Kelly, K. (1978) 'The impact of nineteenth century agricultural settlement on the land', in J. D. Wood (ed.), *Perspectives on Landscape and Settlement in Nineteenth Century Ontario*. McClelland and Stewart: Toronto, 64–77.

Kemeny, J. G. (1959) *A Philosopher Looks at Science*. Prentice-Hall: Englewood Cliffs.

Kibel, B. M. (1972) *Simulation of the Urban Environment*. Association of American Geographers: Washington, Commission on College Geography, Technical Paper No. 5.

Kiefer, W. E. (1969) *Rush County, Indiana: A Study in Rural Settlement Geography*. Geographic Monograph Series, Vol. 2. Indiana University, Department of Geography: Bloomington, Indiana.

Kimble, G. H. T. (1951) 'The inadequacy of the regional concept', in L. D. Stamp and S. W. Wooldridge (eds), *London Essays in Geography*. Longman: London, 151–74.

King, L. J. (1962) 'A quantitative expression of the pattern of urban settlements in selected areas of the United States', *Tijdschrifte voor Economische en Sociale Geografie*, 53, 1–7.

King, L. J. (1969) 'The analysis of spatial form and its relation to geographic theory', *Annals of the Association of American Geographers*, 59, 573–95.

King, L. J. (1976) 'Alternatives to a positive economic geography', *Annals of the Association of American Geographers*, 66, 293–308.

Kirk, W. (1951) 'Historical geography and the concept of the behavioral environment', *Indian Geographical Journal*, 25, 152–60.

Kirk, W. (1975) 'The role of India in the diffusion of early cultures', *Geographical Journal*, 141, 19–34.

Kniffen, F. (1951a) 'The American agricultural fair', *Annals of the Association of American Geographers*, 41, 42–57.

Kniffen, F. (1951b) 'The American covered bridge', *Geographical Review*, 41, 114–23.

Kniffen, F. (1954) 'Whither cultural geography', *Annals of the Association of*

American Geographers, 44, 222–3.

Kniffen, F. (1965) 'Folk housing: key to diffusion', *Annals of the Association of American Geographers*, 55, 549–77.

Kniffen, F. (1968) *Louisiana: Its Land and People*. Louisiana State University Press: Baton Rouge.

Kolars, J. F. and Malin, H. J. (1970) 'Population and accessibility: an analysis of Turkish railroads', *Geographical Review*, 60, 229–46.

Koroscil, P. M. (1971) 'Historical geography: a resurrection', *Journal of Geography*, 70, 415–20.

Kovacik, C. F. and Rowland L. S. (1973) 'Images of colonial Port Royal, South Carolina', *Annals of the Association of American Geographers*, 63, 331–40.

Kreisel, W. (1981) 'Cultivated plants as indicators in the reconstruction of the progression of settlement in Oceania: the example of the sweet potato', *Tijdschrifte voor Economische en Sociale Geografie*, 72, 266–278.

Krog, C. (1977) 'The development of a railroad system north of Green Bay', *Geographical Perspectives*, 39, 27–34.

Kulikoff, A. (1973) 'Historical geographers and social history: a review essay', *Historical Methods Newsletter*, 6, 122–8.

Lachene, R. (1965) 'Networks and the location of economic activities', *Papers of the Regional Science Association*, 14, 187–96.

Lai, C-Y. D. (1979) 'Ethnic groups', in C. N. Forward (ed.), *Vancouver Island: Land of Contrasts*. University of Victoria: Victoria, Western Geographical Series, Vol. 17, 23–47.

Lambert, A. M. (1971) *The Making of the Dutch Landscape: An Historical Geography of the Netherlands*. Seminar Press: London.

Langton, H. H. (ed.) (1950) *A Gentlewoman in Upper Canada*. Clarke, Irwin: Toronto.

Langton, J. (1975) 'Residential patterns in pre-industrial cities: some case studies from seventeenth century Britain', *Transactions of the Institute of British Geographers*, 65, 1–27.

Langton, J. (1977a) 'Review of Amedeo and Golledge: scientific reasoning in geography', *Journal of Historical Geography*, 3, 90–91.

Langton, J. (1977b) 'Late medieval Gloucester: some data from a rental of 1455', *Transactions of the Institute of British Geographers*, 3, 259–277.

Langton, J. (1979) *Geographical Change and Industrial Revolution*. Cambridge University Press: Cambridge.

Lattimore, O. (1962) *Studies in Frontier History, Collected Papers, 1928–1958*. Oxford University Press; London.

Lawton, R. (1978) 'Population and society, 1730–1900', in R. A. Dodgshon and R. A. Butlin (eds), *An Historical Geography of England and Wales*. Academic Press: London, 313–66.

Leaman, J. H. and Conkling, E. C. (1975) 'Transport change and agricultural specialization', *Annals of the Association of American Geographers*, 65, 425–37.

Lee, C. H. (1981) 'Regional growth and structural change in Victorian Britain', *Economic History Review*, 34, 438–52.

Lefferts, H. L. Jnr. (1977) 'Frontier demography: an introduction', in D. H.

Miller and J. O. Steffen (eds), *The Frontier*. University of Oklahoma Press: Norman, 33–55.

Lehr. J. C. (1975) 'The rural settlement behavior of Ukrainian pioneers in Western Canada, 1891–1914', *British Columbia Geographical Series*, 21, 51–66.

Leighly, J. (1978) 'Town names of colonial New England in the West', *Annals of the Association of American Geographers*, 68, 233–48.

Leighly, J. (1979), 'Drifting into geography in the twenties', *Annals of the Association of American Geographers*, 69, 4–9.

Lemon, J. T. (1972) *The Best Poor Man's Country: A Geographical Study of Early South Eastern Pennsylvania*. Johns Hopkins Press: Baltimore.

Leonard, S. (1976) 'Von Thünen in British agriculture', *South Hampshire Geographer*, 8, 23–37.

Le Roy Ladurie, E. (1971) *Times of Feast, Times of Famine: A History of Climate Since the Year 1000*. Doubleday: Garden City, New York.

Le Roy Ladurie, E. (1974) *The Peasants of Languedoc*. University of Illinois Press: Urbana.

Le Roy Ladurie, E. (1979) *The Territory of the Historian*. Harvester Press: Sussex.

Levison, M., Ward, R. G. and Webb, J. W. (1973) *The Settlement of Polynesia: A Computer Simulation*. Oxford University Press: London.

Levi-Strauss, C. (1963) *Structural Anthropology*. Basic Books: New York.

Lewis, A. R. (1958) 'The closing of the medieval frontier, 1250–1350', *Speculum*, 33, 475–83.

Lewis, C. B. (1979a) 'Agricultural evolution on secondary frontiers: a Florida model', in W. W. Savage, Jun. and S. I. Thompson (eds), *The Frontier*, Vol. Two. University of Oklahoma Press: Norman, 205–234.

Lewis, C. B. (1979b), 'Cultural conservatism and pioneer Florida viticulture' *Agricultural History*, 53, 622–36.

Lewis, P. F. (1972) 'Small town in Pennsylvania', *Annals of the Association of American Geographers*, 62, 323–51.

Lewis, P. F. (1975) 'The future of the past: our clouded view of historic preservation', *Pioneer America*, 7, 1–20.

Linge, G. R. J. (1975) 'The forging of an industrial nation: manufacturing in Australia, 1788–1913', in J. M. Powell and M. Williams (eds), *Australian Space, Australian Time*. Oxford University Press: London, 150–81.

Livingstone, D. N. and Harrison, R. T. (1980) 'The frontier: metaphor, myth and model', *Professional Geographer*, 32, 127–32.

London, H. I. (1970) *Non-White Immigration and the 'White Australia' Policy*. New York University Press: New York.

Lösch, A. (1954) *The Economics of Location*, trans. W. H. Woglom. Yale University Press: New Haven.

Louch, A. R. (1969) 'History as narrative', *History and Theory*, 8, 54–70.

Lowe, J. C. and Moryadas, S. (1975) *The Geography of Movement*. Houghton Mifflin: Boston.

Lowenthal, D. (1979) 'Environmental perception: preserving the past', *Progress in Human Geography*, 3, 549–59.

Lowther, G. R. (1959) 'Idealist history and historical geography', *Canadian Geographer*, 14, 30–6.

Lubasz, H. (1963) 'Introduction to the symposium: use of theory in the study of history', *History and Theory*, 3, 3–5.

McCallum, J. (1980) *Unequal Beginnings: Agriculture and Economic Development in Quebec and Ontario Until 1870*. University of Toronto Press: Toronto.

McCarty, H. H. (1954) 'Agricultural geography', in P. E. James and C. F. Jones (eds), *American Geography: Inventory and Prospect*. Syracuse University Press: Syracuse, 258–77.

McClelland, P. D. (1968) 'Railroads, economic growth and the new economic history: a critique', *Journal of Economic History*, 28, 102–23.

McClelland, P. D. (1975) *Causal Explanation and Model Building in History. Economics and the New Economic History*. Cornell University Press: Ithaca.

McCloskey, D. N. (1975) 'The persistence of English common fields', in W. N. Parker and E. L. Jones (eds), *European Peasants and Their Markets*. Princeton University Press: Princeton, 73–119.

McCormick, P. L. (1980) 'Transportation and settlement: problems in the expansion of the frontier of Saskatchewan and Assiniboia in 1904', *Prairie Forum*, 5, 1–18.

Macfarlane, A. (1977) *Reconstructing Historical Communities*. Cambridge University Press: Cambridge.

McIlwraith, T. F. (1970) 'The adequacy of rural roads in the era before railways: an illustration from Upper Canada', *Canadian Geographer*, 4, 344–60.

McInnis, M. (1976) 'Comment on paper by Gagon', *Journal of Economic History*, 36, 142–6.

McIntosh, C. B. (1981) 'One man's sequential land alienation on the Great Plains', *Geographical Review*, 71, 427–45.

McKee, J. O. (1971) 'The Choctaw Indians: a geographical study in cultural change', *Southern Quarterly*, 9, 107–41.

McQuillan, D. A. (1978a) 'Territory and ethnic identity: some new measures of an old theme in the cultural geography of the United States', in J. R. Gibson (ed.), *European Settlement and Development in North America*. University of Toronto Press: Toronto, 136–69.

McQuillan, D. A. (1978b) 'Farm size and work ethic: measuring the success of immigrant farmers on the American grassland, 1875–1925', *Journal of Historical Geography*, 4, 57–76.

Malm, R., Olsson, G. and Wärneryd, O. (1966) 'Approaches to simulation of urban growth', *Geografiska Annaler*, 48B, 9–22.

Mannion, J. (1974) *Irish Settlements in Eastern Canada: A Study of Culture Transfer and Adoption*. University of Toronto: Toronto, Department of Geography, Research Publication No. 12.

Marble, D. F. (1970) *Simulation in Human Geography*. Northwestern University: Evanston, Department of Geography, Research Report No. 58.

Marshall, J. U. and Smith, W. R. (1978) 'The dynamics of growth in a regional urban system in southern Ontario, 1851–1971', *Canadian Geographer*, 22, 22–40.

Martin, R. L. *et al*. (1978) *Towards the Dynamic Analysis of Spatial Systems*. Pion: London.

Mathewson, K. (1977) 'Maya urban genesis reconsidered: trade and intensive agriculture as primary factors', *Journal of Historical Geography*, 3, 203–215.

Mathias, P. (1974) 'Comment on papers by Felix and Eckstein, Chao and Chong', *Journal of Economic History*, 34, 265–272.

May, J. (1970) *Kant's Concept of Geography and Its Relation to Recent Geographic Thought*. University of Toronto: Toronto, Department of Geography, Research Publication No. 4.

Mayhew, A. (1973) *Rural Settlement and Farming in Germany*. Batsford: London.

Mead, W. R. (1959) 'Frontier themes in Finland', *Geography*, 44, 145–56.

Mees, A. I. (1975) 'The revival of cities in medieval Europe: an application of catastrophe theory', *Regional Science and Urban Economics*, 5, 403–25.

Meier, R. C., Newell, W. T. and Pazer, H. L. (1969) *Simulation in Business and Economics*. Prentice-Hall: Englewood Cliffs.

Meinig, D. (1962) 'A comparative historical geography of two railnets: Columbia Basin and South Australia', *Annals of the Association of American Geographers*, 52, 394–413.

Meinig, D. W. (1965) 'The Mormon culture region: strategies and patterns in the geography of the American West, 1847–1964', *Annals of the Association of American Geographers*, 55, 197–220.

Meinig, D. W. (1969) *Imperial Texas: An Interpretive Essay in Cultural Geography*. University of Texas Press: Austin.

Meinig, D. W. (1972) 'American wests: preface to a geographical introduction', *Annals of the Association of American Geographers*, 62, 159–85.

Meinig, D. W. (1978) 'The continuous shaping of America: a prospectus for geographers and historians', *American Historical Review*, 83, 1186–1217.

Mercer, D. C. and Powell, J. M. (1972) *Phenomenology and Related Non-positivistic Viewpoints in the Social Sciences*. Monash Publications in Geography, No. 1: Clayton, Victoria.

Merrens, H. R. (1964) *Colonial North Carolina in the Eighteenth Century*. University of North Carolina Press: Chapel Hill.

Merrens, H. R. (1969) 'The physical environment of early America: images and image makers in colonial South Carolina', *Geographical Review*, 59, 530–56.

Merrens, H. R. (1979) *The Colonial South Carolina Scene: Contemporary Views, 1697–1774*. University of South Carolina Press: Columbia.

Meyer, D. R. (1980) 'A dynamic model of the integration of frontier urban places into the United States system of cities', *Economic Geography*, 56, 120–40.

Mikesell, M. W. (1960) 'Comparative studies in frontier history', *Annals of the Association of American Geographers*, 50, 62–74.

Millman, R. N. (1975) *The Making of the Scottish Landscape*. Batsford: London.

Mills, D. R. (1978) 'The residential propinquity of kin in a Cambridgeshire village, 1841', *Journal of Historical Geography*, 4, 265–76.

Minshull, R. (1967) *Regional Geography: Theory and Practice*. Hutchinson: London.

Mitchell, J. B. (1954) *Historical Geography*. English Universities Press: London.

Mitchell, R. D. (1972) 'The Shenandoah Valley frontier', *Annals of the Association of American Geographers*, **62**, 461–86.

Mitchell, R. D. (1973) 'Agricultural change and the American Revolution: a Virginia case study', *Agricultural History*, **47**, 119–32.

Mitchell, R. D. (1978) 'The formation of early American cultural regions', in J. R. Gibson (ed.), *European Settlement and Development in North America*. University of Toronto Press: Toronto, 66–90.

Monk, J. (1978) 'Review article: race and restrictive immigration', *Journal of Historical Geography*, **4**, 192–6.

Moodie, D. W. (1971) 'Content analysis: a method for historical geography', *Area*, **3**, 146–9.

Moodie, D. W. (1977) 'The Hudson's Bay Company's archives: a resource for historical geography', *Canadian Geographer*, **21**, 268–74.

Moodie, D. W. (1980) 'Agriculture and the fur trade', in C. M. Judd and A. J. Ray (eds), *Old Trails and New Directions: Papers on the Third North American Fur Trade Conference*. University of Toronto Press: Toronto, 272–290.

Moodie, D. W. and Catchpole, A. J. W. (1975) *Environmental Data From Historical Documents by Content Analysis: Freeze Up and Break Up of Estuaries on Hudson Bay, 1714–1871*. Manitoba Geographical Studies No. 5.

Moodie, D. W. and Lehr, J. C. (1976) 'Fact and theory in historical Geography', *Professional Geographer*, **28**, 132–5.

Moodie, D. W., Lehr, J. C. and Alwin, J. A. (1974) 'Zelinksy's pursuit: wild goose or canard', *Historical Geography Newsletter*, **4**, 18–21.

Morgan, M. (1979) *Historical Sources in Geography*. Butterworth: London.

Morrill, R. L. (1963) 'The distribution of migration distances', *Papers and Proceedings of the Regional Science Association*, **11**, 75–84.

Morrill, R. L. (1965a) *Migration and the Spread and Growth of Urban Settlement*. Gleerup: Lund, Lund Studies in Geography No. 26.

Morrill, R. L. (1965b) 'Expansion of the urban fringe: a simulation experiment', *Papers and Proceedings of the Regional Science Association*, **15**, 185–202.

Morrill, R. L. (1970) *The Spatial Organization of Society*. Duxbury: Belmont.

Morrill, R. L. and M. B. Kelley (1970) 'The simulation of hospital use and the estimation of local efficiency', *Geographical Analysis*, **2**, 283–300.

Moyes, A. (1978) 'Transport: 1730–1900', in R. A. Dodgshon and R. A. Butlin (eds), *An Historical Geography of England and Wales*. Academic Press: London, 401–29.

Muller, E. K. (1976) 'Selective urban growth in the middle Ohio Valley, 1800–1860', *Geographical Review*, **66**, 178–99.

Muller, E. K. (1977) 'Regional urbanization and the selective growth of towns in North American regions', *Journal of Historical Geography*, **3**, 21–40.

Muller, E. K. and P. A. Groves (1979) 'The emergence of industrial districts in mid-nineteenth century Baltimore', *Geographical Review*, **69**, 159–78.

Muller, P. O. (1973) 'Trend surfaces of American agriculture patterns: a macro-Thünian analysis', *Economic Geography*, 49, 228–42.

Murton, B. J. (1975) 'Agrarian system dynamics in interior Tamil Nadu before 1800 AD', *National Geographical Journal of India*, 21, 151–65.

Nelson, H. J. (1974) 'Town founding and the American frontier', *Yearbook*, Association of Pacific Coast Geographers, Vol. 36, 7–24.

Newcomb, R. M. (1967) 'Geographic aspects of the planned preservation of visible history in Denmark', *Annals of the Association of American Geographers*, 57, 462–80.

Newcomb, R. M. (1969) 'Twelve working approaches to historical geography', *Yearbook*, Association of Pacific Coast Geographers, Vol. 31, 27–50.

Newcomb, R. M. (1970) 'An example of the applicability of remote sensing in historical geography', *Geoforum*, 2, 89–92.

Newson, L. (1976) 'Cultural evolution: a basic concept for human and historical geography', *Journal of Historical Geography*, 2, 239–56.

Newton, M. B., jun. and Pulliam Di-Napoli L. (1977) 'Log houses as public occasions: a historical theory', *Annals of the Association of American Geographers*, 67, 360–83.

Nisbet, R. (1980) *History of the Idea of Progress*. Basic Books: New York.

Norcliffe, G. B. (1969) 'On the use and limitations of trend surface models', *Canadian Geographer*, 13, 338–48.

Norrie, K. H. (1975) 'The rate of settlement of the Canadian prairies', *Journal of Economic History*, 35, 410–27.

Norrie, K. H. (1977) 'Dry farming and the economics of risk bearing: the Canadian prairies, 1870–1930', *Agricultural History*, 51, 134–48.

Norrie, K. H. (1980) 'Cultivation techniques as a response to risk in early Canadian prairie agriculture', *Explorations in Economic History*, 17, 386–99.

North, D. C. (1961) *The Economic Growth of the United States*. Prentice-Hall: Englewood Cliffs, NJ.

North, D. C. (1974) 'Beyond the new economic history', *Journal of Economic History*, 34, 1–7.

North, D. C. (1977) 'The new economic history after twenty years', *American Behavioral Scientist*, 21, 187–200.

Norton, W. (1974) 'Some investigations of a growth model of innovation diffusion', *South African Geographer*, 4, 383–7.

Norton, W. (1975) 'The process of rural land occupation in Upper Canada', *Scottish Geographical Magazine*, 91, 145–52.

Norton, W. (1976) 'Constructing abstract worlds of the past', *Geographical Analysis*, 8, 269–88.

Norton, W. (1977a) 'A conceptual framework for the process of frontier settlement', *Comparative Frontier Studies*, 9, 3.

Norton, W. (1977b) 'Commentary: frontier agriculture: subsistence or commercial', *Annals of the Association of American Geographers*, 62, 463–4.

Norton, W. (1978) 'Process and form relationships: an example from historical geography', *Professional Geographer*, 30, 128–34.

Norton, W. (1979) 'Urban dispersion in Cape Province, South Africa,

1652–1970', *Geoforum*, **10**, 427–32.

Norton, W. (1982a) 'Historical geography as the evolution of spatial form', in A. R. H. Baker and M. Billinge (eds), *Period and Place: Research Methods in Historical Geography*. Cambridge University Press: Cambridge, 251–7.

Norton, W. (1982b) 'Some comment on late-nineteenth-century agriculture in areas of European overseas expansion', *Ontario History*, **74**, 113–17.

Norton, W. and Conkling, E. C. (1974) 'Land-use theory and the pioneering economy', *Geografiska Annaler*, **56B**, 44–56.

Norton, W. and Cook, J. M. (1976) 'Description and analysis of urban dispersion', *South African Geographer*, **4**, 295–302.

Norton, W. and Smit, P. D. (1977) 'Rural settlement surface evolution: Cape Province, 1865–1970', *Geografiska Annaler*, **56B**, 43–50.

Nostrand, R. C. (1970) 'The Hispanic American borderland: delimitation of an American cultural region', *Annals of the Association of American Geographers*, **60**, 638–61.

Nurkse, R. (1961) *Patterns of Trade and Development*. Blackwell: Oxford.

O'Brien, P. (1977) *The New Economic History of the Railways*. St Martin's Press: New York.

Ogden, P. E. (1980) 'Migration, marriage and the collapse of traditional peasant society', in P. E. White and R. I. woods (eds), *The Geographical Impact of Migration*. Longman: London, 152–79.

Ogilvie, P. G. (1952) 'The time element in geography', *Transactions of the Institute of British Geographers*, **18**, 1–15.

Olsson, G. (1968) 'Complementary models: a study of colonization maps', *Geografiska Annaler*, **50B**, 115–32.

Olsson, G. (1969) 'Trends in spatial model building: an overview', *Geographical Analysis*, **1**, 219–24.

Olsson, G. (1974) 'The dialectics of spatial analysis', *Antipode*, **6**, 50–62.

Olwig, K. R. (1980) 'Historical geography and the society/nature "problematic": the perspective of J. F. Schouw, G. P. Marsh, and E. Reclus', *Journal of Historical Geography*, **6**, 29–45.

Orrman, E. (1981) 'The progress of settlement in Finland during the late Middle Ages', *Scandinavian Economic History Review*, **29**, 129–43.

Osborne, B. S. (1977) 'Frontier settlement in eastern Ontario in the nineteenth century: a study in changing perceptions of land and opportunity', in D. H. Miller and J. O. Steffen (eds), *The Frontier*. University of Oklahoma Press: Norman, 201–26.

Osborne, B. S. and Rogerson, C. M. (1978) 'Conceptualizing the frontier settlement process: development or dependency', *Comparative Frontier Studies*, **11**, 1–3.

Ostergren, R. C. (1980) 'Prairie bound: migration patterns to a Swedish settlement on the Dakota frontier', in F. C. Luebke (ed.), *Ethnicity on the Great Plains*. University of Nebraska Press: Lincoln, 73–91.

Overton, J. D. (1981) 'A theory of exploration', *Journal of Historical Geography*, **7**, 53–70.

Overton, M. (1979) 'Estimating crop yields from probate inventories: an example from East Anglia, 1585–1735', *Journal of Economic History*, 39, 363–78.

Overton, M. (1977) 'Computer analysis of an inconsistent data source: the case of probate inventories', *Journal of Historical Geography*, 3, 317–326.

Owram, D. (1980) *Promise of Eden: The Canadian Expansionist Movement and the Idea of the West, 1856–1900*. University of Toronto Press: Toronto.

Palmer, B. D. (1979) *A Culture in Conflict*. McGill-Queen's University Press: Montreal.

Parker, W. N. and Jones, E. C. (1975) *European Peasants and Their Markets: Essays in Agrarian Economic History*. Princeton University Press: Princeton.

Parkes, D. N. and Thrift, N. J. (1980) *Times, Spaces and Places: A Chronogeographic Perspective*. Wiley: New York.

Parson, H. E. (1977) 'Settlement policy and land evaluation at the turn of the twentieth century in Quebec', *Area*, 9, 290–2.

Passmore, J. (1962) 'Explanation in everyday life, in science and in history', *History and Theory*, 2, 105–23.

Patten, J. (1977) 'Urban occupations in pre-industrial England', *Transactions of the Institute of British Geographers*, 3, 296–313.

Patten, J. (1978) *English Towns: 1500–1700*. Dawson: Folkestone.

Patten, J. (1979) 'Introduction and select bibliography', in J. Patten (ed.), *Pre-Industrial England: Geographical Essays*. Dawson: Folkestone, 9–53.

Pawson, E. (1977) *Transport and Economy*. Academic Press: London.

Pawson, E. (1978) 'The framework of industrial change, 1730–1900', in R. A. Dodgshon and R. A. Butlin (eds), *An Historical Geography of England and Wales*. Academic Press: London, 267–89.

Pawson, E. (1979) *The Early Industrial Revolution: Britain in the Eighteenth Century*. Batsford: London.

Pechuro, E. E. (1965) 'Review of: *History and Theory*, Vol. 1, No. 1, to Vol. 3, No. 2', *History and Theory*, 4, 359–67.

Peet, J. R. (1969) 'The spatial expansion of commercial agriculture in the nineteenth century: a von Thünen interpretation', *Economic Geography*, 45, 283–301.

Peet, J. R. (1970) 'Von Thünen theory and the dynamics of agricultural expansion', *Explorations in Economic History*, 8, 181–201.

Peet, J. R. (1972) 'Influences of the British market on agriculture and related economic development in Europe', *Transactions of the Institute of British Geographers*, 56, 1–20.

Perry, P. J. (1969) 'Working class isolation and mobility in rural Dorset, 1837–1936: a study of marriage distances', *Transactions of the Institute of British Geographers*, 46, 121–41.

Perry, P. J. (1972) 'Where was the "Great Agricultural Depression"? A geography of agricultural bankruptcy in late Victorian England and Wales', *Agricultural History Review*, 20, 30–45.

Perry, P. J. (1975) *A Geography of Nineteenth Century Britain*. Batsford: London.

Perry, T. M. (1963) *Australia's First Frontier*. Cambridge University Press: London.

Peters, B. C. (1972) 'Oak openings or barrens: landscape evaluation on the Michigan frontier', *Proceedings of the Association of American Geographers*, 4, 84–6.

Peters, G. L. and Anderson, B. L. (1976) 'Industrial landscapes: past views and stages of recognition', *Professional Geographer*, 28, 341–8.

Piaget, J. (1971) *Structuralism*. Routledge and Kegan Paul: London.

Piellusch, F. (1975) 'Applied historical geography', *Pennsylvania Geographer*, 13, 7–11.

Pitts, F. R. (1965) 'A graph theoretic approach to historical geography', *Professional Geographer*, 17, 15–20.

Planhol, X. de (1972) 'Historical geography in France', in A. R. H. Baker (ed.), *Progress in Historical Geography*. David and Charles: Newton Abbott, 29–44.

Platt, R. S. (1957) 'A review of regional geography', *Annals of the Association of American Geographers*, 47, 187–90.

Plumb, J. H. (1972) 'History as geography, economics, folklore: as everything that touches the lives of men', *New York Times Book Review*, 31 Dec.

Pollock, N. C. and S. Agnew (1963) *An Historical Geography of South Africa*. Longman: London.

Pomfret, R. (1981) 'The staple theory as an approach to Canadian and Australian economic development', *Australian Economic History Review*, 21, technological knowledge', *Journal of Economic History*, 36, 399–415.

Pomfret, R. (1981) 'The staple theory as an approach to Canadian and Australian economic development', *Australian Economic History Review*, 21, 133–46.

Pooley, C. G. (1977) 'The residential segregation of migrant communities in mid-Victorian Liverpool', *Transactions of the Institute of British Geographers*, 2, 364–82.

Porter, D. H. (1975) 'History as process', *History and Theory*, 14, 297–313.

Porter, R. (1956) 'Approach to migration through its mechanism', *Geografiska Annaler*, 38B, 317–43.

Pounds, N. J. G (1973) *An Historical Geography of Europe, 450 B.C. to 1330A.D.* Cambridge University Press: Cambridge.

Pounds, N. J. G. (1979) *An Historical Geography of Europe, 1500–1840*. Cambridge University Press: Cambridge.

Powell, J. M. (1969) 'The squatting occupation of Victoria, 1834–1860', *Australian Geographical Studies*, 7, 9–27.

Powell, J. M. (1970) *The Public Lands of Australia Felix: Settlement and Land Appraisal in Victoria, 1834–1891*. Oxford University Press: Melbourne.

Powell, J. M. (1977) *Mirrors of the New World: Images and Image Makers in the Settlement Process*. Dawson: Folkestone.

Pred, A. (1966) *The Spatial Dynamics of United States Urban–Industrial Growth, 1800–1914: Interpretation and Theoretical Essays*. Massachusetts Institute of Technology Press: Boston.

Pred, A. (1969) *Behavior and Location: Foundations for a Geographic and Dynamic Location Theory*, Part 2. Gleerup: Lund, Lund Studies in Geography.

Pred, A. (1973) *Urban Growth and the Circulation of Information: The United States System of Cities, 1790–1840*. Harvard University Press: Cambridge, Mass.

Pred, A. (1977) *City Systems in Advanced Economies: Past Growth, Present Processes and Future Management Options*. Wiley: New York.

☛ Pred, A. (1980) *Urban Growth and City Systems in the United States, 1840–1960*. Harvard University Press: Cambridge, Mass.

☛ Pred, A. (1981) 'Production, family and free-time projects: a time geographic perspective on the individual and societal change in nineteenth-century U.S. cities', *Journal of Historical Geography*, 7, 3–36.

Primarck, M L. (1962) 'Land clearing under nineteenth-century techniques', *Journal of Economic History*, 22, 484–97.

Prince, H. C. (1967) 'Historical Geography', in J. W. Watson (ed.), *Congress Proceedings: Twentieth International Geographical Congress*. Nelson: London, 164–72.

Prince, H. C. (1969) 'Progress in historical geography', in R. U. Cooke and J. H. Johnson (eds), *Trends in Geography. An Introductory Survey*, Pergamon: New York, 110–122.

Prince, H. C. (1971) 'Real, imagined and abstract worlds of the past', in C. Board *et al.* (eds), *Progress in Geography*, Vol. 3. Edward Arnold: London, 1–86.

Prince, H. C. (1977) 'Richard Cobb: a spy in revolutionary France', *Journal of Historical Geography*, 3, 363–72.

Prince, H. C. (1978) 'Time and historical geography', in T. Carlstein, D. N. Parkes and N. J. Thrift (eds), *Timing Space and Spacing Time*, Vol. 1. Edward Arnold: London, 17–37.

Prince, H. C. (1980) 'Historical geography in 1980', in E. H. Brown (ed.), *Geography: Yesterday and Tomorrow*. Oxford University Press: Oxford.

Prince, H. C. (1982) 'Modernization, restoration, preservation: changes in tastes for antique landscape', in A. R. H. Baker and M. Billinge (eds), *Period and Place: Research Methods in Historical Geography*. Cambridge University Press: Cambridge, 33–43.

Prithvish, N. (1980) 'Current trends of historical approaches in geographical researches in India', in *Historical Geography, 19*. Institute of Czechoslovak and World History of the Czechoslovak Academy of Sciences: Prague, 25–35.

Pryce, W. T. R. (1975) 'Migration and the evolution of culture areas: cultural and linguistic frontiers in North-east Wales, 1750–1851', *Transactions of the Institute of British Geographers*, 65, 79–108.

Pyle, G. F. (1969) 'Diffusion of cholera in the United States', *Geographical Analysis*, 1, 59–75.

Quastler, I. E. (1978) 'Some major unanswered questions about the historical geography of American railroads', *Historical Geography*, 8, 1–9.

Raby, S. C. (1973) 'Indian land surrenders in southern Saskatchewan', *Canadian Geographer*, 17, 36–52.

● Radford, J. P. (1976) 'Race, residence and ideology: Charleston South Carolina, in the mid-nineteenth century', *Journal of Historical Geography*, 2, 329–46.

Ramesar, M. D. (1976) 'Patterns of regional settlement and economic activity by immigrant groups in Trinidad: 1850–1900', *Social and Economic Studies*, 25, 187–215.

Rashevsky, N. (1968) *Looking at History Through Mathematics*. MIT Press: Cambridge, Mass.

Redlich, F. (1965) 'New and traditional approaches to economic history and their interdependence', *Journal of Economic History*, 25, 480–95.

Relph, E. (1970) 'An inquiry into the relations between phenomenology and geography', *Canadian Geographer*, 14, 193–201.

Reps, J. W. (1979) *Cities of the American West: A History of Frontier Urban Planning*. Princeton University Press: Princeton.

Reynolds, H. C. (1980) 'The land, the explorers and the Aborigines', *Historical Studies*, 19, 213–26.

Rice, J. G. (1978a) 'The effect of land alienation on settlement', *Annals of the Association of American Geographers*, 68, 61–72.

Rice, J. G. (1978b) 'Indicators of social change in rural Sweden in the late nineteenth century', *Journal of Historical Geography*, 4, 23–34.

Richerson, P. J. (1979) 'Ecology and the origins of agriculture: a review essay', *Agricultural History*, 53, 637–43.

Richtik, J. M. (1975) 'The policy framework for settling the Canadian West, 1870–1880', *Agricultural History*, 49, 613–28.

Ricoeur, P. (1980) *The Contribution of French Historiography to the Theory of History*. Clarendon Press: Oxford.

Rimmer, P. J. (1967) 'The search for spatial regularities in the development of Australian seaports, 1861–1961/2', *Geografiska Annaler*, 49B, 42–54.

Roberts, B. K. (1968) 'A study of medieval colonization in the Forest of Arden, Warwickshire', *Agricultural History Review*, 16, 101–13.

Roberts, B. K. (1976) 'The anatomy of settlement', in P. H. Sawyer (ed.) *Medieval Settlement*. Edward Arnold: London, 295–326.

Robinson, G. (1981) 'A statistical analysis of agriculture in the Vale of Evesham during the "Great Agricultural Depression"', *Journal of Historical Geography*, 7, 37–52.

Robinson, M. E. (1974) 'The Robertson Land Acts in New South Wales, 1861–84', *Transactions of the Institute of British Geographers*, 61, 17–33.

Rodger, R. G. (1979) 'The building cycle and the urban fringe in Victorian cities: another comment', *Journal of Historical Geography*, 5, 72–8.

Rogers, E. M. (1962) *Diffusion of Innovations*. Free Press: New York.

Rose, C. (1981) 'William Dilthey's philosophy of historical understanding: a neglected heritage of contemporary humanistic geography', in D. R. Stoddart (ed.), *Geography, Ideology and Social Concern*. Barnes and Noble: Totowa, 99–133.

Roseman, C. C. (1971) 'Migration as a spatial and temporal process', *Annals of the Association of American Geographers*, 61, 589–598.

Ross, R. (1975) 'The "White" population of South Africa in the eighteenth century', *Population Studies*, 29, 217–30.

Rothstein, M. (1975) 'West coast farmers and the tyranny of distance: agriculture on the fringes of the world market', *Agricultural History*, 49, 272–80.

Rowland, D. T. (1977) 'Theories of urbanization in Australia', *Geographical Review*, 67, 167–76.

Rowney, D. K. and Graham, J. O. (eds) (1969) *Quantitative History*. Dorsey Press: New York.

Roy, W. T. (1970) 'Immigration policy and legislation' in K. W. Thomson and A. D. Trlin (eds), *Immigrants in New Zealand*. Massey University: Palmerston North, 15–24.

Royle, E. (1977) 'Social stratification from early census returns: a new approach', *Area*, 9, 215–19.

Rozman, G. (1978) 'Urban networks and historical stages', *Journal of Interdisciplinary History*, 9, 65–92.

Ruggles, R. I. (1971) 'The west of Canada in 1763: imagination and reality', *Canadian Geographer*, 15, 235–61.

Russwurm, L. H. and Thakur, B. (1981) 'Hierarchical and functional stability and change in a strongly urbanizing area of southwestern Ontario, 1871–1971', *Canadian Geographer*, 25, 149–66.

Rutten, A, (1980) 'But it will never be science, either', *Journal of Economic History*, 40, 137–42.

Saarinen, T. F. (1974) 'Environmental perception', in I. R. Manners and M. W. Mikesell (eds), *Perspectives on Environment*. Association of American Geographers: Washington, Commission on College Geography, Publication No. 13, 252–89.

Sabloff, J. A. (ed.) (1981) *Simulation in Archaeology*. University of New Mexico Press: Albuquerque.

Sack, R. D. (1972) 'Geography, geometry and explanation', *Annals of the Association of American Geographers*, 62, 61–78.

Samuels, M. S. (1971) 'Continuity and change in Chinese frontier values: the North west, 1820–1884', *Proceedings of the Association of American Geographers*, 3, 194.

Sargent, C. G. (1972) 'Toward a dynamic model of urban morphology', Economic Geography, 48, 357–74.

Sargent, C. G. (1975) 'Towns of the Salt River Valley, 1870–1930', *Historical Geography Newsletter*, 5 (2), 1–9.

Sarly, R. M. (1972) 'A model for the location of rural settlement', *Papers of the Regional Science Association*, 29, 87–104.

Sauer, C. O. (1941) 'Foreword to historical geography', *Annals of the Association of American Geographers*, 31, 1–24.

Sauer, C. O. (1952) *Agricultural Origins and Dispersals*. American Geographical Society: New York.

Sauer, C. O. (1963) 'The morphology of landscape', in J. Leighly (ed.), *Land and Life*. University of California Press: Berkeley, 315–50.

Sauer, C. O. (1966) *The Early Spanish Main*. University of California Press: Berkeley.

Savage, W. W. Jnr. and Thompson, S. I. (1979) 'The comparative study of the frontier: an introduction', in W. W. Savage, jun. and S. I. Thompson (eds), *The Frontier*, Volume Two. University of Oklahoma Press: Norman, 3–24.

Sawyer, P. H. (1976) 'Introduction: early medieval English settlement', in P. H. Sawyer (ed.), *Medieval Settlement*. Arnold: London, 1–10.

Schaefer, D. and Weiss, T. (1971), 'The use of simulation techniques in historical analysis: railroads versus canals', *Journal of Economic History*, 31, 854–84.

Schaeffer, F. K. (1953) 'Exceptionalism in geography: a methodological examination', *Annals of the Association of American Geographers*, 43, 226–49.

Schlebecker, J. T. (1960) 'The world metropolis and the history of American agriculture', *Journal of Economic History*, 20, 187–208.

Schnore, L. F. (1975) *The New Urban History*. Princeton University Press: Princeton.

Senda, M. and Tanioka, T. (1980) 'Current trends of historical approach in geographical research in Japan', in *Historical Geography*, Vol. 19. Institute of Czechoslovak and World History of the Czechoslovak Academy of Sciences: Prague, 13–24.

Sharpless, J. B. and Warner, S. B. jnr. (1977) 'Urban history', *American Behavioral Scientist*, 21, 221–44.

Shaw, D. J.B. (1976) 'Data and theory in historical geography: some problems of explanation in data scarce situations', in V. V. Annenkov (ed.), *International Geography*. Pergamon: Toronto, 79–83.

Sitwell, O. F. G. (1976) 'Pioneer attitudes as revealed by the township of Strathcona, Alberta', in B. S. Osborne (ed.), *The Settlement of Canada: Origins and Transfer*. Queens University Press: Kingston, 236.

Sitwell, O. F. G. (1980) 'Why did the grain elevator become the chief symbol of the Canadian prairies', *Albertan Geographer*, 16, 3–11.

Sjoberb, G. (1960) *The Pre-Industrial City: Past and Present*. Free Press: Glencoe, Ill.

Small, A. (1968) 'The historical geography of the Norse Viking colonization of the Scottish Highlands', *Geografisk Tidsskrift*, 22, 1–16.

Smith, C. T. (1965) 'Historical geography: current trends and prospects', in R. J. Chorley (ed.), *Frontiers in Geographical Teaching*. Methuen: London, 118–43.

Smith, C. T. (1967) *An Historical Geography of Western Europe Before 1800*. Longman: London.

Smith, E. G. (1967) 'An urban interpretation of American settlement', *Yearbook*, Association of Pacific Coast Geographers, Vol. 29, 43–52.

Sommer, J. W. (1975) 'Review of A. Pred, "Urban growth and the circulation of information: the United States System of cities, 1790–1840"', *Journal of Historical Geography*, 1, 316–18.

Spencer, J. E. and Thomas, W. L. (1973) *Introducing Cultural Geography*. Wiley: New York.

Stamp, L. D. (ed.) (1937–47) *The Land of Britain: The Final Report of the Land Utilization Survey of Britain.* 9 vols. Geographical Publications: London.

Stamp, L. D. (1964) *Man and the Land.* Collins: London.

Stevenson, I. (1981) 'Review of "E. LeRoy Ladurie, The Territory of the Historian"', *Journal of Historical Geography*, 7, 196–7.

Stiverson, G. A. (1976) 'Early American farming: a comment', *Agricultural History*, 50, 37–44.

Stoianovich, T. (1976) *French Historical Method: The Annales Paradigm.* Cornell University Press: Ithaca.

Stone, K. H. (1965) 'The development of a focus for the geography of settlement', *Economic Geography*, 41, 346–56.

Stone, L. (1979) 'The revival of narrative: reflections on a new old history', *Past and Present*, 85, 3–24.

Supple, B. (1981) 'Economic history in the 1980s: old problems and new directions', *Journal of Interdisciplinary History*, 12, 199–205.

Sutter, R. E. (1973) *The Next Place You Come To.* Prentice-Hall: Englewood Cliffs, NJ.

Swanson, J. and Williamson, J. G. (1971) 'Explanations and issues: a prospectus for quantitative economic history', *Journal of Economic History*, 31, 43–57.

Swauger, J. (1978) 'Pittsburgh's residential pattern in 1851', *Annals of the Association of American Geographers*, 68, 265–277.

Swierenga, R. J. (ed.) (1970) *Quantification in American History.* Atheneum: New York.

Swierenga, R. J. (1973) 'Towards the "New rural history": a review essay', *Historical Methods Newsletter*, 6, 111–22.

Taafe, E. J., Garner, B. J. and Yeates, M. H. (1963) *The Peripheral Journey to Work: A Geographical Consideration.* Northwestern University Press: Evanston.

Taafe, E. J. *et al.* (1963) 'Transport expansion in underdeveloped countries: a comparative analysis', *Geographical Review*, 53, 503–29.

Taylor, G. R. (1967) 'American urban growth preceding the railway age', *Journal of Economic History*, 27, 309–39.

Taylor, H. W. (1973) 'Sao Paulo's hollow frontier', *Revista Geographica*, 79, 149–66.

Temin, P. (1981) 'Economic history in the 1980s: the future of the new economic history', *Journal of Interdisciplinary History*, 12, 179–97.

Thirsk, J. (1964) 'The common fields', *Past and Present*, 29, 3–25.

Thirsk, J. (1966) 'The origin of the common fields', *Past and Present*, 33, 142–7.

Thompson, E. P. (1968) *The Making of the English Working Class.* Penguin: Harmondsworth.

Thompson, I. B. (1978) 'Settlement and conflict in Corsica', *Transactions of the Institute of British Geographers*, 3, 259–73.

Thompson, K. C. (1975) 'The perception of the agricultural environment', *Agricultural History*, 49, 230–7.

Thompson, R. (1974) 'Seventeenth-century English and colonial sex ratios', *Population Studies*, **28**, 153–165.

Thomson, G. M. (1975) *The North West Passage*. Futura: London.

Thrift, N. (1977) 'Time and Theory in human geography: Part 1', *Progress in Human Geography*, **1**, 65–101.

Thrower, N. J. W. (1966) *Original Survey and Land Subdivision*. Rand McNally: Chicago.

Todd, W. (1972) *History as Applied Science*. Wayne State University Press: Detroit.

Topolski, J. (1976) *Methodology of History*. D. Reidel: Boston.

Tracie, C. J. (1973) 'Land of plenty or poor man's land: environmental perception and appraisal respecting agricultural settlement in the Peace River country, Canada', in B. W. Blouet and M. P. Lawson (eds), *Images of the Plains*. University of Nebraska Press: Lincoln, 115–22.

Tuan, Yi-Fu (1974) 'Space and place: humanistic perspectives', in C. Board *et al*. (eds), *Progress in Geography*, Vol. 6. Arnold: London, 211–52.

Turner, F. J. (1961) *Frontier and Section*. R. A. Billington (ed.). Prentice-Hall: Englewood Cliffs, NJ.

Turner, W. H. K. (1972) 'Flax cultivation in Scotland: an historical geography', *Transactions of the Institute of British Geographers*, **55**, 127–43.

Tyman, J. C. (1973) 'Subjective surveyors: the appraisal of farm lands in western Canada, 1870–1930', in B. W. Blouet and M. P. Lawson (eds), *Images of the Plains*. University of Nebraska Press: Lincoln, 75–97.

Usher, P. J. (1975) 'The growth and decay of the trading and trapping frontiers in the Western Canadian Arctic', *Canadian Geographer*, **19**, 308–20.

Vance, J. E. (1970) *The Merchant's World: The Geography of Wholesaling*. Prentice-Hall: Englewood Cliffs, NJ.

Vance, J. E. (1971) 'Land assignment in pre-capitalist, capitalist and post-capitalist societies', *Economic Geography*, **47**, 101–20.

Vance, J. E. (1978) 'Institutional forces that shape the city', in D. T. Herbert and R. J. Johnston (eds), *Social Areas in Cities*, Wiley: London, 83–109.

Vedder, R. K. and Galloway, L. E. (1972), 'The geographical distribution of British and Irish emigrants to the United States After 1800', *Scottish Journal of Political Economy*, **19**, 19–35.

Vicero, R. D. (1971) 'French Canadian settlement in Vermont prior to the Civil War', *Professional Geographer*, **23**, 290–4.

Vorob'yev, V. V. (1975) 'The settling of eastern Siberia before the Revolution', *Soviet Geography*, **16**, 75–85.

de Vorsey, L. J. (1973) 'Florida's seaward boundary', *Professional Geographer*, **25**, 214–20.

Wacker, P. O. (1968) *The Musconetcong Valley of New Jersey: A Historical Geography*. Rutgers University Press: New Brunswick.

Wacker, P. O. (1975) *Land and People: A Cultural Geography of Pre-Industrial New Jersey: Origins and Settlement Patterns*. Rutgers University Press: New Brunswick.

Wade, R. C. (1959) *The Urban Frontier, 1790–1830*. Harvard University

Press: Cambridge, Mass.

Wagner, P. L. (1975) 'The themes of cultural geography rethought', *Yearbook*, Association of Pacific Coast Geographers, Vol. 37, 7–14.

Wagner, P. L. and Mikesell, M..W. (1962) 'The themes of cultural geography', in P. L. Wagner and M. W. Mikesell, (eds), *Readings in Cultural Geography*. University of Chicago Press: Chicago, 1–24.

Wagstaff, J. M. (1978a) 'A possible interpretation of settlement pattern evolution in terms of "catastrophe theory"', *Transactions of the Institute of British Geographers*, 3, 165–78.

Wagstaff, J. M. (1978b) 'War and settlement desertion in the Morea, 1685–1830', *Transactions of the Institute of British Geographers*, 3, 295–308.

Wagstaff, J. M. (1980) 'Dialectical materialism, geography and catastrophe theory', *Area*, 12, 326–32.

Walker, G. (1972) 'Two settlement simulations', in W. P. Adams and F. M. Helleiner (eds), *International Geography*, Vol. 2. IGU: Montreal, 773–4.

Walker, G. (1975) 'Migrants and place of birth: a methodological note', *Professional Geographer*, 27, 58–64.

Wall, G. (1977) 'Nineteenth-century land use and settlement on the Canadian Shield frontier', in D. H. Miller and J. O. Steffen (eds), *The Frontier*. University of Oklahoma Press: Norman, 227–42.

Walsh, M. (1978) 'The spatial evolution of the mid-western pork industry, 1835–75', *Journal of Historical Geography*, 4, 1–22.

Walton, J. R. (1978) 'Agriculture, 1730–1900', in R. A. Butlin and R. A. Dodgshon (eds), *An Historical Geography of England and Wales*. Academic Press: London, 239–65.

Ward, D. (1971) *Cities and Immigrants*. Oxford University Press: New York.

Ward, D. (1975a) 'The debates on alternative approaches in historical geography', *Historical Methods Newsletter*, 8, 82–87.

Ward, D. (1975b) 'Victorian cities: how modern?', *Journal of Historical Geography*, 1, 135–51.

Ward, D. (1976) 'The Victorian slum: an enduring myth?', *Annals of the Association of American Geographers*, 66, 323–36.

Warkentin, J. (1978) 'Epilogue', in J. R. Gibson (ed.), *European Settlement and Development in North America*. University of Toronto Press: Toronto, 208–20.

Warner, S. B. (1968) *The Private City: Philadelphia in Three Periods of its Growth*. University of Pennsylvania Press: Philadelphia.

Warnes, T. (1977) 'Evolving urban system', *Area*, 9, 207–8.

Warren, K. (1970) *The British Iron and Steel Sheet Industry Since 1840*. Bell: London.

Warren, K. (1973) *The American Steel Industry, 1850–1970: A Geographical Interpretation*. Clarendon: Oxford.

Warren, K. (1976) *The Geography of British Heavy Industry Since 1800*. Oxford University Press: London.

Watson, A. M. (1974) 'The Arab agricultural revolution and its diffusion, 700–1100', *Journal of Economic History*, 34, 8–35.

Watson, J. W. (1955) 'Geography: a discipline in distance', *Scottish Geographical Magazine*, 71, 1–13.

Watts, S. J. and Watts, S. J. (1978), 'The idealist alternative in geography and history', *Professional Geographer*, 30, 123–7.

Webb, W. P. (1964) *The Great Frontier*. University of Texas Press: Austin.

Webber, M. J. (1972) 'Population growth and town location in an agricultural community: Iowa 1840–1960', *Geographical Analysis*, 4, 134–55.

Weber, A. (1929) *Theory of the Location of Industries*, trans. C. Friedrich. University of Chicago Press: Chicago.

Wessel, T. R. (1976) 'Agriculture, Indians and American history', *Agricultural History*, 50, 9–20.

Whebell, C. F. J. (1979) 'The concept of frontier in the politico-territorial evolution of New World settlement systems', paper presented to CUKAN-ZUS, An International Conference for Historical Geographers, Los Angeles.

White, L. (1959) *The Evolution of Culture*. McGraw-Hill: New York.

White, R. W. (1974) 'Sketches of a dynamic central place theory', *Economic Geography*, 50, 219–27.

White, R. W. (1977) 'Dynamic central place theory: results of a simulation approach', *Geographical Analysis*, 9, 226–43.

Whitehand, J. W. R. (1975) 'Building activity and the intensity of development of the urban fringe: the case of a London suburb in the nineteenth century', *Journal of Historical Geography*, 1, 211–24.

Whitehand, J. W. R. (1977) 'The basis for an historico-geographical theory of urban form', *Transactions of the Institute of British Geographers*, 2, 400–16.

Whittlesey, D. (1929) 'Sequent occupance', *Annals of the Association of American Geographers*, 19, 162–5.

Whittlesey, D. (1945) 'The horizon of geography', *Annals of the Association of American Geographers*, 35, 1–38.

Whyte, I. (1981) 'The evolution of rural settlement in lowland Scotland in medieval and early modern times: an exploration', *Scottish Geographical Magazine*, 97, 4–16.

Widgren, M. (1979) 'A simulation model of farming systems and land use in Sweden during the early Iron Age, c. 500 B.C.–A.D. 500', *Journal of Historical Geography*, 5, 21–32.

Wild, M. T. and Shaw, G. (1971) 'Locational behavior of urban retailing during the nineteenth century: the case of Kingston upon Hull', *Transactions of the Institute of British Geographers*, 61, 101–18.

Wild, M. T. and Shaw, G. (1976) 'Population distribution and retail provision: the case of the Halifax–Calder Valley area of West Yorkshire during the second half of the nineteenth century', *Journal of Historical Geography*, 2, 193–210.

Wilkie, R. W. (1974) 'The process method versus the hypothesis method: a nonlinear example of spatial perception and behavior', in M. H. Yeates (ed.) *Proceedings of the I.G.U. Commission on Quantitative Geography*. McGill–Queen's University Press: Montreal, 1–31.

Williams, A. (1977) 'Family, household and residence since the eighteenth century', paper presented to the Second Anglo-Canadian Historical Geography Conference, Danbury, England.

Williams, M. (1970) 'Places, periods and themes: a review and prospectus of Australian historical geography', *Australian Geographer*, 11, 403–16.

Williams, M. (1971) 'The enclosure and reclamation of the Mendip Hills, 1770–1870', *Agricultural History Review*, 19, 65–81.

Williams, M. (1974) *The Making of the South Australian Landscape*. Academic Press: London.

Williams, M. (1975) 'More and smaller is better: Australian rural settlement, 1788–1914', in J. M. Powell and M. Williams (eds), *Australian Space, Australian Time*. Oxford University Press: London, 61–103.

Williams, O. (1972) 'The goldfields of South Africa: a study in the exploitation of fortuity', in W. P. Adams and F. M. Helleiner (eds), *International Geography, Vol. 1*. IGU: Montreal, 601–3.

● Williamson, J. G. (1974) *Late Nineteenth Century American Development*. Cambridge University Press: London.

● Williamson, J. G. and Swanson, J. A. (1966) 'The growth of cities in the Northeast, 1820–1870', *Explorations in Entrepreneurial History*, Second Series, 4, Supplement.

Wills, M. W. (1979) 'The California–Victoria irrigation frontiers, 1880–1900', in W. W. Savage, jun. and S. I. Thompson (eds), *The Frontier, Volume Two*. University of Oklahoma Press: Norman, 235–50.

Wilson, A. G. (1980) 'Theory in human geography: a review essay', in E. H. Brown (ed.), *Geography: Yesterday and Tomorrow*. Oxford University Press: Oxford, 201–15.

Wilson, A. G. (1981) *Catastrophe Theory and Bifurcation*. Croom Helm: London.

Wilson, A. (1981) 'Inferring attitudes from behavior', *Historical Methods*, 14, 143–4.

Winters, C. (1981) 'The urban systems of medieval Mali', *Journal of Historical Geography*, 7, 341–55.

Wisdom, J. O. (1976) 'General explanation in history', *History and Theory*, 15, 257–66.

Wishart, D. (1976) 'Cultures in cooperation and conflict: Indians in the fur trade on the northern Great Plains, 1807–1840', *Journal of Historical Geography*, 311–28.

Wishart, D. (1979) 'The dispossession of the Pawnee', *Annals of the Association of American Geographers*, 69, 382–401.

Wolforth, J. (1974) 'Residential concentration of non-British minorities in nineteenth-century Sydney', *Australian Geographical Studies*, 12, 207–18.

Wonders, W. C. (1979) 'Log dwellings in Canadian folk architecture', *Annals of the Association of American Geographers*, 69, 187–207.

Wood, C. J. B. (1966) 'Settlement in the Long Point Region', unpublished Master's Thesis. Department of Geography, McMaster University, Hamilton.

Wood, J. D. (1974) 'Simulating pre-census population distribution' *Canadian Geographer*, 18, 250–64.

Wood, L. J. (1974) 'Glottochronology and research in historical geography', *Area*, 6, 251–3.

Woodham-Smith, C. (1963) *The Great Hunger*. Harper and Row: New York.

Woods, R. I. (1978) 'Mortality and sanitary conditions in the "best governed city in the world": Birmingham, 1870–1910', *Journal of Historical Geography*, 4, 35–56.

Wright, J. K. (1947) 'Terra incognitae: the place of imagination in geography', *Annals of the Association of American Geographers*, 37, 1–15.

Wrigley, E. A. (1966) 'Family limitation in pre-industrial England', *Economic History Review*, 19, 82–109.

Wrigley, E. A. (1981) 'Population history in the 1980s', *Journal of Interdisciplinary History*, 12, 207–26.

Wrigley, E. A. and Schofield, R. S. (1981) *The Population History of England: A Reconstruction*. Harvard University Press: Cambridge, Mass.

Wynn, G. (1979) 'Notes on society and environment in old Ontario', *Journal of Social History*, 13, 49–65.

Yelling, J. A. (1969) 'The combination and rotation of crops in East Worcestershire, 1540–1660', *Agricultural History Review*, 17, 23–43.

Yelling, J. A. (1970) 'Probate inventories and the geography of livestock farming: a study of East Worcestershire, 1540–1750', *Transactions of the Institute of British Geographers*, 51, 111–26.

Yelling, J. A. (1977) *Common Field and Enclosure in England, 1450–1850*. Macmillan: London.

Yelling, J. A. (1978) 'Agriculture, 1500–1730', in R. A. Butlin and R. A. Dodgshon (eds), *An Historical Geography of England and Wales*. Academic Press: London, 151–72.

Yeung, Y. M. (1974) 'Periodic markets: comments on spatial temporal relationships', *Professional Geographer*, 26, 147–51.

Zelinsky, W. (1973a) *The Cultural Geography of the United States*. Prentice-Hall: Englewood Cliffs, NJ.

Zelinsky, W. (1973b) 'In pursuit of historical geography and other wild geese', *Historical Geography Newsletter*, 3, 1–5.

Zimmerman, L. J. (1978) 'Simulating prehistoric locational behaviour', in I. Hodder (ed.), *Simulation Studies in Archaeology*. Cambridge University Press: London, 27–37.

Index

p.100.